Windows
Operating System
Fundamentals

Windows

Operating System
Fundamentals

Crystal Panek

This book is dedicated to my loving husband, William Panek, and to my two wonderful daughters, Alexandria and Paige. Thank you all for your love and support. I love you all more than anything!

Acknowledgements

I would like to thank my husband and best friend, Will, because without him I would not be where I am today - Thank you! I would also like to express my love to my two daughters, Alexandria and Paige, who have always shown nothing but love and support. Thank you all!

I would like to thank everyone on the Sybex team, especially my Associate Acquisitions Editor, Devon Lewis, who helped make this the best book possible. It's imperative to have the very best technical expert supporting you. I would like to thank Katie Wisor, who was the production editor.

Finally, I also want to thank everyone behind the scenes that helped make this book possible. Thank you all for your hard work and dedication.

About the Author

 **Crystal Panek**   holds the following certifications: MCP, MCP+I, MCSA, MCSA+ Security and Messaging, MCSE-NT (3.51 & 4.0), MCSE 2000, 2003, 2012/2012 R2, 2016, MCSE+Security and Messaging, MCDBA, MCTS, MCITP.

For many years she trained as a contract instructor teaching at such places as MicroC, Stellacon Corporation and the University of New Hampshire. She then became the vice-president for a large IT training company and for 15 years she developed training materials and courseware to help 1000's of students get through their certification exams. She currently works on a contract basis creating courseware for several large IT training facilities.

She currently resides in New Hampshire with her husband and two daughters. In her spare time, she likes to camp, hike, shoot trap and skeet, golf, bowl, and snowmobile.

Contents

Introduction

What Does This Book Cover?

Chapter 1: Installing and Upgrading Client Systems   This chapter covers identifying Windows operating system editions, identifying hardware and compatibility requirements, determine the appropriate editions per device type. Covers identifying different upgrade paths, how to identify upgrade paths from previous Windows versions and application compatibility. This chapter also covers understanding installation types, how to perform a clean install, upgrade using Windows Update, migrate from previous Windows versions, perform removable media installation and how to perform network installation. As well as, understanding operating system architecture, understanding the kernel mode and user mode; understand memory, IRQs, drivers, CPUs, and UI; and understanding 32-bit versus 64-bit architecture.

Chapter 2: Understanding Operating System Configurations   This chapter covers how to configure user account control (UAC), understanding standard user versus administrative user, understand types of UAC prompts and levels. Also covers how to configure Control Panel options, configure administrative tools, configure accessibility options, configure power settings, as well as how to configure File Explorer settings. This chapter delves into how to configure desktop settings, profiles, display settings, and shortcuts. How to configure and customize the Start Menu; configure Task Bar settings and configuring toolbars. You will also learn about libraries, how to configure libraries, add multiple local locations to a library, and adding networked locations.

Chapter 3: Understanding Native Applications, Tools, Mobility, and Remote Management and Assistance Designing for Technical Requirements   This chapter covers how to configure Windows SmartScree as well as how to configure Microsoft Edge, configure Cortana, and configure computer management. You will learn how to configure mobility settings, configure Sync Center, Windows Mobility Center, and Remote Desktop. This chapter also discusses how to configure and use management tools, configure MMC, configure the Windows PowerShell console and Windows PowerShell ISE. You will also learn about offline files.

Chapter 4: Managing Applications, Services, and Disks   This chapter covers configuring applications, understand local versus network applications, configure desktop applications, configure app startup options, configure Windows features, configure application removal, and how to configure Windows Store apps. You will also learn about services, understand service start-up types, service accounts, and service dependencies. You will learn to configure settings using MSCONFIG, configure processes and applications using Task Manager. This chapter also discusses understanding storage, different disk types, security (encryption), storage device types (eSATA, USB, IEEE 1394, iSCSI, InfiniBand), and storage drive types (basic, primary, extended, logical, dynamic disk, VHDs). This chapter delves into understanding file systems, FAT32, NTFS, and ReFS as well as, understanding encryption using BitLocker and Encrypting File Systems (EFS).

Chapter 5: Managing Devices   This chapter covers connecting devices, how to connect, enable, and disable plug-and-play and Bluetooth devices, connect and disconnect printers, install third-party software for devices and install device drivers. This chapter also discusses cloud storage options. You will learn about printing devices, understanding local printers, network printers, print queues, print-to-file, and Internet printing. This chapter will also delve into system devices, understanding video, audio, and infrared input devices and discussing Device Manager.

Chapter 6: Understanding File and Print Sharing   This chapter covers file and print sharing, how to configure File System permissions, configure Share Permissions, configure HomeGroup settings, configure print drivers, configure effective permissions, create shares, and create mapped drives.

Chapter 7: Maintaining, Updating, and Protecting Windows 10   This chapter covers using maintenance tools, such as Disk Defragmenter, Disk Cleanup, Task Scheduler, and System Information. You will learn how to configure updates, configure Windows Update options, implement Insider Preview, Current Branch, and Current Branch for Business scenarios as well as manage update history and utilize roll back updates. This chapter also discusses how to optimize drives. You will learn how to also configure antivirus settings, how to set up Windows Defender and the Malicious Software Removal tool. This chapter will also teach you how to configure notifications.

Chapter 8: Understanding Backup and Recovery Methods   This chapter covers backup and recovery methods, such as configuring System Restore, configure a recovery drive, configure recovery boot options, and various Safe Mode options and how to recover files from OneDrive.

Interactive Online Learning Tools

Studying the material in *Windows Operating System Fundamentals* is an important part of self-learning but we provide additional tools to help you prepare.

To start using these tools to jump start your self-study for go to www.wiley.com/go/windowsosfundamentals.

How to Contact the Publisher

If you believe you've found a mistake in this book, please bring it to our attention. At John Wiley & Sons, we understand how important it is to provide our customers with accurate content, but even with our best efforts an error may occur.

In order to submit your possible errata, please email it to our Customer Service Team at wileysupport@wiley.com with the subject line "Possible Book Errata Submission".

Lesson 1

Installing and Upgrading Client Systems

Objective Domain Matrix

Technology Skill	Objective Domain Description	Objective Domain Number
Understanding Windows Systems	Identify Windows operating system editions	2.1
	Understand operating system architecture	2.4
Understanding Installation Types	Understand installation types	2.3
	Identify upgrade paths	2.2

Key Terms

AppLocker

Assigned Access 8.1

BitLocker

BranchCache

Business Store

clean installation

Client Hyper-V

cloud

command-line interface (CLI)

Continuum

Cortana

Credential Guard

Current Branch for Business

desktop PC

device driver

Device Guard

DirectAccess

Encrypting File System (EFS)

Enterprise Mode Internet Explorer
(EMIE)

graphical user interface (GUI)

Group Policy management

hardware interrupts (IRQ)

High Touch Installation (HTI)

hybrid computer

joining to a domain

kernel mode

laptop

Lite Touch Installation (LTI)

LoadState.exe

Long-Term Servicing Branch

Private catalog

Remote Desktop

RemoteApp

ScanState.exe

smartphone

tablet

text user interface (TUI)

upgrade installation

User Experience control and lockdown

user interface (UI)

user mode

User State Migration Tool (USMT)

UsmtUtils.exe

virtual desktops

Windows 10

Windows 10 Education

Windows 10 Enterprise

Windows 10 Home

Windows 10 Media Creation tool

Windows 10 Pro

Windows Deployment Services

Windows Hello

Windows Spotlight

Windows To Go

Windows Update

Windows Update for Business

x64

x86

Zero Touch Installation (ZTI)

Real World Scenario

Lesson 1 Case

You work as an IT technician for Interstate Snacks, Inc., a mid-market food service and vending company. Management has decided to standardize on Windows 10 Pro and has asked your IT group to evaluate all existing computers to determine if they can support the operating system. Any newly acquired computers should have Windows 10 Pro installed. You need to learn as much as possible about Windows 10 system requirements, types of installations, and upgrade paths.

Understanding Windows Systems

The client version of Windows is the version that is purchased and installed on personal computers such as desktop computers, laptops, workstations, and tablets. Windows Server operating systems are purchased and installed on stand-alone physical servers, blade servers, and virtual machines.

Windows XP merged the consumer-oriented Windows 9x series with Windows NT/2000, while introducing a redesigned user interface that included the Start menu, Internet Explorer 6, and Remote Assistance functionality. As a result, Windows XP became one of the most popular client operating systems in history.

Microsoft attempted to replace Windows XP with Windows Vista, which had an updated graphical user interface and improved security. Unfortunately, Windows Vista was not well received, and it failed to overtake Windows XP. To overcome the shortcomings of Windows Vista, Microsoft released Windows 7, which offered increased performance, a more intuitive interface, and fewer User Account Control pop-ups. Windows 7 included some terrific new features as well, such as large and animated task thumbnails, HomeGroups, Jump Lists, libraries, and Windows XP Mode.

The next version of Windows introduced was Windows 8, which was upgraded to support desktop computers, mobile computers, and tablets, while optimized for touch screens. Windows 8 replaced the Start button and menu with the Start screen, a new platform for developing apps, and the Windows Store. Unfortunately, the new interface made it confusing and difficult to learn. To address some of these concerns, Microsoft released Windows 8.1, which improved the Start screen.

There are some common threads throughout all editions of Windows. For example, every edition contains the same integrated applications, such as Network and Sharing Center, Control Panel, and Windows Media Player. The different editions also include many of the same multimedia features. All Windows editions support 32-bit systems, and all editions except Windows 7 Starter support 64-bit systems.

Windows 10 is the newest client operating system. After the failure of Windows 8, Microsoft listened to customer complaints to develop Windows 10. To distance the new version of Windows from Windows 8/8.1, Microsoft skipped Windows 9 and went to Windows 10. Unlike previous versions of Windows, Windows 10 is released as an "operating system as a service," which means that it will receive ongoing updates to its features and functionality.

As client operating systems are developed and released, Microsoft also develops and releases server operating systems, as shown in Table 1.1. Until Windows 10, the client operating system and server operating system were introduced together. While both client and server operating systems can provide and request services, server operating systems can provide additional services and can service many more clients simultaneously.

TABLE 1.1   Client and Server Operating Systems

Client Operating Systems	Server Operating Systems	Version Number
Windows 10	Windows Server 2016	10.0
Windows 8.1	Windows Server 2012 R2	6.3
Windows 8	Windows Server 2012	6.2
Windows 7	Windows Server 2008 R2	6.1
Windows Vista	Windows Server 2008	6.0
Windows XP	Windows Server 2003/Windows Server 2003 R2	5.1/5.2
Windows 2000 Professional	Windows 2000 Server	5.0
Windows NT 4.0 Workstation	Windows NT 4.0 Server	4.0

Understanding User Interfaces

A *user interface (UI)* is the part of the operating system, program, or device that users use to input and receive data, and to tell the computer what to do. For example, to play a video, navigate to the folder where the video file is located, and double-click the file. Windows typically identifies the program, opens a video player, and plays the file.

User interfaces are organized into two types:

- *Graphical user interface (GUI)*: Performs functions by clicking and moving buttons, icons, and menus with a pointing device, such as a mouse or track pad.
- *Text user interface (TUI)/command-line interface (CLI)*: Performs functions by using a keyboard to type commands.

Most operating systems have a GUI, as do Windows 10 and Windows Server 2016. These operating systems include a Start menu with program groups, a taskbar showing the programs currently in use, a desktop, and various icons and quick-launch icons.

Early operating systems, such as UNIX and Microsoft DOS, were text user interface operating systems, in which you would type commands to perform tasks. However, even GUI operating systems include a text user interface that you can access to perform functions that may or may not also be available with the GUI. For example, when using Windows 10, you can use the command prompt (which allows you to type commands similar to Microsoft DOS) or Windows PowerShell. Use the command prompt or Windows PowerShell to create scripts, which can be used for repetitive tasks or for automation.

Determining Appropriate Editions Per Device Type

Like previous client version operating systems, Windows 10 offers multiple editions. The barest version is Windows 10 Home, which has the fewest number of features. Windows 10 Pro includes more features, and Windows 10 Enterprise and Windows 10 Education have the most features. Of course, Windows 10 Home is the least expensive edition, whereas Windows 10 Enterprise is the most expensive edition.

Before installing Windows, you should do a little bit of planning and ask the following questions:

1. What will the computer be used for?
2. What type of environment will the computer run in?
3. Does the computer need to be portable?

Determining what the computer will be used for will help you determine what hardware you need. For example, for a computer-aided design (CAD) system, you need a fast processor, lots of memory, and a fast video card. In addition, a CAD system would greatly benefit from a solid-state drive.

Examining the computer's environment will help you determine if you need special equipment to keep the computer clean. If the computer is in a dusty environment, dust will accumulate, which can cause systems to overheat.

Today, being mobile brings its own challenges. You want a system that can give you long battery life as well as sufficient power to perform the necessary tasks. In addition, your requirements will help determine what portable hardware you might need. For example, does the system need external or high-quality loud speakers, or do you need to work with a large screen? In some situations, you might only need a smaller computer (such as a small laptop or notepad) that enables you to check emails, take notes, write reports, and construct spreadsheets.

Now that you understand how the computer will be used, you can determine its form factor, which specifies the size, configuration, and physical arrangement of a computing device. Common form factors include:

- *Desktop PC* A desktop PC is the traditional PC that comes in a box and either lies down (desktop) or stands upright (tower). Desktops can be inexpensive systems that handle basic office tasks, or they can be very expensive systems that provide maximum performance for uses such as CAD or video editing. Because desktop PCs tend to be large, they are not very portable.

- *Laptop* A laptop is a portable computer that provides mobility for traveling users or users who might work from home. Although laptops tend not to be as powerful as desktop PCs, today's laptops can provide superior performance. Laptops can be enhanced with docking stations, external keyboards, mice, and monitors. Recently, laptop sales have surpassed desktop PC sales.

- *Tablet* A tablet is a smaller version of the laptop, with a screen that makes up the body of the computer. Tablets can be used for reading emails, doing presentations, creating reports, taking notes, and so forth.

- *Hybrid Computer* A hybrid computer is a laptop that can convert to a tablet. These devices typically offer better performance than tablets and include a keyboard for faster typing.

- *Smartphone* A smartphone is a small device with a screen that can be used to read email, keep track of tasks, access calendar information, manage address books, and run a wide range of applications.

Another device worth mentioning is a gaming console, such as Xbox. Although this system is designed to run games, it might also have additional applications and features.

Windows 10 has multiple editions and versions. The desktop editions of Windows 10 include:

- *Windows 10 Home* The Home edition is designed for consumer-based personal computers and tablets.

- *Windows 10 Mobile* Windows 10 Mobile is designed to deliver user experience on smaller, mobile, touch-centric devices like smartphones and tablets. It offers the same Windows apps that are included in Windows 10 Home, as well as a version of Office.

- *Windows 10 Pro* The Pro edition is designed for personal computers and tablets for small and medium-sized businesses, and for advanced users. It is similar to Windows 10 Home, but has extra features to meet the needs of small businesses. It includes BitLocker Drive Encryption, Encrypting File System (EFS), domain join, and Group Policy Management.

- *Windows 10 Enterprise* The Enterprise edition is designed for personal computers and tablets for large enterprises. It builds on Windows 10 Pro by adding advanced features designed to meet the demands of medium- and large-sized organizations. It includes AppLocker, BranchCache, and DirectAccess. Windows 10 Enterprise is only available to Volume Licensing customers.

- *Windows 10 Education*   The Education edition is designed for personal computers and tablets aimed at schools (including staff, administrators, teachers, and students). Windows 10 Education has the same features as Windows 10 Enterprise. Windows 10 Education is only available through academic Volume Licensing.

- *Windows 10 Mobile Enterprise*   Windows 10 Mobile Enterprise is designed to deliver an outstanding experience to business customers using smartphones and tablets. It is available to Volume Licensing customers.

Some of the features that are available in Windows 10 include:

- *AppLocker*   A feature that allows you to specify which groups or users can run, or not run, a particular application in your organization

- *Assigned Access 8.1*   A setting that lets you restrict a specific standard account to using only one Windows Store app, for use as a kiosk station

- *BitLocker*   A feature that encrypts a volume to protect a system from being accessed if the system is lost or stolen

- *BranchCache*   A wide area network bandwidth optimization technology that allows the local caching of shared folders and websites so that you don't always have to access data over a slower WAN link

- *Business Store*   A feature that allows administrators to find, acquire, manage, and distribute apps to Windows 10 devices

- *Client Hyper-V*   Virtualization technology that allows you to run virtual machines so that you can run older applications on older operating systems or run a different operating system on the same machine as Windows 10

- *Continuum*   A feature that allows you to turn your phone into a big-screen projector or attach a keyboard or mouse to your phone

- *Cortana*   A voice-activated personal assistant

- *Credential Guard*   A feature that stores credentials, such as NTLM hashes and Kerberos tickets, and provides them to the necessary applications; the credentials are stored in a secured isolated container, which uses Hyper-V and virtualization-based security (VBS).

- *Current Branch for Business*   A feature that allows you to delay upgrades (new versions) and updates, so that you can perform pilot testing before deploying updates

- *Device Guard*   A feature that helps protect a system by locking a device so that it can only run trusted applications

- *DirectAccess*   An advanced VPN technology that allows remote users to securely access internal network file shares while connected to the Internet

- *Encrypting File System (EFS)*   A feature that provides transparent file-level encryption

- *Enterprise Mode Internet Explorer (EMIE)*   A compatibility mode that runs Internet Explorer 11 or higher and lets websites render using a modified browser configuration that's designed to emulate either Windows Internet Explorer 7 or 8, avoiding the common compatibility problems associated with Web Apps written and tested on older versions of Internet Explorer

- *Group Policy Management*   An infrastructure that allows you to centrally manage computer settings and configuration
- *Joining to a Domain*   A feature that allows you to join an Active Directory domain
- *Long-Term Servicing Branch*   An option for organizations that only want to receive features updates every two to three years, so that the current systems can be stable
- *Private Catalog*   A feature that provides a list of applications that users within the organization can download apps from
- *Remote Desktop*   A program or feature that allows you to connect to a remote computer and access the desktop and applications as if you were accessing the machine directly
- *RemoteApp*   A feature that enables you to run a program remotely through Remote Desktop Services, although the application appears to be running on your local machine
- *User Experience Control and Lockdown*   A feature that allows you to customize and lock down the Windows 10 user interface
- *Virtual Desktops*   A feature that allows you to run and switch between multiple desktops
- *Windows Hello*   A credential technology that provides multi-factor authentication, including a personal identification number (PIN) or biometrics (face, iris, or fingerprint)
- *Windows Spotlight*   An option that displays a new image on the lock screen each day
- *Windows To Go*   A feature that allows you to boot and run Windows from USB mass storage devices such as USB flash drives and external hard disk drives
- *Windows Update for Business*   A free service for Windows 10 Pro, Enterprise, and Education editions that can provide updates to your users based on distribution rings

Table 1.2 shows some of the common features available for the various editions of Windows 10.

TABLE 1.2   Features Based on Windows 10 Editions

Feature	Windows 10 Home	Windows 10 Pro	Windows 10 Enterprise	Windows 10 Education
AppLocker	No	No	Yes	Yes
Assigned Access 8.1	No	Yes	Yes	Yes
BitLocker	No	Yes	Yes	Yes
BranchCache	No	No	Yes	Yes
Business Store	No	Yes	Yes	Yes

Feature	Windows 10 Home	Windows 10 Pro	Windows 10 Enterprise	Windows 10 Education
Client Hyper-V	No	64-bit SKUs only	64-bit SKUs only	64-bit SKUs only
Continuum	Yes	Yes	Yes	Yes
Cortana*	Yes	Yes	Yes	Yes
Credential Guard	No	No	Yes	Yes
Current Branch for Business	No	Yes	Yes	Yes
Device Guard	No	No	Yes	Yes
DirectAccess	No	No	Yes	Yes
Encrypting File System (EFS)	No	Yes	Yes	Yes
Enterprise Mode Internet Explorer (EMIE)	No	Yes	Yes	Yes
Group Policy management	No	Yes	Yes	Yes
Joining to a domain	No	Yes	Yes	Yes
Long-Term Servicing Branch	No	No	Yes	No
Private catalog	No	Yes	Yes	Yes
Remote Desktop	Client only	Client and host	Client and host	Client and host
RemoteApp	Client only	Client only	Client and host	Client and host
User Experience control and lockdown	No	No	Yes	Yes
Virtual desktops	Yes	Yes	Yes	Yes
Windows Hello	Yes	Yes	Yes	Yes
Windows Spotlight	Yes	Yes	Yes	Yes
Windows To Go	No	No	Yes	Yes
Windows Update for Business	No	Yes	Yes	Yes

*Cortana is currently available in Windows 10 only for the United States, United Kingdom, China, France, Italy, Germany, and Spain.

Understanding Processor and Memory Architecture

The processor of a Windows computer runs in two different modes: kernel mode and user mode. The *kernel mode* has complete and unrestricted access to the underlying hardware, while the *user mode* does not have direct access to the hardware or reference memory.

Certification Ready

What is the advantage of having programs run in user mode instead of kernel mode?
Objective 2.4

Kernel mode is generally reserved for the most trusted part of the operating system. Code that crashes in kernel mode will cause catastrophic errors such as the dreaded Stop error or "blue screen of death."

Most programs that you install and use on a daily basis are stored in user mode. When programs run in user mode, they are isolated from other programs. Therefore, when a program crashes, it usually only affects the individual program.

Windows 10 supports two platforms:

- IA-32—Designed to run on systems with the 32-bit x86 processors. IA-32 can only access up to 4 GB of memory.

- X86-64—Designed to run on the x86-64 processors. Windows 10 can support up to 128 GB of memory, while the other desktop editions can support up to 2048 GB of memory.

Windows runs on a desktop computer that has an Intel or Intel-compatible processor based on the *x86* (32-bit) or *x64* (64-bit) architecture.

32-bit and 64-bit refer to the CPU, or processor. Computer processors are typically rated by speed. The speed of the processor is rated by the number of clock cycles that can be performed in 1 second. This is usually conveyed in gigahertz (GHz). One GHz is one billion cycles per second.

The 32-bit and 64-bit architectures determine how data is processed and how much memory can be accessed. A 64-bit architecture can process larger numbers or larger chunks of data, allowing for faster processing. In addition, a 32-bit processor can access up to 4 GB of memory, while a 64-bit processor can theoretically access up to 16 exabytes (16 billion gigabytes) of memory, although you will most likely be limited by the motherboard and software. The 32-bit versions of Windows 10 support up to 4 GB of memory. The 64-bit version of Windows 10 Home supports up to 128 GB of memory and the 64-bit versions of Windows 10 Pro and Windows 10 Enterprise editions support up to 512 GB.

To install a 32-bit version of Windows, you can use an x86 or x64 processor. To install a 64-bit version of Windows, you can use only a 64-bit processor. Software written for a 64-bit architecture does not work on a 32-bit architecture. Most programs designed for 32-bit versions of Windows will work on a 64-bit version of Windows by using Windows on Windows 64 (WoW64). However, some 32-bit system software, such as an antivirus program, does not operate on a 64-bit architecture. In addition, 64-bit hardware requires 64-bit drivers. Drivers designed for 32-bit versions of Windows do not run on 64-bit versions of Windows, and drivers designed for 64-bit versions of Windows do not run on 32-bit versions of Windows. If you transition from a 32-bit version architecture to a 64-bit architecture, you may not find 64-bit drivers for all your devices, particularly for older devices.

If you want to use 64-bit Windows, keep the following in mind:

- 16-bit applications (applications generally written for Windows 9x) or 32-bit kernel drivers will fail to start or function properly on a 64-bit edition of Windows 10.
- Installation of 32-bit kernel drivers will fail on the 64-bit system.
- Installation of 64-bit unsigned drivers will fail by default on the 64-bit system.

Finally, many computers today have multi-core processors. A 32-bit version of Windows 10 supports up to 32 processor cores; a 64-bit version of Windows 10 supports up to 256 processor cores.

Determine Whether Your PC Is Running 32-Bit Windows or 64-Bit Windows

To find out if your computer is running a 32-bit version of Windows 10 or a 64-bit version of Windows 10, perform the following steps:

1. Right-click Start and choose System. The System window opens.
2. Look in the System area to view the system type (see Figure 1.1).

FIGURE 1.1   Viewing system information

An alternative method is to check the System Information window. To do so, perform the following steps:

1. Click Start, type system info in the Search programs and files search box, and then click System Information in the resulting list.

2. Make sure System Summary is selected in the Navigation pane on the left.

3. Look at the System Type value in the right pane (see Figure 1.2):

   ▪ "x86-based PC" displays for a 32-bit operating system.

   ▪ "x64-based PC" displays for a 64-bit operating system.

FIGURE 1.2   Viewing the System Type value in the System Information window

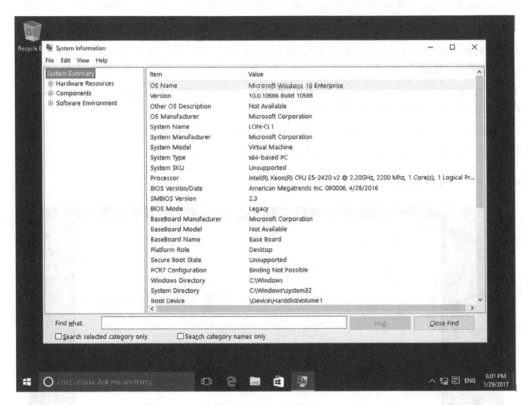

Understanding Drivers

A computer is a collection of hardware devices, each of which requires a piece of software called a device driver in order to function. Windows 10 includes a large library of device drivers, but it is still sometimes necessary to obtain them yourself.

Certification Ready

How does a device get the attention of the processor? Objective 2.4

Certification Ready

Which software component allows a hardware component to interface with the operating system? Objective 2.4

As most people know, a PC is a collection of hardware devices, all of which are connected together and installed in a single case. Disk drives, keyboards, mice, modems, and printers are all types of devices. To communicate with the operating system running on the computer, each device also requires a software element called a *device driver.* The device driver provides the operating system with information about a specific device.

For example, when you use a word-processing application to save a file to a hard disk, the application issues a generic WriteFile function call to the operating system. The application knows nothing specific about the disk drive hardware; it just issues an instruction to store a particular file there. When the operating system processes the function call, it accesses the device driver for the hard disk drive, which provides detailed information about how to communicate with the drive. If the user selects a different target location for the file, the operating system accesses the device driver for that location, whether it's a hard drive, a floppy drive, or a USB flash drive.

Device drivers run in the kernel mode or in user mode. A driver that runs in user mode provides for a more stable system, because poorly written user mode device drivers cannot crash the entire system. However, drivers that run in user mode are slower than drivers that run in kernel mode.

A driver communicates with the device through the computer bus or communications subsystem. *Hardware interrupts (IRQ)* are used by devices that require attention from the operating system. For example, every time you press a key on a keyboard or move the mouse, you trigger a hardware interrupt that causes the processor to read and process the keystroke or mouse position. So, basically, a hardware interrupt is used by devices to communicate that they need attention from the operating system. Interrupts are also used for asynchronous events, such as the arrival of data from an external network. Hardware interrupts are delivered straight to the CPU by using a small network of interrupt management and routing devices.

Understanding Windows 10 System Requirements

Software manufacturers, including Microsoft, list the system requirements needed to run their products. The specifications are usually minimum requirements; recommended requirements—which allow for much better performance of the OS and applications—are often much higher (in the case of memory, processor speed, or hard disk space) or involve more recent technology.

Certification Ready

What is the minimum amount of RAM a computer must have in order to run Windows 10 on a 32-bit processor? Objective 2.1

The system requirements for Windows 10 include the following:

- Processor: 1 GHz or faster processor
- RAM: 1 GB for 32-bit or 2 GB for 64-bit
- Hard disk space: 32 GB or larger hard disk
- Graphics card: DirectX 9 or later with WDDM 1.0 driver
- Display: 800 × 600
- Internet connection: Internet connectivity is necessary to perform updates and to download and take advantage of some features.

Regarding the hard disk space needed for Windows 10, the size of the Windows operating system that comes with a device and the amount of space needed to download and install Windows updates are variable, as they depend on a wide variety of factors. The factors include:

- The versions of Windows that were previously installed on the machine
- The amount of disk space available to reuse from Windows files, such as the virtual memory pagefile or hibernation file
- What applications are installed on the device and how those applications store data

Starting with the May 2019 Update, the system requirements for hard drive size for clean installs of Windows 10 as well as new PCs changed to a minimum of 32 GB. The 32 GB or larger drive requirement is to allow for users to install apps and to keep data on the device.

Installing Windows or updating from a previous version of Windows on devices with less than 32 GB storage will still work, but only if the device has enough free space available. Windows will attempt to automatically free up enough hard drive space and walk the user through the process of freeing up more space if the automatic cleanup is not sufficient during an update.

A *clean installation* of Windows is when you install Windows where there are no operating system, data, or programs stored on the hard drive, or you perform the installation of Windows while reformatting the current hard drive, so that you are installing Windows on an empty hard drive. An *upgrade installation* of Windows is when you have a system that is running Windows 7 or Windows 8/8.1, and you run the Windows installation program, replacing the Windows 7 or Windows 8/8.1 operating system with Windows 10.

The minimum hardware specifications usually mean the software will run, but might not result in an optimal user experience. When preparing to run Windows 10, it's best to exceed the processor, RAM, and hard disk space requirements, if possible. For example, a user who wants to simultaneously run a web browser, an email client, and productivity software (such as a word processor and a spreadsheet application) will have a good user experience on a computer with a 2 GHz dual-core processor, 4 GB of RAM, and at least a 250 GB hard drive. A user who needs to run memory-intensive graphic programs along with other applications will find the computer highly responsive with at least 8 GB of RAM and 500 GB or more of hard disk space. Computers that don't have access to shared storage space on a network may also need secondary storage, such as an external flash hard drive. This is especially important if the user has a large number of image, video, or audio files, which tend to consume much more disk space than ordinary document files require.

In addition, Microsoft lists the following items as required for using specific features or for optimal performance:

- BitLocker Drive Encryption (available with Windows 10 Pro or Windows 10 Enterprise only)—requires a Trusted Platform Module (TPM) 1.2 or higher and Trusted Computing Group (TCG)-compliant BIOS or UEFI. BitLocker can be used on devices without TPM, but you will need to save a startup key on a removable device such as a USB flash drive. TPM 2.0 and InstantGo support are required when you want to automatically encrypt the local drive when joining a device to Azure Active Directory (AAD). Check with your PC manufacturer to confirm if your device supports the correct TPM version and InstantGo for the scenario you want to enable.

- BitLocker To Go—requires a USB flash drive (available in Windows 10 Pro and Windows 10 Enterprise only)

- Client Hyper-V—requires a 64-bit system with second level address translation (SLAT) capabilities and an additional 2 GB of RAM (available in Windows 10 Pro and Windows 10 Enterprise only)

- Cortana—is only currently available on Windows 10 for the United States, United Kingdom, China, France, Italy, Germany, Brazil, Mexico, Japan, Canada, Spain, Australia and India.

- A Microsoft account—is required for some features.

- Miracast—requires a display adapter which supports Windows Display Driver Model (WDDM) 1.3 and a Wi-Fi adapter that supports Wi-Fi Direct.

- Movies & TV application—is not available in all regions.

- Secure boot—requires firmware that supports UEFI v2.3.1 Errata B and has the Microsoft Windows Certification Authority in the UEFI signature database.

- Skype—is available only in select countries and regions. Calling to select countries and regions only.

- Snap—the number of applications that can be snapped will depend upon the minimum resolution for the application with a limit of two applications in Tablet mode and four applications in Desktop mode.

- Speech recognition—will vary by device microphone. For a better experience will need a high fidelity microphone array and a hardware driver with microphone array geometry exposed.

- Tablet mode—is available on tablets and 2-in-1s with GPIO indicators, or those who have a laptop and slate indicator will be able to be configured to enter "tablet mode" automatically.

- Touch—To use touch, you need a tablet or a monitor that supports multi-touch.

- Two-factor authentication—requires the use of a PIN, biometric (fingerprint reader or illuminated infrared camera), or a phone with Wi-Fi or Bluetooth capabilities.

- Windows Hello—requires a camera configured for near infrared (IR) imaging or fingerprint reader for biometric authentication. Devices without biometric sensors can use Windows Hello with a PIN or a portable Microsoft compatible security key.

- Xbox application—requires an Xbox Live account, which is not available in all regions.

- Wi-Fi Direct Printing—requires a Wi-Fi adapter that supports Wi-Fi Direct and a device that supports Wi-Fi Direct Printing.

Feature Deprecations and Removals

When upgrading to Windows 10 from a previous version of Windows, such as Windows 7 or Windows 8.1, or when installing a newer update to Windows 10, some features have been deprecated or removed. These include:

Desktop Messaging App   The messaging app on Desktop has a sync feature that can be used to sync SMS text messages received from Windows Mobile and keep a copy of them on the Desktop. Starting with the May 2019 Update (Windows 10, version 1903), the sync feature has been removed from all devices. Due to this change, you will only be able to access messages from the device that received the message.

Wi-Fi WEP and TKIP   Starting with the May 2019 Update (Windows 10, version 1903), a warning message will appear when connecting to Wi-Fi networks secured with WEP or TKIP, which are not as secure as those using WPA2 or WPA3. In a future release, any connection to a Wi-Fi network using these old ciphers will be disallowed. Wi-Fi routers should be updated to use AES ciphers, available with WPA2 or WPA3.

Windows To Go   This feature is no longer being developed. It does not support feature updates and requires a specific type of USB that is no longer supported by many device manufacturers.

Phone Companion   As of the October 2018 Update (Windows 10, version 1809), Phone Companion is removed from your PC. Use the Phone page in the Settings app to sync your mobile phone with your PC. It includes all the Phone Companion features.

HomeGroup   HomeGroup was removed starting with the April 2018 Update (Windows 10, version 1803), but you still have the ability to share printers, files, and folders. When you update from an earlier version of Windows 10, you won't see HomeGroup in File Explorer, the Control Panel, or Troubleshoot (Settings ➤ Update & Security ➤ Troubleshoot). Any printers, files, and folders you shared using HomeGroup will continue to be shared. Instead of using HomeGroup, you can now share printers, files, and folders by using features that are built into Windows 10:

- Share your network printers
- Share files in File Explorer
- For Xbox 360 and HomeGroup users

People App   In Windows 10, the People app shows mail from Office 365 contacts and contacts from your school or work organization under Conversations. Starting with the April 2018 Update (Windows 10, version 1803), in order to see new mail in the People app from these specific contacts, you need to be online, and you need to have signed in with either an Office 365 account or, for work or school organization accounts, through the Mail, People, or Calendar apps. Please be aware that you'll only see mail for work and school organization accounts and some Office 365 accounts.

Reader App   The Reader app was removed from Windows 10 starting with the Fall Creators Update (Windows 10, version 1709). For reading PDF files, Microsoft Edge is the recommended replacement app and offers similar functionality as well as additional features, including improved accessibility support, improved Inking, and support for AskCortana. Similarly, Windows XPS Viewer is recommended when reading XPS files and the Windows Photos app for viewing TIFF files. Note that users of earlier Windows 10 versions can continue using the Reader app.

Windows Journal   Windows Journal was removed starting with the Windows 10 Anniversary Update (Windows 10, version 1607). After Windows Journal is removed, you will no longer be able to open or edit Journal files (with .JNT or .JTP extensions). In place of Windows Journal, we encourage you to switch to OneNote. If you need to open or edit your journal files, more information is available here.

Windows Media Digital Rights Management (WMDRM)   WMDRM is no longer supported starting with the Windows 10 Anniversary Update (Windows 10, version 1607). You are no longer able to play music or video files that were protected by this rights management technology.

For an updated list of Windows 10 specifications, systems requirements, and deprecations/removals, go to https://www.microsoft.com/en-us/windows/windows-10-specifications.

Understanding Installation Types

There are many different types of Windows 10 installations, from the manual DVD method to a fully automated setup effort over a network. Learn the various ways in which you can install Windows 10 and select the most efficient method for your needs.

Microsoft provides many different ways to install Windows 10, from manual methods like inserting a DVD to fully automated, "non-touch" installations performed over a network or even via the cloud. (The *cloud* generally refers to the Internet or to a server accessible over the Internet.) The method you choose depends mainly on the number of computers on which you need to install Windows and how much time you have to devote to the project.

Certification Ready

Perform a network installation. Objective 2.3

Installing Windows 10

Windows 10 can be installed either from the bootable DVD or by using a network installation by using files that have been copied to a network share point or USB device. Can also use the setup.exe file to upgrade the operating system.

To start the installation, just restart the computer and boot to the DVD. The installation process will begin automatically. The installation will guide you through the steps.

If installing Windows 10 from the network, you need a distribution server and a computer that has a network connection. A distribution server is a server that has the Windows 10 distribution files copied to a shared folder. The following steps are used to install Windows 10 over the network:

1. Boot the target computer.
2. Attach to the distribution server and access the share that has the files copied to it.
3. Launch setup.exe.
4. Complete the Windows 10 installation using either the clean install method or the upgrade method.

Installing Windows 10 from removable media is common in smaller enterprise or home environments. When you think of removable media, you might think of DVDs, but many installations are performed from USB drives as well. Using a DVD or USB drive is considered a manual method of installation. If you're installing Windows on one, two, or even ten computers, a manual method works well. If you must install Windows on many computers, you'll want to understand automated methods, in order to save time (and, thus, money).

Certification Ready

What are the types of removable media installations? Objective 2.3

The following are categories that correspond to the level of interaction required during an installation:

- High Touch Installation (HTI)
- Lite Touch Installation (LTI)
- Zero Touch Installation (ZTI)

High Touch Installation (HTI) may include retail media or a standard image (ISO file). Using this method, you use an installation DVD or USB drive and manually install the operating system on every computer. You must then also manually configure each system.

An image file is an exact replica of the contents of a hard disk, saved to a file with an .iso extension or a .wim extension if it's a Windows Imaging Format image.

In a larger environment, where you have, say, 25 or more computers that require Windows 10 installations, you could use a tool called the Windows Assessment and Deployment Kit (ADK) to create bootable media. ADK includes Deployment Image Servicing and Management (DISM), which allow you to modify disk images. You would perform these general steps:

1. Install Windows 10 on a clean hard disk.
2. Configure it with settings that will apply to all computers.
3. Use the Sysprep utility to create an image of the installation.
4. Boot to the Windows Preinstallation Environment (WinPE) and use DISM to save the image to a DVD, a USB drive, or whatever type of media you plan to use.
5. Install the image on the remaining computers.

Lite Touch Installation (LTI) requires some human intervention in the early phase of the installation but is automated (or unattended) from that point on. This installation method works well in environments with more than 150 computers.

You need the Windows ADK, Windows Deployment Services, and the Microsoft Deployment Toolkit for LTIs. *Windows Deployment Services* is a server role for Windows Server 2008 or higher. It allows a user to press the F12 key, log on, and select an image for installation. After that, the installation can be automated. For example, you can use an answer file to configure Windows settings during installation. The answer file contains all the settings that are required for an unattended installation. The Microsoft Deployment Toolkit is a free download used to automate high-volume operating system deployments.

Zero Touch Installation (ZTI) is a fully automated, "touchless" method of installing Windows. You need System Center Configuration Manager (SCCM) for ZTIs. You use SCCM to deploy and update servers, client computers, and all kinds of devices on a network.

The ZTI method is geared for environments with more than 500 computers, involves a fairly steep learning curve, and requires a considerable budget compared to HTIs.

Performing a Clean Install of Windows 10

The simplest way to perform a clean install (a new installation) of Windows 10 is to boot from a bootable Windows 10 installation disk or USB drive, which will start the setup program. You can also search for and find the *Windows 10 Media Creation tool*, which can be used to create a copy of your Windows 10 ISO file on a USB flash drive or DVD. You can then use the USB flash drive to install Windows 10.

A clean installation of Windows 10 allows you to start as if the machine were new. If you decide to perform a clean installation on a machine that already has Windows 7 or Windows 8/8.1 installed, you will remove any existing corrupted files, problem programs, or erroneous settings. However, if you perform a clean installation, you have to then install all programs, copy over desired data files from a backup, and reconfigure the system.

Install Windows 10 from a Windows 10 Installation DVD

To install Windows 10 from a Windows 10 installation DVD, perform the following steps:

Before you start, you need to make sure that your system can boot from the DVD drive, which may need to be configured using the BIOS Setup program. The BIOS Setup program is usually accessed by pressing the Del key, F10 key, or similar key during boot up.

1. Turn on the computer and insert the Windows 10 installation disc into the DVD drive. Press any key to boot from the DVD (if necessary).

2. The computer switches to the Windows graphical interface and the Windows Setup page appears, as shown in Figure 1.3. Using the drop-down lists, choose the appropriate "Language to install," the "Time and currency format," and the "Keyboard or input method." Click Next.

3. On the Windows 10 Install now page, click Install Now.

4. On the License Terms page, select the "I accept the license terms" check box and click Next.

5. Click the "Custom: Install Windows only (advanced)" option.

6. On the License Terms page, select the "I accept the license terms" check box and click Next.

7. The "Where do you want to install Windows?" page appears, as shown in Figure 1.4. From the list, click the partition on which you want to install Windows 10, or click an area of unallocated disk space where the Setup program can create a new partition. Click Next.

FIGURE 1.3   The Windows Setup page

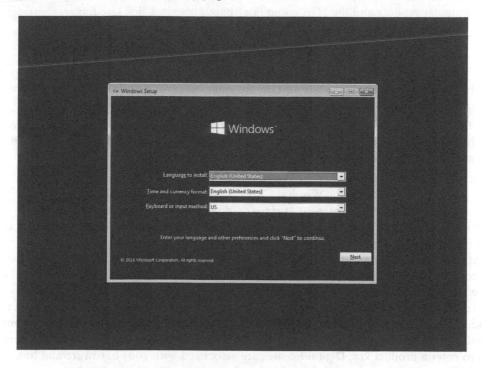

FIGURE 1.4   The "Where do you want to install Windows?" page

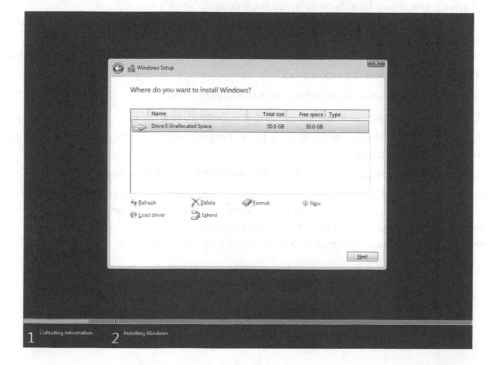

8. After several minutes, during which time the Setup program installs Windows 10, the computer reboots and the "Get going fast" page appears. Click Use Express Settings.

9. On the "Choose how you'll connect" page, click Join A Domain and click Next.

10. On the "Create an account for this PC" page, in the "Who's going to use this PC?" text box, type User1.

11. In the Enter Password text box and the Re-enter Password text box, type **Pa$$w0rd**. In the Password Hint box, type **Default**. Click Next.

12. The Networks pane opens on the right side of the Windows desktop. When you are prompted to confirm that you want to allow your PC to be discoverable by other PCs and devices on the network, click Yes.

At this point, you can remove the installation disc from the drive.

If you need to upgrade from Windows 7 or Windows 8/8.1, you can navigate to https://www.microsoft.com/en-us/software-download/windows10 and click the Download Tool Now button. You would then launch the Download Tool to create installation media or to upgrade a PC with the older operating system.

After you install Windows, you should activate Windows 10. Activation helps verify that the copy of Windows is genuine, and that it is not in use on more devices than the number for which you own licenses.

Depending on how you got your copy of Windows 10, you'll need either a 25-character product key or a digital license to activate it. A digital license (called a digital entitlement in Windows 10, Version 1511) is a method of activation in Windows 10 that doesn't require you to enter a product key. Digital licenses are associated with your hardware and linked to your Microsoft account, so there's nothing to find on your PC. You're all set once your PC is connected to the Internet and you log in to your Microsoft account. However, without one of these, you won't be able to activate your device.

If you have a retail, OEM, or some volume license keys, you will need to type a valid 25-character product key.

A Windows 10 product key looks similar to:

xxxxx-xxxxx-xxxxx-xxxxx-xxxxx

but is composed of letters and numbers. It is usually located:

▪ On the installation disc holder inside the Windows package

▪ On a sticker on the back or bottom of your computer if the operating system came pre-installed on the computer

▪ In a confirmation email if you purchased and downloaded Windows 10 online

During installation, you must enter the product key exactly as printed. (If you are off by even one character, the installation fails.) After you enter the product key correctly, the product key is then written to the Windows registry in an encrypted format, making it unreadable (for security purposes). Therefore, it's important to keep your Windows 10 installation media and printed product key in a safe location after initial installation, in case you need to reinstall or repair the operating system at some point.

Activate Windows 10 Using a Product Key

To activate Windows 10, perform the following steps:

1. Click Start ➢ Settings.
2. In the Settings window, click Update & Security ➢ Activation. In the Activate Windows section, click the Activate button.

    Alternatively, you can open System Properties by right-clicking Start and choosing Control Panel, then clicking System and Security ➢ System. In the System window, click Activate Windows.
3. Click Change Product Key.
4. In the Enter A Product Key window, in the Product Key text box, type the 25-character product key. The system will automatically activate over the Internet.

Upgrading to Windows 10

If you need to upgrade from Windows 7 or Windows 8/8.1 to Windows 10, you can use a Windows 10 bootable DVD or bootable USB drive. You can also upgrade Windows 10 by using the Windows 10 Media Creation tool.

Certification Ready

Which type of upgrade path is necessary to upgrade from Windows 7 or 8/8.1 to Windows 10? Objective 2.2

Before you upgrade to Windows 10, you need to ensure that your software will run on Windows 10. To help check application compatibility, you can visit the Windows Dev Center site (https://developer.microsoft.com/en-us/windows/ready-for-windows#/), and search for the desired software.

An upgrade to Windows 10 is a time-saving feature that will allow you to keep your programs, files, and settings. After the upgrade, you will be able to use the same programs and access your data. However, if you have corrupt non-Windows files, problematic programs, or erroneous settings, you may still experience those problems after the upgrade. Sometimes, the upgrade does not go smoothly (usually caused by incompatible programs or device drivers), and it could make your system unusable. If you are using a legacy device, the device may not run under Windows 10. Of course, before you perform an upgrade, you should always make sure you have a current backup in case you need to roll back device drivers or recover lost programs and data.

You can upgrade from Windows 7 or Windows 8/8.1 to like versions of Windows 10. For example:

- If you have Windows 7 Starter, Windows 7 Home Basic, Windows 7 Home Premium, Windows 8, or Windows 8.1, you can upgrade to Windows 10 Home.

- If you have Windows 7 Pro, Windows 7 Ultimate, Windows 8.1 Pro, or Windows 8.1 Pro for Student, you can upgrade to Windows 10 Pro.

- If you have Windows 7 Enterprise or Windows 8/8.1 Enterprise, you can upgrade to Windows 10 Enterprise.

If you want to migrate to a different edition (such as from Windows 8.1 Pro to Windows 8.1 Enterprise), you will have to perform a clean installation.

In addition, you can only upgrade from a 32-bit version of Windows 7 or Windows 8/8.1 to a 32-bit version of Windows 10; or from a 64-bit version of Windows 7 or Windows 8/8.1 to a 64-bit version of Windows 10. If you want to have a 64-bit version, and you want to upgrade to a newer 32-bit version, or from a 32-bit version to a newer 64-bit version, you will have to perform a clean installation.

Before you perform any upgrade, you should always make sure that you have a current backup of all programs, settings, and data files. You should also make sure that the backup is stored away from the machine you are trying to upgrade.

Upgrade to Windows 10 from a Windows 10 Installation DVD

To upgrade from Windows 7 or Windows 8/8.1 to Windows 10 using a Windows 10 installation DVD, perform the following steps:

1. Turn on the computer and log on to the computer that is running Windows 7 or Windows 8/8.1.

2. Insert the Windows 10 installation disc into the DVD drive.

3. Click Start ≻ Computer. The Computer window opens.

4. Double-click the DVD/Blu-Ray drive.

5. In the Windows 10 Setup program, on the Get Important Updates page, keep the "Download and install updates (recommended)" option selected, and click Next.

6. On the License Terms page, click Accept. The Windows 10 Setup program will download any available updates.

7. On the Ready To Install page, click "Choose what to keep."

8. On the Choose What To Keep page (as shown in Figure 1.5), click one of the following options and click Next:
   - Keep personal files, apps, and Windows settings
   - Keep personal files only
   - Nothing

FIGURE 1.5   Specifying what to keep during a Windows 10 upgrade

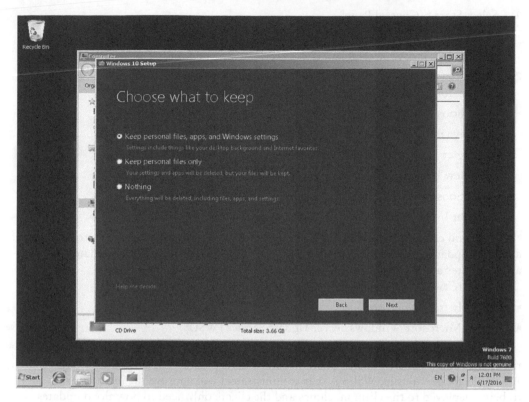

9. On the Ready to install page, click Install.

    After a few minutes, Windows will reboot and complete the upgrade.

    When Windows 10 was initially released, Microsoft offered a free upgrade from Windows 7 or Windows 8/8.1 to Windows 10 for the first year. These free upgrades are done over the Internet with Windows Update. In addition, because Windows 10 is released as an "operating system as a service," Windows 10 machines will receive ongoing updates to its features and functionality.

Using Windows Update

Windows Update is a utility that connects to the Microsoft website and checks if a machine has the most up-to-date versions of Microsoft products. Some of the common update categories include:

- Critical updates
- Drivers
- Service packs

Use the following steps to configure Windows Update:

1. Select Start ➤ Control Panel.

   - From Windows Icons View, select Windows Update.

   - From Windows Category View, select System And Security ➤ Windows Update.

2. Configure the options you want to use by clicking the Advanced Options link. The options for Windows Update include:

   - Choose how updates are installed

   - Give me updates for other Microsoft products

   - Defer Upgrades

   - View Update History

   - Choose how updates are delivered

   - Get Insider Builds

When you click on the Check For Updates button, Windows Update will retrieve a list of available updates. You can then click View Available Updates to see what updates are available. Updates are marked as Important, Recommended, or Optional.

There are two ways a user can receive updates:

- Directly from Microsoft

- Using Microsoft Windows Server Update Service (WSUS)

WSUS runs on a Windows server and goes out to the Microsoft website and downloads the updates for you. This allows client machines to receive their updates from a local server. A few advantage to using WSUS is that administrators can approve the updates prior to being deployed to the client machines and the clients only need to download updates locally, without using the Internet bandwidth.

Migrating to Windows 10 from Previous Versions of Windows

Sometimes, you might want to move a user from one system to another, including moving a user from a computer running Windows 7 or Windows 8/8.1 to a computer running Windows 10. One of the most time-consuming tasks you will perform as an administrator is to move user files and settings between computers and operating systems. The User State Migration Tool (USMT) eases this burden. The USMT 10 tool is part of the Windows Assessment and Deployment Kit for Windows 10.

Certification Ready

How can you migrate from previous versions of Windows? Objective 2.2

The *User State Migration Tool (USMT)* is a command-line tool that migrates user data from a previous installation of Windows to a new installation of Windows. It provides you with the ability to customize the user-profile migration experience. This means you can copy selected user data and exclude any data that you do not want to migrate. USMT captures user accounts, user files, operating system settings, and application settings to migrate to your new Windows installation.

The USMT includes three command-line tools:

- *ScanState.exe* scans the source computer, collects the files and settings, and creates a store that contains the user's files and settings.

- *LoadState.exe* loads the files and settings onto the destination computer.

- *UsmtUtils.exe* deletes hardlink folders in use by applications no longer removable through normal measures, checks the store file's consistency, and restores selected files. A hardlink folder provides a way for the New Technology File System (NTFS) to point to the same file from multiple locations on the same volume. The store file contains the user state migration data. UsmtUtils can be used to check for corrupted files or a corrupted catalog in the store file.

The ScanState.exe and LoadState.exe programs use a similar syntax, in which you specify the location of the migration store, the scripts you want to use to specify what to migrate, which user accounts you want to migrate, and how the program should store the data.

Table 1.3 lists some of the most common command-line options for ScanState and LoadState and their functions.

TABLE 1.3   SMT Command-Line Options

Command-Line Option	ScanState or LoadState	Description
StorePath	Both	Specifies the location where the program should create or from which it should read the migration store
/o	ScanState	Overwrites any existing data in the migration store
/vsc	ScanState	Uses the Volume Shadow Copy Service to migrate files that are locked open, eliminating some errors
/hardlink	ScanState	Creates a hardlink migration store at the location specified in the StorePath variable
/encrypt:*algorithm*	ScanState	Creates an encrypted migration store, using the specified algorithm
/decrypt	LoadState	Decrypts the migration store as it restores the user state

TABLE 1.3 SMT Command-Line Options *(continued)*

Command-Line Option	ScanState or LoadState	Description
/key:*keystring*	Both	Uses the key specified by the *keystring* variable to encrypt or decrypt the migration store
/keyfile:*filename*	Both	Uses the key specified in the file identified by the filename variable to encrypt or decrypt the migration store
/nocompress	ScanState	Disables the default data compression used when creating a migration store
/i:*filename*	Both	Specifies the name of an XML file that the program should use to determine what to migrate
/genconfig:*filename*	ScanState	Creates a Config.xml file containing all of the migratable data on the computer, but does not create the migration store
/config:*filename*	Both	Specifies the Config.xml file the program should use when creating or reading the migration store
/localonly	ScanState	Creates a migration store containing only the files on local, fixed drives
/c	Both	Causes the program to continue running, even if nonfatal errors occur
/all	Both	Migrates all user accounts on the computer
/ui:*domain\user* /ui:*computer\user*	Both	Migrates a specific user account
/ue:*domain\user* /ue:*computer\user*	Both	Excludes a specific account from migration
/uel:*<numberofdays>* /uel:*<YYYY/MM/DD>* /uel:0	Both	Migrates only the users who have logged on to the computer within a specified number of days or since a specific date or who are currently logged on to the computer

USMT also includes the following modifiable .xml files. Use these files with ScanState and LoadState if you want to perform a targeted migration:

- MigApp.xml includes rules to migrate application settings.
- MigDocs.xml includes rules to migrate user documents from the source computer.
- MigUser.xml includes rules to migrate user profiles and user data.

When you use USMT, you should use the following three-step process:

Step 1: Plan the migration.

- Determine whether to refresh or replace your system, identify what you want to migrate (application settings, operating system settings, files, and/or folders), determine where to store it (remotely, locally in a hardlink migration store, or directly on the destination computer), and determine which files will be included in the migration.
- If necessary, modify the MigApp.xml and MigDocs.xml files or create and modify a config.xml file. In general, it's best to leave the original .xml files in place and create and modify a config.xml file to keep your changes separate from the default .xml files.

Step 2: Collect the files and settings from the source computer.

- Back up the source computer and close all applications before running ScanState; otherwise, USMT might not be able to migrate all the data.
- Run ScanState to collect the files and settings using an account with administrative privileges. Specify all .xml files you want the command to use:

```
ScanState \\server\migration\mystore /config:config.xml /i:migdocs.xml
/:migapp.xml /v:13 /l:scan.log
```

- After the store is completed, run UsmtUtils with the /verify switch to ensure that the store you created was not corrupted. Replace X with the store location and mystore with the actual name of the store:

```
UsmtUtils /verify x:\mystore\store.img
```

Step 3: Prepare the destination computer and restore the files and settings.

- Install the operating system on the destination computer, install any applications that were on the source computer, and then close any open applications.
- Run the LoadState command on the destination computer to migrate the files and settings. Make sure you specify the same .xml files you used when you ran ScanState during the collection process in Step 2:

```
LoadState \\server\migration\mystore /config:config.xml /i:migdocs.xml
/i:migapp.xml /v:13 /l:load.log
```

- After completing the LoadState process, you must log off and then log back on the machine to see if some of the settings changed (for example, the screen saver, the fonts, the wallpaper, and so on).

Create a Custom Config.xml File and Exclude Content from the My Pictures Folder

To create a custom config.xml file and exclude content from the My Pictures folder, log on as an administrator to a computer running Windows 10 Enterprise, and then perform the following steps:

 To complete this exercise, you must have USMT installed on your Windows 10 Enterprise computer.

1. On LON-CL1, press the Windows logo key+r. In the Run dialog box, in the Open text box, type **cmd**. Click OK.
2. From the search results list, right-click Command Prompt and choose Run As Administrator.
3. Change to the directory that contains the USMT tools. In a default installation, this would be found by executing the cd command as shown.

    ▪ For 32-bit machines:

    ```
    cd "c:\Program Files\Windows Kits\10.0\Assessment and Deployment Kit\User
    State Migration Tool\x86"
    ```

    ▪ For 64-bit machines:

    ```
    cd "c:\Program Files (x86)\Windows Kits\10.0\Assessment and Deployment
    Kit\User State Migration Tool\amd64"
    ```

4. To create a config.xml file, execute the following command:

    ```
    scanstate /i:migapp.xml /i:miguser.xml /genconfig:config.xml /v:13
    ```

    Log messages regarding the creation of the file will be sent to the scanstate.log file. Both the log file and the config.xml file will be created in the directory from which you ran the ScanState command.

5. To exclude the My Pictures folder from the migration, change migrate="yes" to **migrate="no"**. (The following code is an excerpt from the config.xml file created in Step 4.)

    ```
    <?xml version="1.0" encoding="UTF-8"?>
    <Configuration>
    <Documents>
    <component displayname="My Pictures" migrate="yes" ID="http://www.microsoft
    .com/migration/1.0/migxmlext/miguser/my pictures/data"/>
    </Documents>
    ```

6. Save the file.

This file can now be used with ScanState to collect information from the source computer and with LoadState to prepare the destination computers.

Skill Summary

In this lesson, you learned:

- Windows 10 is the newest client operating system. Unlike previous versions of Windows, Windows 10 is released as an "operating system as a service," which means that it will receive ongoing updates to its features and functionality.

- Windows 10 supports two platforms: IA-32 and X86-64. IA-32 is designed to run on systems with the 32-bit x86 processors. IA-32 can only access up to 4 GB of memory. X86-64 is designed to run on the x86-64 processors. Windows 10 can support up to 128 GB of memory, while the other desktop editions can support up to 2048 GB of memory.

- A clean installation of Windows is when you install Windows where there is no operating system, data, or programs stored on the hard drive, or you perform the installation of Windows while reformatting the current hard drive, so that you are installing Windows on an empty hard drive.

- An upgrade installation of Windows is when you have a system that is running Windows 7 or Windows 8/8.1, and you run the Windows installation program, replacing the Windows 7 or Windows 8/8.1 operating system with Windows 10. You can upgrade from Windows 7 or Windows 8/8.1 to like versions of Windows 10.

- The User State Migration Tool (USMT) is a command-line tool that migrates user data from a previous installation of Windows to a new installation of Windows. Installation methods fall into three main categories: High Touch Installation (HTI), Lite Touch Installation (LTI), and Zero Touch Installation (ZTI). HTI is mostly manual, and ZTI is almost completely automated.

Knowledge Assessment

You can find the answers to the following sections in the Appendix.

Multiple Choice

1. Which of the following Windows 10 editions allow you to join the system to a domain? (Choose all that apply.)

    A. Windows 10 Home

    B. Windows 10 Pro

    C. Windows 10 Enterprise

    D. Windows 10 Education

2. Which of the following tools can be used to download Windows 10 installation files and create a bootable USB flash drive so that it can be used to install Windows 10?

    A. Windows 10 Media Creation tool

    B. Setup.exe program

    C. USB Create tool

    D. Express tool

3. Which edition of Windows 10 requires a volume license agreement with Microsoft? (Choose all that apply.)

    A. Home

    B. Pro

    C. Education

    D. Enterprise

4. Which of the following features is not included in Windows 10 Pro?

    A. Encrypting File System

    B. BranchCache

    C. Support for joining domains

    D. BitLocker

5. Which of the following tools or features can be used to determine if a copy of Windows is genuine?

    A. An antivirus program

    B. Activation

    C. USB/DVD Download tool

    D. Device Manager

6. Which Windows 10 installation method uses System Center Configuration Manager for deployment across a network?
   A. HTI
   B. LTI
   C. ZTI
   D. Windows Anytime Upgrade

7. Which Windows 10 installation method requires some human interaction but uses Windows Deployment Services to automate most of the installation?
   A. HTI
   B. LTI
   C. ZTI
   D. Windows Anytime Upgrade

8. The upgrade installation method can be used when upgrading from Windows 7 Home Premium to which of the following? (Choose all that apply.)
   A. Windows 10 Enterprise
   B. Windows 10 Home
   C. Windows 10 Pro
   D. Windows 10 Education

9. Which of the following are common methods for determining whether your computer is running a 32-bit version of Windows 10 or a 64-bit version of Windows 10? (Choose two answers.)
   A. Run Windows 7 Upgrade Advisor.
   B. Open the Computer window.
   C. Open the System window.
   D. Run the System Information utility.

10. Which of the following describes where you might find a Windows 10 product key? (Choose all that apply.)
    A. On the installation disc holder inside the Windows package
    B. On a sticker on the back or bottom of your computer
    C. On the installation media itself
    D. In a confirmation email received after purchasing and downloading Windows 10 online

Fill in the Blank

1. A(n) _____ is the set of options you have to upgrade from one Windows operating system to another.

2. _____ is the process of verifying that your copy of Windows is genuine and that it is not in use on more computers than the number for which you own licenses.

3. A _____-bit computer is also designated as x86.

4. A(n) _____ installation replaces your current version of Windows with Windows 10 while retaining your files, settings, and programs.

5. The _____ method involves manual installation of Windows 10 from media such as a DVD or USB drive.

6. Windows 10 _____ edition is targeted mainly toward small business users.

7. Windows 10 _____ edition includes all Windows 10 features aimed at corporations and advanced users.

8. _____ is a fully automated, touchless method of installing Windows.

9. _____ is a server role for Windows Server 2008 or higher that allows for mostly automated installation of Windows 10 over a network.

10. Windows 10 is released as a(n) _____, which means that Windows 10 will receive ongoing updates to its features and functionality.

True/False

1. A custom installation must be performed in order to upgrade from Windows 7 to Windows 10.

2. A 1 GHz or faster 32-bit (x86) processor is required to run Windows 10 64-bit edition.

3. Windows 10 must be registered before it can be run.

4. The purpose of a Windows 10 product key is to help avoid illegal installations.

5. Windows 10 will always remain a free upgrade for Windows 8.1 systems.

Case Scenarios

You can find the answers to the following sections in the Appendix.

Scenario 1-1: Troubleshooting a Compatibility Problem

You need to replace an aging Windows 7 computer with a new computer that runs Windows 10, ensuring the programs, settings, and data files are transferred to the new computer. Describe your recommended solution.

Scenario 1-2: Converting a Small Office to Windows 10

Danielle provides IT support for Swish It Away, a small cleaning service in the Pacific Northwest. The company has eight computers. Four of the computers run Windows 8.1 Pro and the other four computers run Windows 7 Pro. The company president has asked her to make sure all eight computers are running Windows 10 Pro by the beginning of the next quarter. What type of installations must Danielle perform, and what additional steps (if any) must Danielle take to retain the users' files and settings?

Scenario 1-3: Selecting the Right Computer and Operating System

Swish It Away is beginning to grow. The president now wants Danielle to acquire computers for three new staff members. Randi has been hired as the president's personal assistant and will need to run a word processor, spreadsheet application, a web browser, and an email client. Pooja will provide marketing and graphics services, such as press releases, brochures, flyers, advertisements, and graphics for the new website. Stan is the new salesperson who will travel locally each day. When he's in the office, he will share a desktop computer with another salesperson, but Stan needs to be able to check email and access the Internet while he's out of the office. Which computer specifications should be recommended, and which editions of Windows 10 should run on each computer?

Scenario 1-4: Installing Windows 10

You are an administrator of an organization that has 150 client computers. 60 systems are running Windows 7 Enterprise, 60 systems are running Windows 7 Pro, and 30 systems are running Windows 8.1 Pro. You also need to purchase 25 more systems, which will run Windows 10. Which edition and version of Windows 10 should be recommended? Describe how to deploy Windows 10.

Lesson

2

Understanding Operating System Configurations

Objective Domain Matrix

Technology Skill	Objective Domain Description	Objective Domain Number
Understanding User Accounts	Configure user account control (UAC)	3.2
Configuring and Optimizing User Account Control (UAC)	Configure user account control (UAC)	3.2
Configuring Windows 10	Configure Control Panel options	1.1
	Configure desktop settings	1.2
	Understand libraries	4.4
Configuring Hyper-V	None	None

Key Terms

accessibility options

Administrative Tools

Administrator account

checkpoint

Control Panel

desktop

differencing virtual disk

Documents library

domain

Dynamic Memory

Ease of Access Center

elevated permissions

File Explorer

Guest account

hibernate mode

host

hybrid mode

Hyper-V Manager

Hyper-V Virtual Machine Connection

hypervisor

Jump List

library

Microsoft Management Console (MMC)

Music library

Pictures library

pin

power plan

Recycle Bin

resolution

sleep mode

sleep settings

Standard user account

startup RAM

user account

User Account Control (UAC)

user profile

user state

Videos library

virtual disk

Windows 10 Settings

workgroup

Understanding User Accounts

A *user account* is a collection of information that defines the actions that can be taken on a computer and which files and folders can be accessed (rights, policies, and permissions). An account also keeps track of user preferences, such as the desktop background, window color, and screen saver. Several users can share a computer, but each user should have his own account. With separate accounts, each user can personalize her desktop, keep her files and settings protected from other users, and so on.

There are three types of user accounts in Windows 10:

- Administrator
- Standard user
- Guest

Each account has a different level of control over the computer.

Certification Ready

What are the differences between a Standard user account and an Administrator user account? Objective 3.2

The *Guest account* type is simply an account with few permissions and no password that allows a user to access a computer without requiring a unique user account. The Guest account is disabled by default and, when enabled, is intended for a user who needs temporary access to a computer.

The *Standard user account* type has fewer permissions than an Administrator account, but enough permissions to be productive. You should use a Standard user account for day-to-day work. When you're logged on to a Standard user account, you can surf the web, read email, create documents, listen to music, and perform other basic tasks.

The *Administrator account* type provides the broadest permissions and, therefore, the most control over the computer. When you're logged on as an administrator, you can change all settings, install programs, and modify the Windows registry. Use an Administrator account only when you need to make changes or perform maintenance that requires elevated permissions. *Elevated permissions* generally refer to administrative-level permissions. Using an Administrator account for ordinary (standard-level) computing tasks leaves the computer at a much greater risk of attack. For example, if you visit a malicious website by accident, the site can easily install and execute a Trojan horse program on the computer because of the broad permissions of the Administrator account.

A computer administrator can use a Standard user account for most tasks and use the Run as administrator command to start certain tasks or programs with full administrator-level permissions. For example, let's say you want to run a program but get an Access Denied error message. Depending on the program, you might be able to right-click the program's menu item or icon and then choose Run as administrator from the shortcut menu. The program will run with full administrator rights. Before running any tasks or programs with elevated privileges, make sure the computer is protected by a firewall and an up-to-date antivirus program or that it's disconnected from the Internet.

Another special account type that you should be aware of is the default Administrator account. It is the name of the default administrative-level account that's created when you install Windows. Think of it as the ultimate master local (i.e., non-domain) account in Windows. Use this account only for troubleshooting or for specific activities that you can't perform with any other account.

The default Administrator account is automatically hidden (disabled) in Windows 10, but you can enable it if necessary. You must first open a command prompt window in Administrator mode by clicking Start, typing **cmd**, right-clicking cmd.exe in the resulting list, and then choosing Run As Administrator. In the command prompt window, type **net user administrator /active:yes** and press Enter. When you're finished using the account and want to disable it, open a command prompt window as described and type **net user administrator /active:no**.

When you create a new user account or modify an existing account, you can choose Standard or you can choose Administrator. The Guest account type does not show up as an option in the Create a New Account window.

Create a User Account

To create a new user account, perform the following steps:

1. Click Start ➤ Settings.
2. On the Settings page, click Accounts.
3. On the Accounts page (see Figure 2.1), click Family & Other People.

FIGURE 2.1   Managing user accounts

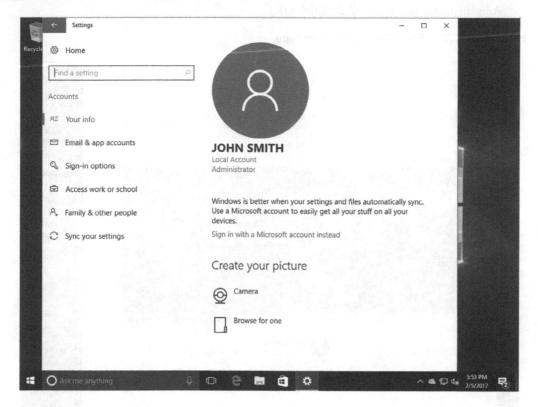

4. In the Other People section, click "Add someone else to this PC."

5. On the "How will this person sign in?" page, click "I don't have this person's sign-in information."

6. On the "Let's create your account" page, click "Add a user without a Microsoft account."

7. On the "Create an account for this PC" page, in the "Who's going to use this PC?" text box, type **DJoel**.

8. In the Enter Password text box and the Re-enter Password text box, type **Pa$$w0rd**.

9. In the Password Hint text box, type **default** and click Next.

10. On the Settings page, click the DJoel account and click Change Account Type.

11. In the Change Account Type dialog box, in the Account Type drop-down list, click Administrator (see Figure 2.2). Click OK.

FIGURE 2.2   Specifying an account type

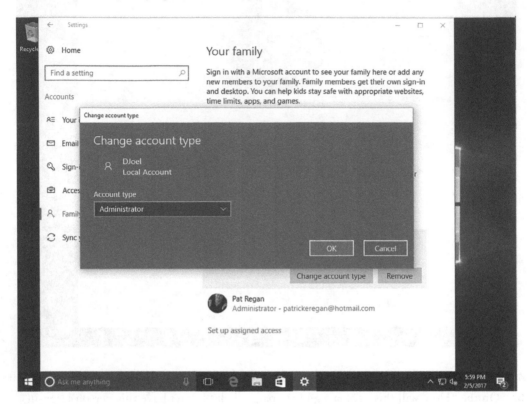

12. Close the Settings page.

Configuring and Optimizing User Account Control (UAC)

User Account Control (UAC) is a technology used with Windows Vista, 7, 8/8.1, and 10 to enhance system security by detecting and preventing unauthorized changes to the system. Some applications might not run properly using a standard user credential if the application needs to access restricted files or registry locations.

With UAC, when a user logs on to Windows 10, the system issues a token, which indicates the user's access level. Standard users receive a standard user token and members of the Administrators group receive two tokens, a standard user token and an administrator token. Normally, both types of users use the standard user token. However, if you need to perform an administrative task, UAC prompts indicate that a change needs to be made. If you are an administrator, click Yes to continue. If you are not an administrator, you must log on with an Administrator account. If malicious code tries to access your system and make changes without your knowledge, the UAC prompts notify you, and you can stop the program from making those changes.

In Windows 10, the number of operating system applications and tasks that require elevated permission is lower when compared with older versions of Windows. The default UAC setting allows a standard user to perform the following tasks without receiving a UAC prompt:

- View Windows settings
- Pair Bluetooth devices with the computer
- Reset the network adapter and perform other network diagnostic and repair tasks
- Establish a local area network (LAN) connection or wireless connection
- Modify display settings
- Play and burn CD/DVD media
- Change the desktop background for the current user
- Open Date and Time in Control Panel and change the time zone
- Use Remote Desktop to connect to another computer
- Change the user's own password
- Configure battery power options
- Configure accessibility options
- Restore a user's backup files
- Set up computer synchronization

UAC will prompt you and require elevation to an Administrator account for the following tasks:

- Install and uninstall applications
- Install a driver for a device
- Install Windows updates

- Install an ActiveX control
- Open Windows Firewall in Control Panel
- Change a user's account type
- Configure Remote Desktop access
- Add or remove a user account
- Copy or move files into the Program Files directory or the Windows directory
- Schedule automated tasks
- Restore system backup files
- Configure Automatic Updates
- Browse to another user's directory

In Windows 10, four UAC settings are available through Control Panel:

- **Always Notify Me.** The user is always prompted when changes are made to the computer and the desktop is dimmed.
- **Notify Me Only When Apps Try to Make Changes to My Computer (Default).** When a program makes a change, a prompt appears and the desktop dims. Otherwise, the user is not prompted.
- **Notify Me Only When Apps Try to Make Changes to My Computer (Do Not Dim My Desktop).** When a program makes a change, a prompt appears and the desktop does not dim.
- **Never Notify Me.** UAC is off.

To configure UAC through Control Panel, use the following procedure.

Review UAC Settings

To review UAC settings, log on to Windows 10 using an account with administrator privileges and then perform the following steps:

1. Click Start. Type **uac** and then from the results list, click Change User Account Control Settings. The User Account Control Settings dialog box opens, as shown in Figure 2.3.

2. Read the current setting and then drag the slider up and down to each setting to review its description:

    - Always notify me
    - Notify me only when apps try to make changes to my computer (default)
    - Notify me only when apps try to make changes to my computer (do not dim my desktop)
    - Never notify me

3. In the User Account Control Settings dialog box, click Cancel.

FIGURE 2.3   Reviewing UAC settings

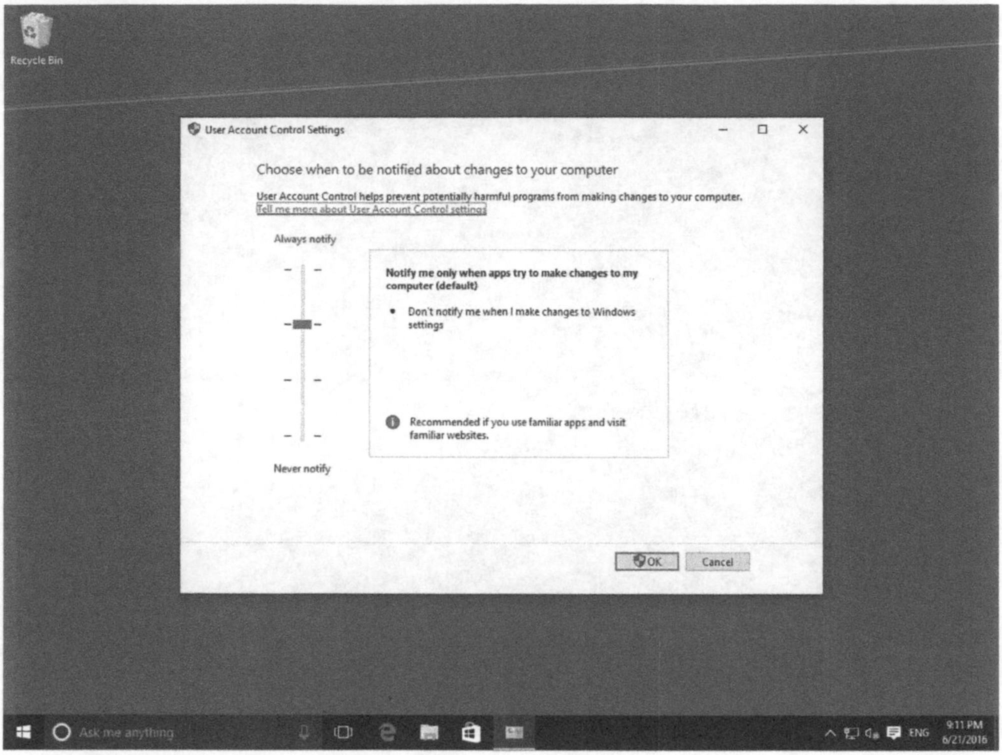

Configuring Windows 10

Windows 10 is a robust and flexible operating system that is made to work on and support a wide range of hardware. For example, Windows 10 can work on a tablet, a laptop, or a desktop computer. Windows 10 also supports mobile devices so that you can take your computer or device with you while accessing your files and programs.

The *desktop* (as shown in Figure 2.4) is the main screen area that you see when you first start the computer and log on to Windows. Like the top of an actual desk, it is where you perform your work by opening and running one or more applications. The desktop also includes the *Recycle Bin*, which is used to recover files that have been previously deleted.

FIGURE 2.4   Viewing the Windows 10 desktop

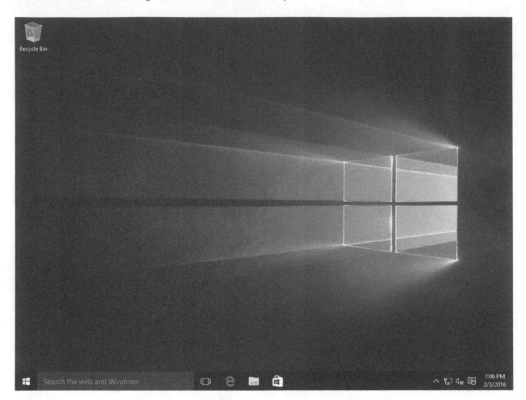

At the bottom of the desktop, the taskbar displays icons that indicate which programs are running and allows you to switch between those running programs. The Start button displays on the left side of the taskbar.

When you click the Start button, the Windows 10 Start menu opens, as shown in Figure 2.5. The Windows 10 Start menu is a blend of the Windows 7 Start menu and the Windows 8 Start screen.

The left side of the Windows 10 Start menu lists the most used programs, and provides access to File Explorer, Settings, and other applications. When you right-click an installed application, you can choose Pin to Start, which will attach the application to the Start menu, or you can choose More ➢ Pin to attach the application to the taskbar.

When you have multiple windows open, you may want to minimize the windows by clicking the Show desktop button (on the far right side of the taskbar), or by right-clicking the taskbar and choosing Show the desktop. If you grab a window's title bar (at the top of the window) and shake it around, all other windows will minimize.

The right side of the Windows 10 Start menu displays tiles, which are larger than the icons found on the Windows desktop. Unlike the static desktop icons, tiles can contain dynamic content provided by the software they represent. For example, the tile for a web browser can contain a thumbnail of the currently open website, while the Messaging tile can display part of your latest incoming email. Tiles in Windows 10 that contain this type of dynamic content are called *live tiles*.

FIGURE 2.5　Opening the Windows 10 Start menu

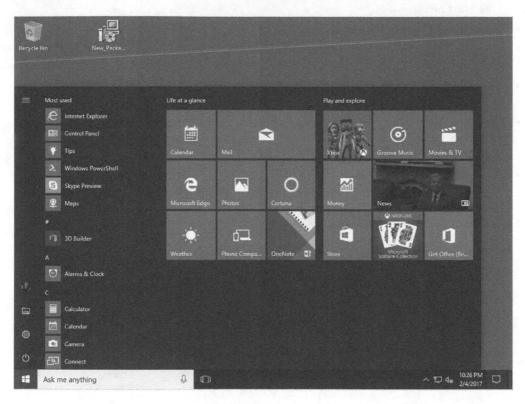

The tiles on the Start menu are configurable in a number of ways. Users can move the tiles around, change their size, change their groupings, and control whether they display live content. It is also possible to remove seldom-used tiles and add new tiles for applications, files, and shortcuts on the computer.

Introducing Windows 10 Settings

In Windows 10, many of the Windows configurations are done within the Settings application. These settings can be accessed by clicking the Start button and clicking Settings.

Click the Settings option on the Start menu to open the Settings application and access common Windows settings. The Settings application is based on the Modern UI interface, as shown in Figure 2.6. These settings are divided into the following categories:

- **System:** Allows you to configure the display, notifications & actions, apps and features, multitasking, tablet mode, power & sleep options, and default apps.

- **Devices:** Provides quick access to hardware devices, such as printers, which you can use with the currently selected app.

- **Network & Internet:** Keeps track of Wi-Fi connections and allows you to configure VPN, dial-up connections, Ethernet connections, and proxy settings.

- **Personalization:** Provides settings for the background, colors, lock screen, themes, and the Start menu.

- **Accounts:** Allows you to change the profile picture and add accounts.

- **Time & Language:** Allows you to configure date & time, region & language, and speech settings.

- **Ease of Access:** Provides settings for Narrator, Magnifier, high contrast, closed captions, keyboard, and mouse.

- **Privacy:** Allows you to configure camera, microphone, speech, account information, contacts, calendar, messaging, and application radios control settings for Wi-Fi and Bluetooth connections.

- **Update & Security:** Allows you to configure Windows Update, activate Windows, perform backups and recoveries, and configure Windows Defender.

FIGURE 2.6   Accessing Windows settings

Cortana is Microsoft's new personal assistant that will help you find things on your PC, manage your calendar, locate files, chat with users, and search the Internet. To see the search results, just type the desired text in the Ask me anything text box, as shown in Figure 2.7.

FIGURE 2.7 Using Cortana

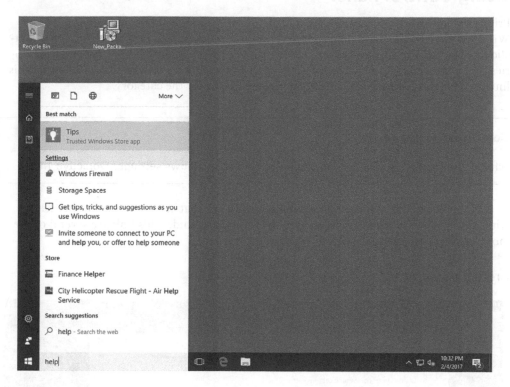

Using a Touch Screen

Windows 10 can be used with a pointing device such as a mouse, or by using a touch screen. Operating a touch screen requires a familiarity with certain finger gestures, such as the following:

Tap: Press a fingertip to the screen and release it. The function is identical to that of a mouse click.

Double-Tap: Press a fingertip to the screen twice in quick succession on the same spot. The function is identical to that of a double mouse click.

Press and Hold: Tap a point on the screen and press down for approximately two seconds. The function is the same as that of mousing over a designated spot and hovering.

Slide: Press a point on the screen and draw your finger across it without pausing. The function is the same as clicking and dragging with a mouse.

Swipe: Draw a finger across the screen in the indicated direction.

Using Control Panel

Prior to Windows 10, *Control Panel* was the primary graphical utility to configure the Windows environment and hardware devices. In Windows 10, it can be accessed by right-clicking the Start button and choosing Control Panel (see Figure 2.8). Of the eight categories that are listed in Control Panel, each category includes a top-level link, and under this link are several of the most frequently performed tasks for the category.

Certification Ready

What is the traditional tool used to configure general Windows settings? Objective 1.1

Clicking a category link provides a list of utilities in that category. Each utility listed within a category includes a link to open the utility, and under this link are several of the most frequently performed tasks for the utility.

FIGURE 2.8   Opening Control Panel

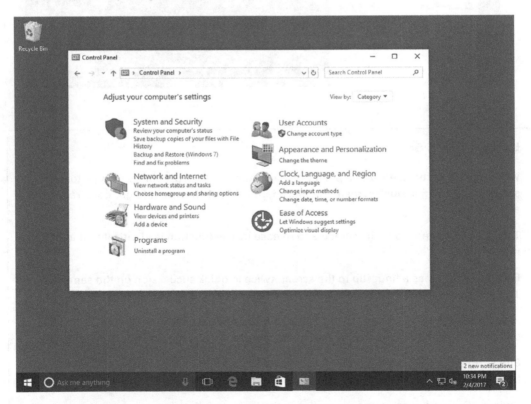

As with current and previous versions of Windows, you can change from the default Category view to Classic view (Large icons view or Small icons view). Icons view is an alternative view that provides the look and functionality of Control Panel in Windows 2000 and earlier versions of Windows, in which all options were displayed as applets or icons.

The *Microsoft Management Console (MMC)* is one of the primary administrative tools used to manage Windows and many of the network services provided by Windows. It provides a standard method to create, save, and open the various administrative tools provided by Windows. When you open Administrative Tools, most of these programs are MMC.

Administrative Tools is a folder in Control Panel that contains tools for system administrators and advanced users. To access the Administrative Tools, right-click Start and choose Control Panel. Click System and Security ➤ Administrative Tools while in Category view or click the Administrative Tools applet while in icons view. There are also quick links to the administrative tools that can be accessed by clicking the Start button and clicking Windows Administrative Tools.

Some common administrative tools in this folder (as shown in Figure 2.9) include:

- **Component Services:** Configures and administers Component Object Model (COM) components. Component Services is designed for use by developers and administrators.

- **Computer Management:** Manages local or remote computers by using a single, consolidated desktop tool. Using Computer Management, you can perform many tasks, such as monitoring system events, configuring hard disks, and managing system performance.

- **Defragment and Optimize Drives:** Disk Defragmenter in Windows rearranges fragmented data so your disks and drives can work more efficiently. Disk Defragmenter runs on a schedule, but you can also analyze and defragment your disks and drives manually.

- **Disk Cleanup:** Use this tool to remove temporary files and old logs, empty the Recycle Bin, and delete redundant Windows Update files.

- **Event Viewer:** Shows information about significant events, such as programs starting or stopping, or security errors that are recorded in event logs.

- **iSCSI Initiator:** Configures advanced connections between storage devices on a network.

- **Hyper-V Manager:** Allows the user to manage his virtualization platform where available.

- **Local Security Policy:** Shows and enables you to edit Group Policy security settings.

- **ODBC Data Sources:** Uses Open Database Connectivity (ODBC) to move data from one type of database (a data source) to another.

- **Performance Monitor:** Shows advanced system information about the processor, memory, hard disk, and network performance.

- **Print Management:** Manages printers and print servers on a network and performs other administrative tasks.

- **Resource Monitor:** A powerful tool for understanding how system resources are used by processes and services. In addition to monitoring resource usage in real time, Resource Monitor can help analyze unresponsive processes, identify which applications are using files, and control processes and services.

- **Services:** Manages the different services that run in the background on your computer.
- **System Configuration:** Identifies problems that might be preventing Windows from running correctly.
- **System Information:** Shows details about your computer's hardware configuration, computer components, and software, including drivers.
- **Task Scheduler:** Schedules programs or other tasks to run automatically.
- **Windows Firewall with Advanced Security:** Helps protect computers on a network. Includes a stateful firewall that determines which network traffic is permitted to pass between a computer and the network. It also includes connection security rules that use Internet Protocol security (IPsec) to protect traffic as it travels across the network.

Windows Firewall with Advanced Security is designed for administrators of a managed network to secure network traffic in an enterprise environment. Home users should use the Windows Firewall program in Control Panel instead.

- **Windows Memory Diagnostic:** Checks your computer's memory to see whether it is functioning properly.

FIGURE 2.9   Opening the Administrative Tools folder

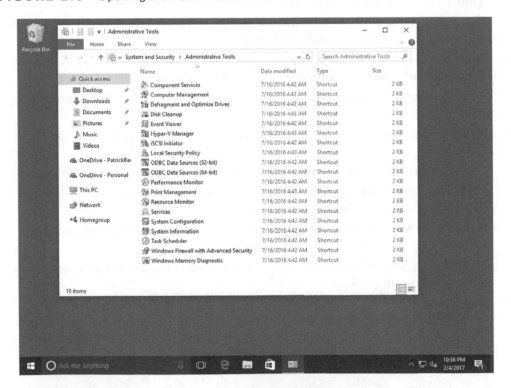

When you use these tools, you might assume that they are used only to manage the local computer. However, many of these tools can be used to manage remote computers as well. For example, you can use the Computer Management console to connect to and manage other computers if you have administrative rights to those computers.

There are a number of ways to open the Administrator Tools. You can:

- Open from Start Menu
- Open from Settings
- Open from Control Panel
- Open using PowerShell Command

Open Administrative Tools from Start Menu: Click the Start button on the taskbar to open the Start menu in Windows 10 and go to Windows Administrative Tools in the All Apps view. Expand the Administrative Tools group.

Open Administrative Tools from Settings: Open Settings and go to System ➤ About. In Related Settings, click on the link Additional Administrative Tools.

Open Administrative Tools from Control Panel: Open Control Panel and go to Control Panel ➤ System and Security ➤ Administrative Tools. All the tools will be listed here.

Open Administrative Tools with Shell Command: Press Win + R on the keyboard and type or paste the following in the Run box: shell:common administrative tools.

Configuring System Options

Some of the most important configuration settings for a user are the system settings within Control Panel. These include gathering generation information about your system, changing the computer name, adding the computer to a domain, accessing the Device Manager, configuring remote settings, configuring startup and recovery options, and configuring overall performance settings.

To access the system settings, you can do one of the following:

- In Control Panel, if you are in Category view, click System and Security, and then click System or click View amount of RAM and processor speed.
- In Control Panel, if in classic view, click the System applet.
- In File Explorer, right-click This PC and choose Properties.
- Right-click Start and choose System.

In Windows, there are often several ways to do the same thing.

At the top of the System window, you see the Windows edition you have and the system type. If Windows comes in 64-bit, it will show 64-bit Operating System in the middle of the window. Toward the bottom of the window, you will see the computer name and domain (if any) if Windows is activated and the Product ID. See Figure 2.10.

FIGURE 2.10   Displaying System settings

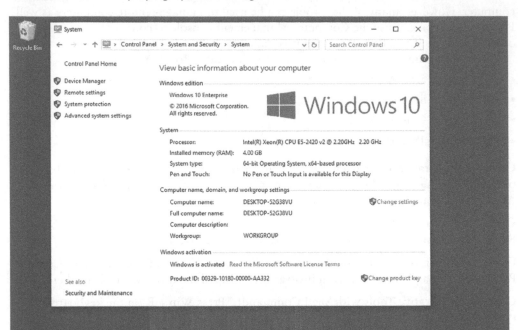

To help identify computers, you should assign a meaningful name to each computer. This can be done in the System settings within Control Panel. You can also add a computer to a domain or workgroup.

Every computer assigned to a network must have a unique computer name. If two computers have the same name, one or both of the computers will have trouble communicating on the network. To change the computer name, open System from Control Panel, or open System by right-clicking Start and choosing System. Then click the Change settings option in the Computer name, domain, and workgroup settings area. In the System Properties dialog box, on the Computer Name tab, click the Change button. See Figure 2.11. Any changes to the computer name or workgroup/domain name will require a reboot.

By default, a computer is part of a workgroup. A *workgroup* is usually associated with a peer-to-peer network in which user accounts are decentralized and stored on each individual computer. If several users need to access the computer (while requiring unique usernames and passwords), you will need to create a user account for each user. If you want those users to access another stand-alone computer, you will have to create the same computer accounts and passwords on that computer as well. As you can imagine, with several computers, this can become a lot of work as you keep creating and managing accounts on each individual computer.

FIGURE 2.11   Displaying System Properties

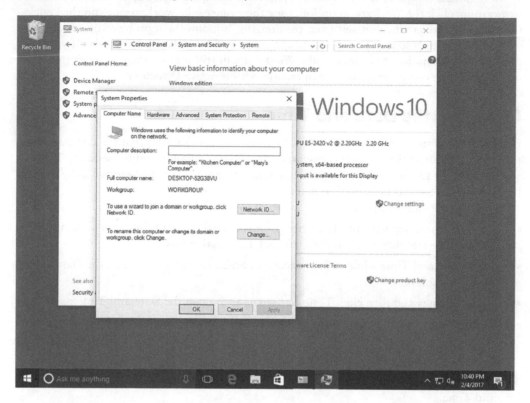

A *domain* is a logical unit of computers that define a security boundary, and it is usually associated with Microsoft's Active Directory Domain Services (AD DS). The security of the domain is generally centralized and controlled by Windows servers acting as domain controllers. As a result, you can manage the security much more easily for multiple computers while providing better security.

When a computer is added to a domain, a computer account is created to represent the computer. In addition, information stored on the computer is used to uniquely identify the computer. When these items match, it shows that a computer is correctly identified, which contributes to a more secure work environment.

To add the computer to the domain, open System Properties and click Change. Next, click the Domain option, type the name of the domain, and then click OK. Windows will prompt you to log on with a domain account that has the capability to add computers to the domain. This is typically a domain administrator or account administrator. After you enter the credentials (username and password), a Welcome dialog box opens. Click OK to close the Welcome dialog box. When you close the System Properties dialog box, Windows will prompt you to reboot the computer.

To remove a computer from a domain, join an existing workgroup, or create a new workgroup, click the Workgroup option, type the name of the workgroup, and then click OK. If you are removing yourself from the domain, Windows will prompt you for administrative credentials so that your account can be deleted from Active Directory. If you don't specify administrative credentials, Windows will still remove the computer from the domain, but the computer account will remain within Active Directory.

Changing the Date and Time

One of the easiest but most essential Windows tasks is making sure that the computer has the correct date and time, which is essential for logging purposes and for security. If a secure packet is sent with the wrong date or time, the packet may be automatically denied because the date and time is used to determine if the packet is legit.

To access the date and time settings, perform one of the following methods:

- Click Clock, Language, and Region in Control Panel while in Category view and click Set the time and date to open the Date and Time dialog box.
- Click Date and Time while in Large icons or Small icons view to open the Date and Time dialog box.
- Open Settings and then click Time & Language to open the Date and Time page.
- Right-click the date or time on the taskbar and choose Adjust Date/Time to open the Date and Time page.

To set the date or clock, follow these steps:

1. In the Date and Time dialog box, click the Date and Time tab and click Change Date and Time.
2. To change the clock, double-click the hour, minutes, or seconds, and click the arrows to increase or decrease the value.
3. To change the date, click the left or right arrows to change the month and then click the correct day of the month.
4. When you are finished changing the time settings, click OK.

To change the time zone, on the Date and Time tab, click Change Time Zone and then click your current time zone in the drop-down list. Click OK.

If you are part of a domain, the computer should be synchronized with the domain controllers. If you have a computer that is not part of a domain, you can synchronize with an Internet time server by clicking the Internet Time tab, clicking Change Settings, and then selecting the Synchronize with an Internet Time Server check box. Select a time server and then click OK.

Configuring the Desktop and Taskbar Settings

Windows desktop settings is a broad term that refers to many different settings you can configure to personalize Windows, such as the Windows theme, the desktop background, mouse clicks and pointer speeds, shortcuts, and more. All settings are customizable—choosing the right mix will make your Windows experience more enjoyable and more productive.

The Windows desktop is a flexible, configurable part of the Windows environment. You can grab the taskbar and move it to either side of the screen, to the top, or back to its default location at the bottom. The taskbar must be unlocked to move it—right-click the taskbar and, if Lock the taskbars is checked, choose Lock the taskbars to deselect it.

To modify it further, open Settings and then click Personalization ➢ Taskbar to open the Taskbar page (see Figure 2.12). Options on this page include hiding the taskbar, using small taskbar buttons, and replacing Command Prompt with Windows PowerShell, among other selections. When you scroll down, you can modify the notification area (including selecting which icons appear on the taskbar) and you can turn system icons on or off.

FIGURE 2.12   Opening the Taskbar page

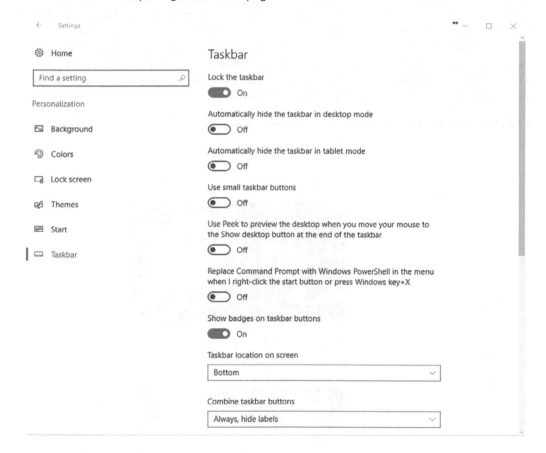

The Toolbars tab allows you to specify which toolbars can be added to the taskbar. The default available toolbars include:

- **Address:** Allows you to type a Uniform Naming Convention (UNC) or Uniform Resource Locator (URL). The UNC uses a \\servername\sharefolder format; a URL is a website address.

- **Links:** Displays Microsoft Edge favorites.
- **Desktop:** Allows you to access all shortcuts on the desktop and File Explorer, including Libraries, This PC, Control Panel, and Recycle Bin.

With Windows 10, you can *pin* program shortcuts directly to the taskbar. When you pin a program, the icon for that program displays on the taskbar even when the program isn't running. This provides you with quick access to your frequently used programs. Shortcuts for Task View, Microsoft Edge, File Explorer, and Store appear there by default. You can unpin programs from the taskbar as well. You'll learn about shortcuts later in the lesson.

When you open a program in Windows 10, an icon for that program displays on the taskbar. To activate a program, just click its icon on the taskbar. If you have several programs open at once, Windows allows you to hover the mouse pointer over an icon in the taskbar to see a thumbnail preview of the window. This thumbnail preview is called a *Jump List*. You can also press and hold the Alt key and then press the Tab key repeatedly to switch between windows and see *live previews* of the window for each open program.

Many Windows 10 desktop settings are available when you right-click a blank area of the desktop and choose Personalize. The Personalization window is shown in Figure 2.13. The main part of the window displays various themes you can use. Just click the theme of your choice and see the changes take effect immediately.

FIGURE 2.13   The Personalization window

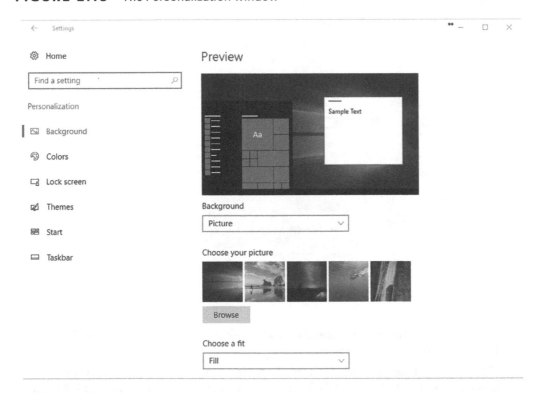

You can also change the background of any theme. In the Personalization window, click Background. In the Background window, open the Picture drop-down list, and then select a picture, a solid color, or a slideshow.

When you click the Themes option and then click Advanced sound settings, the Sound dialog box opens (see Figure 2.14). From here you can choose different sounds to accompany Windows events, such as when you connect a device or when you close Windows. The computer's sound volume must be set at an appropriate level to actually hear the sound.

FIGURE 2.14   The Sound dialog box

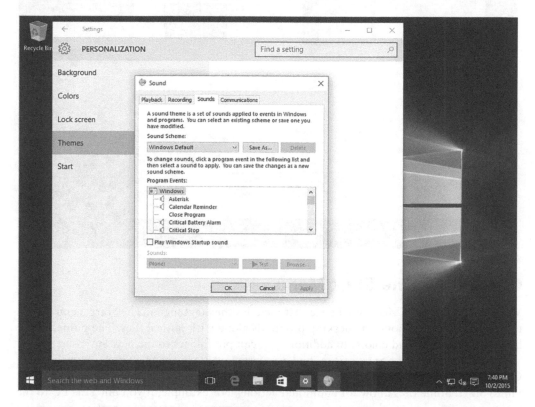

In the Personalization window, click the Lock screen option and click the Screen saver settings option. The Screen Saver Settings dialog box opens (see Figure 2.15). In the Screen saver drop-down list, click a screen saver and click OK.

FIGURE 2.15   Configuring the screen saver

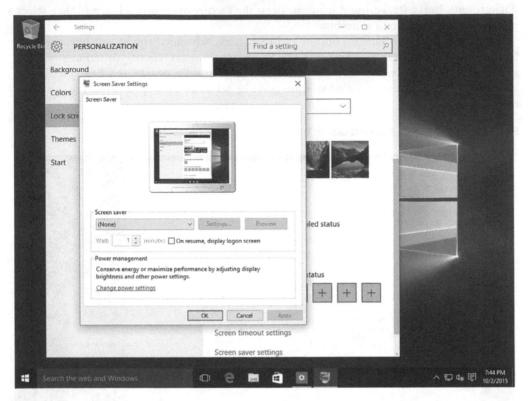

Configuring the Start Menu

Windows 10 uses the Modern UI style that includes the Start menu. The Start menu contains a list of applications and desktop programs along with pinned tiles. The pinned tiles have different sizes and colors. In addition, you can pin folders to the new Start screen.

To pin an item to the Start screen, find a program or file in the Start menu by using Cortana or File Explorer. Then right-click the program, application, or folder and choose Pin to Start. Some tiles allow for additional actions. For example, if you pin This PC to the Start menu, you can quickly open Computer Management or System Properties, or connect/disconnect network drives.

Configuring File Explorer Settings

File Explorer, previously known as Windows Explorer, is the file manager that is included with Windows operating systems. It provides a graphical user interface to access and manage the file system, including opening files, moving and copying files, and deleting files.

To open File Explorer, click the File Explorer tile on the taskbar, or double-click any folder on the desktop. To configure File Explorer, open the Folder Options dialog box.

Configure File Explorer Settings

Log on to Windows 10 using an account with Administrator privileges.

1. To open File Explorer, click the File Explorer icon on the taskbar.
2. In the File Explorer window, click the View tab.
3. At the end of the View tab, click Options. The Folder Options dialog box opens with the General tab active (see Figure 2.16).

FIGURE 2.16 Configuring folder options

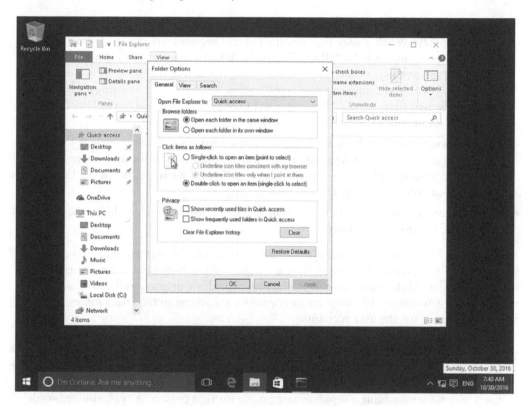

4. To configure each folder to open in its own window, click the "Open each folder in its own window" option.
5. Click the View tab.
6. To show hidden files, folders, and drives, click the "Show hidden files, folders, and drives" option.
7. To show the file extensions, click to deselect the "Hide extensions for known file types" check box.
8. To close the Folder Options dialog box, click OK.

Configuring User Profiles

When a user logs on to Windows, the user has a user state that is captured in his or her profile. A *user state* is the collection of data and settings that pertains to each user. It describes settings and data that determine the user environment. The user state separates the user environment, files, and settings from the files and settings that are specific to the installed operating system and those that belong to installed applications. When a user logs on, the user state is kept separate from other users on the same computer. The user state includes users' data and their application or operating system configuration settings.

The user state includes the following components:

- **User Registry:** When a user logs on, the current settings are copied from HKEY_USERS to HKEY_CURRENT_USER. When a user logs off, those settings, including any settings that were changed during the current session, are copied back to HKEY_USERS. On computers that run Windows 10, each user's settings are stored in that user's own files, named Ntuser.dat and Usrclass.dat, located in the Users folder on the boot volume (usually the C:\Users folder).

- **Application Data:** The AppData folder contains mostly application settings that are specific to a user. The AppData folder provides separation for user-related and computer-related application settings. The AppData folder is located in the Users folder on the boot volume (usually the C:\Users folder).

- **User Data:** User-specific data is stored in multiple folders, which include Documents, Favorites, Pictures, and Music.

A *user profile* is a series of folders associated with a specific user account that contains personal documents, user-specific registry settings, desktop theme, Internet favorites, and other personalized information—everything that provides a user's familiar working environment. On a Windows 10 computer, user profiles are stored in the Users folder, within subfolders named for the user accounts.

On computers running Windows 10, user profiles automatically create and maintain the desktop settings for each user's work environment on the local computer in a folder beneath C:\Users. The system creates a new user profile for each user logging on at the computer for the first time.

Each user folder contains a separate user profile for that person. A typical user profile (as shown in Figure 2.17) consists of the following folders, some of which are hidden, plus a hidden registry file:

- AppData
- Contacts
- Desktop
- Documents
- Downloads
- Favorites
- Links

- Music
- Pictures
- Saved Games
- Searches
- Videos

FIGURE 2.17   Viewing a user's profile in the Users folder

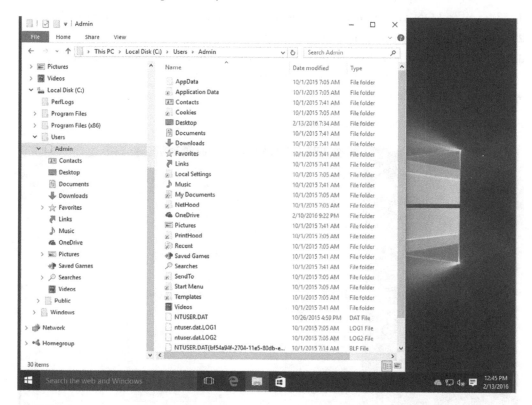

When a user logs on at the workstation using a local or domain account, the system loads that individual's profile and uses it throughout the session until the user logs off. During the session, the Documents folder in the user's profile becomes the operative Documents folder for the system, as do all the other folders in the profile.

Configuring Folder Locations

You can change the location of your personal folders, such as Documents, Music, or Pictures, by specifying a different folder location. Therefore, if one or more of these personal folders grows or the primary drive becomes filled up, you can move the location to another drive or a shared network folder.

When you redirect the folder by specifying a different folder location, you will still be able to access the folder the same way you did before. The following exercise shows you how to manually change the folder location on the local system.

Configure a Folder Location

To configure a folder location in Windows 10, perform the following steps:

1. Log on to LON-CL1 as **adatum\administrator** with the password of **Pa$$w0rd**.

2. Click the File Explorer icon on the taskbar.

3. Right-click the folder that you want to redirect (such as the Desktop, Documents, Pictures, Music, or Videos folder) and choose Properties.

4. Click the Location tab, as shown in Figure 2.18.

FIGURE 2.18   Specifying folder locations

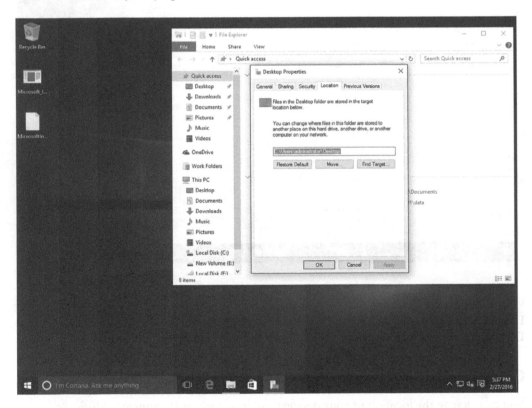

5. Click Move.

6. In the Select A Destination dialog box, browse to and click the location. You can also specify a local path or network path in the Folder text box and press Enter. Next, click Select Folder.

7. Click a folder in the new location where you want to store the files, click Select Folder, and then click OK.

To restore the folder back to the default location, click the Restore Default button on the Location tab.

Configuring Libraries

Libraries were introduced in Windows 7. A library looks like an ordinary folder, but is a virtual folder that simply points to files and folders in different locations on a hard disk, network drive, or external drive.

Certification Ready

Which default libraries are included with Windows 10? Objective 4.4

In Windows 10, a *library* is a virtual folder that can display content from different locations (folders, for example) on your computer or an external drive. Libraries are nothing more than a collection of shortcuts to the original file and folder locations. The locations can either be on the local computer or on a network drive. A library looks like an ordinary folder but simply points to files and folders that are located elsewhere. You access libraries in File Explorer, just like you do files and folders.

To show libraries in File Explorer, click the View tab, and then click Navigation pane ➤ Show Libraries. Windows 10 includes the following default libraries (see Figure 2.19):

- *Documents library*: Stores word-processing documents, spreadsheets, and similar files.
- *Music library*: Stores audio files, such as those you've downloaded from the web, transferred from a portable device (music player), or ripped from a CD.
- *Pictures library*: Stores digital image files.
- *Videos library*: Stores video files.

If multiple users share a Windows 10 system, each user will have his or her own separate libraries and folders, which are stored in the C:\Users*username* folder.

When creating a new library, you must include at least one folder within the library for organizational purposes. You can then copy, move, or save files to the folder in the library. You can add a location such as a folder on your C: drive, a second hard drive in your computer, or an external drive to an existing library.

FIGURE 2.19   Default libraries in Windows 10

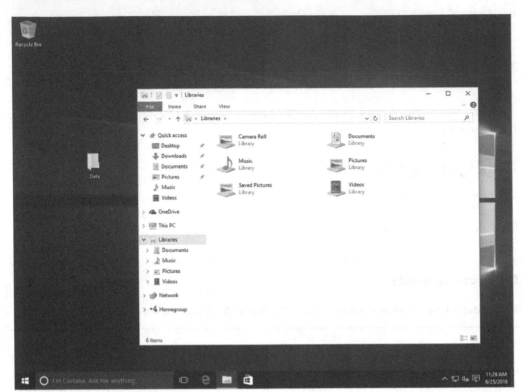

Add a Folder to a Library

To add a folder to a library, perform the following steps:

1. Click the File Explorer icon on the taskbar.

2. When File Explorer opens, locate and click the folder you want to include in a library. The folder cannot already be included in another library.

3. Right-click the folder, choose Include In Library, and then click a library (such as Documents, Music, Pictures, or Videos).

You can also include external drives in a library, as long as the folder is indexed for search or available offline. Make sure the external hard drive is connected to your computer and that your computer recognizes the device. You can't include content on removable media, such as a CD or DVD, in a library. Some USB flash drive devices don't work with libraries either.

To remove a folder, navigate to the library in the File Explorer navigation pane, right-click the folder you want to remove and then choose Remove location from library.

You can also create your own library.

Create a Library

To create a library, perform the following steps:

1. Click the File Explorer icon on the taskbar.

2. If the Libraries don't appear in the navigation pane, click the View tab and then click Navigation pane ➤ Show Libraries.

3. In the Navigation pane, right-click Libraries and choose New ➤ Library.

4. A Library node will appear with the default name New Library. Rename the Library to whatever you choose, such as **Personal Library**.

5. Click the new library.

6. Because the Library was just created, it is empty. Click the Include A Folder button.

7. In the Include Folder In New Library dialog box, navigate to the desired folder and click Include Folder.

To share files and folders, users would typically map shared folders to their computer from another computer to access or store different files. Windows 10 includes Libraries, which is a way to group different storage locations logically.

Sometimes an issue arises when trying to add a network location to a library: users receive a "This network location can't be included because it is not indexed" error message.

This happens because the user is trying to add a mapped folder, which the operating system thinks is a local storage, and mapped drives don't get indexed. This can be fixed by using the UNC path instead.

How to add network shared folder to Libraries:

1. Open File Explorer and expand the Libraries folder.

2. Select the library, right-click on it, and click Properties.

3. On Properties, click Include A Folder.

4. Click on Network from the left pane.

5. Double-click the computer where the shared folder is located.

6. Double-click the folder you want to add to your library, and click Include Folder.

7. Click Apply.

8. Click OK to complete the task.

If you want to add more network shared locations, simply repeat.

Configuring Display Settings

Windows 10 has several display settings. The settings you'll most likely modify include the resolution, color depth, and font size. You can modify each setting to suit a particular application.

When you right-click the desktop and choose Display Settings, the Display page appears, allowing you to change the orientation and the size of the text (see Figure 2.20).

FIGURE 2.20 Opening the Settings Display page

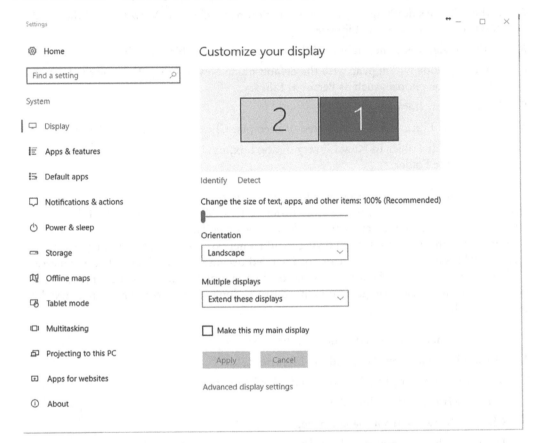

To open the Windows 10 Advanced Display Settings page (as shown in Figure 2.21), click Advanced display settings. This is where you choose which monitor to use (if your computer is connected to two or more monitors) and whether to display content in a landscape orientation or a portrait orientation. You can also configure settings to connect a projector to your computer. Three other important display settings you might want to adjust for specific purposes are resolution, color depth, and font size.

FIGURE 2.21   Opening the Advanced Display Settings page

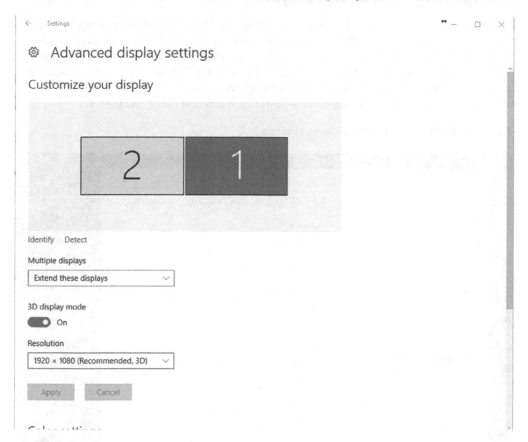

Resolution refers to the number of pixels that create the image, that is, everything you see on the screen. *Resolution* has a horizontal value and a vertical value, such as 1200 × 768 or 1600 × 900. The Windows desktop expands itself to fit whatever resolution you select, so you always have a full background. Similarly, the taskbar stretches across the bottom of the screen, regardless of the resolution you choose.

You might need to change a computer's screen resolution for a variety of reasons, such as when you're accommodating a visually impaired user or when you're using an external projector. Your computer's monitor has a minimum and a maximum resolution it can display, so Windows 10 gives you a range of resolutions from which to choose.

Screen fonts are usually measured in dots per inch (dpi). You can enhance the appearance of your desktop by adjusting font size dpi to improve the readability of pixelated or illegible fonts.

Configuring Power Settings

In Windows 10, simple power management settings can be accessed by opening Settings and clicking System ➤ Power & Sleep, as shown in Figure 2.22. The screen settings allow you to specify how long the screen will remain on if you are not actively using your computer when the computer is using battery power or when it is using AC power (plugged in). The *sleep settings* will specify how long the computer will operate before going into sleep mode when the computer is using battery power or when it is using AC power.

FIGURE 2.22 Configuring Power settings

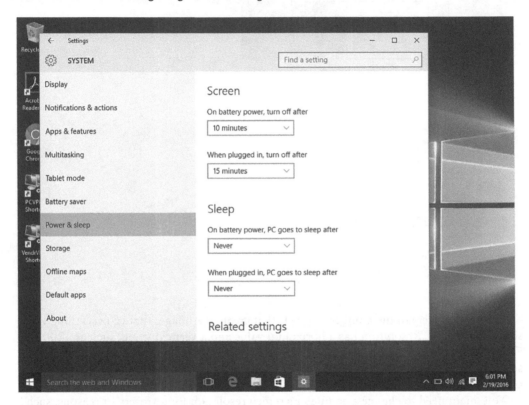

Sleep mode is a low-power mode for computers that uses a minimum amount of power so that the system can be quickly restored back to the previous state without rebooting the computer. Sleep mode is useful when you want to stop working for a short period of time and quickly pick up where you left off. For older versions of Windows and other operating systems, sleep mode is referred to as Stand By mode, Suspend mode, or Suspend to RAM.

Before continuing to the next section, you should understand the difference between sleep mode, hibernate mode, and hybrid sleep. *Hibernate mode* saves all computer operational data on the hard disk to a hibernation file (Hiberfil.sys) before turning the computer completely off. In other words, hibernate mode is a suspend to disk. When the computer is turned back on, the computer is restored to its previous state with all programs and files open and unsaved data intact. Hibernate mode will be discussed later in this lesson.

Hybrid mode is a combination of sleep mode and hibernate mode. Hybrid mode writes information to the hibernation file when the computer enters a sleep state, which allows for a fast wake time. If the system loses power completely and suddenly, you can restore operations from the hibernation file.

Power management is balancing power consumption with performance. Windows 10 includes extensive power management capabilities, including supporting the Advanced Configuration and Power Interface (ACPI), which can be configured using power plans. The power plans can be configured using Control Panel Power Options, using Group Policy, or via the command prompt.

Power Options is the primary interactive power configuration interface that can be used to select the power plan, modify the settings for the default power plans, and create new, custom power plans.

A *power plan* is a collection of hardware and system settings that manage how a computer uses power. Windows 10 includes three default power plans:

- **Balanced (Recommended):** Balances performance with power-saving features.

- **Power Saver:** Saves power by reducing PC performance and screen performance so that you can maximize battery life.

- **High Performance:** Maximizes screen brightness and PC performance.

Table 2.1 shows the default power plan settings.

TABLE 2.1   Default Power Plan Settings

Power Setting	Power Saver	Balanced	High Performance
Wireless adapter power-saving mode	Maximum Power Saving (battery) Maximum Performance (AC)	Medium Power Saving (battery) Maximum Performance (AC)	Maximum Performance (battery) Maximum Performance (AC)
Dim the display	1 minutes (battery) 2 minutes (AC)	2 minutes (battery) 5 minutes (AC)	5 minutes (battery) 10 minutes (AC)
Turn off the display	2 minutes (battery) 5 minutes (AC)	5 minutes (battery) 10 minutes (AC)	10 minutes (battery) 15 minutes (AC)
Put the computer to sleep	10 minutes (battery) 15 minutes (AC)	45 minutes (battery) Never (AC)	Never (battery) Never (AC)
Adjust plan brightness	40% (battery) 100% (AC)	50% (battery) 100% (AC)	100% (battery) 100% (AC)
Turn off hard disk	5 minutes (battery) 20 minutes (AC)	10 minutes (battery) 20 minutes (AC)	20 minutes (battery) 20 minutes (AC)

TABLE 2.1 Default Power Plan Settings *(continued)*

Power Setting	Power Saver	Balanced	High Performance
Minimum processor state	5% (battery)	5% (battery)	5% (battery)
	5% (AC)	5% (AC)	100% (AC)
System cooling policy	Passive (battery)	Passive (battery)	Active (battery)
	Passive (AC)	Active (AC)	Active (AC)
Maximum processor state	100% (battery)	70% (battery)	100% (battery)
	100% (AC)	100% (AC)	100% (AC)

To select one of the default power plans, you can use either of the following procedures:

- Open the Windows Mobility Center and, in the Battery Status tile, click one of the plans from the drop-down list.

- Open Control Panel, click Hardware and Sound ≻ Power Options, and then click the radio button for the desired plan, as shown in Figure 2.23. To display the Power Saver option, you must click the Show additional plans down arrow. If these options are grayed out, click the Change settings that are currently unavailable option.

FIGURE 2.23 Viewing the Power Options page

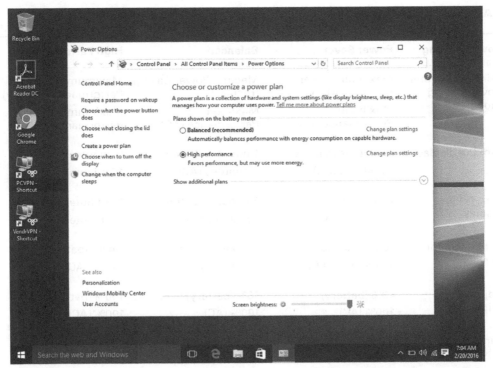

You can use Control Panel Power Options to modify a power plan or to create a new power plan. To create a custom power plan, use the following procedure.

Create a Custom Power Plan

Log on to Windows 10 using an account with Administrator privileges and perform the following steps:

1. O LON-CL1, open Control Panel and then click Hardware and Sound ≻ Power Options.

2. On the Power Options page, click Create A Power Plan.

3. In the Create A Power Plan Wizard, click the radio button for the default power plan that will be the basis for your new plan.

4. In the Plan Name text box, type a name for your power plan and click Next.

5. On the Change Settings For The Plan page, modify the display and sleep settings as desired for the On Battery and Plugged In power states and click Create. The Choose Or Customize A Power Plan page appears.

6. For the new plan, click the Change Plan Settings option.

   The Change Settings for the Plan page appears again.

7. When the Change Settings for the Plan page opens, click Change Advanced Power Settings. The Power Options dialog box opens with the Advanced Settings tab shown (see Figure 2.24).

FIGURE 2.24   Configuring advanced power settings

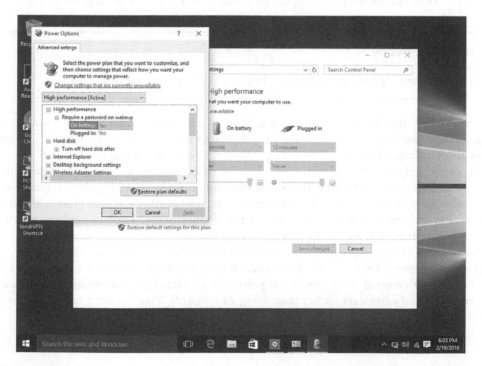

8. Modify any of the settings as desired and click OK.

9. Click Save Changes to close the Change Settings For The Plan page.

The Advanced settings give you a high degree of control for the power plans. Some of the options include:

- **Hard Disk: Turn Off Hard Disk After:** Specifies the amount of time of inactive use before a mechanical disk will stop spinning.

- **Wireless Adapter Settings: Power Savings Mode:** Allows you to control power by selecting one of the following options: Maximum Performance, Low Power Saving, Medium Power Saving, and Maximum Power Saving. If you need a fast Internet connection, click the Maximum Performance or Low Power Saving option. If you don't need Wi-Fi, turn your Wi-Fi antenna off when you aren't using it.

- **Sleep After:** Specifies how long a machine will sleep after inactive use.

- **Allow Hybrid Sleep:** Enables Hybrid sleep mode.

- **Hibernate:** Specifies when a machine goes into hibernation.

- **Allow Wake Timers:** Allows a system to be woken up from sleep mode to perform tasks at certain times, such as Windows updates.

Configuring Accessibility Options

Microsoft has built many features into Windows 10 that work with assistive technologies or as stand-alone features that improve the user experience for the visually and hearing impaired. Most accessibility features can be configured in the Ease of Access Center.

Certification Ready

What is the primary purpose of Windows 10's accessibility options? Objective 1.1

The *Ease of Access Center* (see Figure 2.25) provides many *accessibility options*, which help visually and hearing impaired users use Windows more easily and efficiently. The primary tools include Magnifier, Narrator, On-Screen Keyboard, and High Contrast.

Magnifier helps visually impaired users see a selected portion of the screen or the entire screen more clearly by increasing the size of text and graphics. The Magnifier application window is quite small and provides you with access to Magnifier settings. Here you can set a certain magnification level and choose how the magnification "lens" follows the mouse pointer and text cursor. The lens looks like a magnifying glass icon on the screen.

Narrator is a text-to-speech program that reads aloud the actions you take, such as clicking and typing. This feature can also narrate certain events, such as error messages.

On-Screen Keyboard (see Figure 2.26) presents a keyboard on your screen from which you can type and enter data (rather than using a keyboard). You can use a mouse, stylus, or another pointing device to "press" keys.

FIGURE 2.25   The Ease of Access Center tools

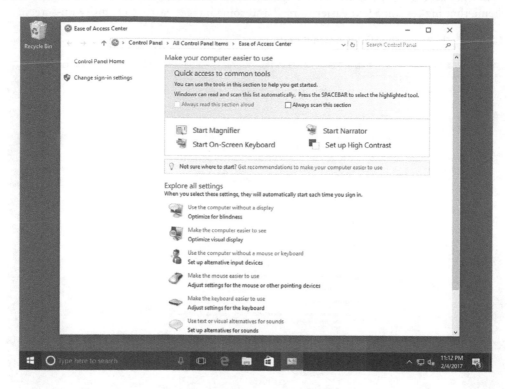

FIGURE 2.26   The On-Screen Keyboard presents a fully functional keyboard

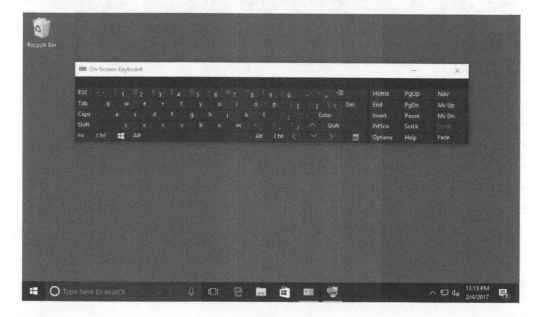

Another accessibility feature is the High Contrast theme (see Figure 2.27), a color scheme that makes some text easier to read and some images easier to identify on-screen.

FIGURE 2.27   The High Contrast settings

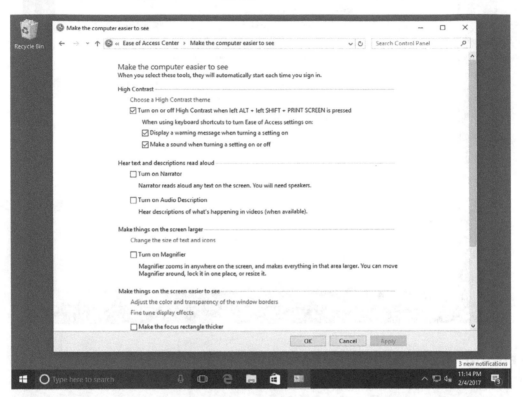

The bottom portion of the Ease of Access Center window includes other accessibility options you can configure for visually or hearing impaired users, including:

- Using the computer without a display
- Making the computer easier to see
- Using the computer without a mouse or keyboard
- Making the mouse easier to use
- Making the keyboard easier to use
- Using text or visual alternatives for sounds
- Making it easier to focus on tasks

Speech Recognition is an accessibility feature that you access in the Ease of Access category in Control Panel. This tool allows a user to speak commands into a microphone, which Windows then processes. All speech recognition programs require a sometimes-lengthy training period in which the user "teaches" the computer to recognize the user's voice. You can learn more about the Windows Speech Recognition feature in Help and Support (click Start, type **speech recognition** in the search box, and then press Enter).

Use Accessibility Features

To enable accessibility features, open the Ease of Access Center in Control Panel and then perform the following steps:

1. To use Magnifier, click Start Magnifier. When the application name displays, click it. A small application window displays a magnifier glass icon. Click the level of magnification in the window and then move the magnifier glass icon around the screen.

2. To use Narrator, click Start Narrator. The Narrator Settings dialog box opens (see Figure 2.28). Now when you type text or navigate text on the screen, Narrator reads it aloud. To turn Narrator off, click Exit in the Microsoft Narrator and then click OK.

FIGURE 2.28   Configuring Narrator settings

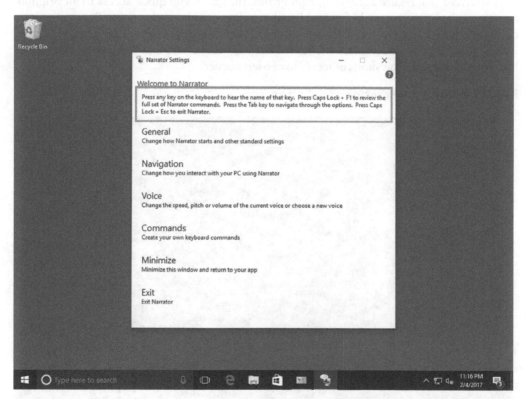

The steps are similar for On-Screen Keyboard and High Contrast. Just click Start On-Screen Keyboard or Set up High Contrast and follow the prompts.

Creating and Managing Shortcuts

Shortcuts are icons you can click to start a program or go to a location without requiring any extra steps. Shortcuts save time because you don't have to use several keystrokes or click several menus or commands.

Certification Ready

What is a shortcut? Objective 1.2

An icon is a small, visual symbol of a computer resource, such as a program, folder, file, or drive. To access an actual computer resource, click or double-click its icon. Some icons are located on the desktop, others are in the Start menu, and still others might appear in the list of files and folders in File Explorer.

A *shortcut* (see Figure 2.29) is an icon or link that gives you quick access to an original resource. The links you see in Control Panel are also considered shortcuts. Because a shortcut only points to a resource, deleting a shortcut does not delete the actual item. You can usually distinguish a shortcut icon from the original item it refers to because the shortcut has a small arrow in the shortcut icon's lower-left corner.

FIGURE 2.29   An example of a shortcut icon

If you regularly access a particular folder, for example, you can create a shortcut to that folder on the desktop. Whenever you want to open that folder, double-click the icon instead of launching File Explorer and navigating to the folder to open it.

Create and Delete a Shortcut

To create a folder shortcut on the desktop, perform the following steps:

1. In File Explorer, point to the folder for which you want to create a shortcut.
2. Right-click the folder and choose Send To ➤ Desktop (Create Shortcut) (see Figure 2.30). The shortcut now displays on your desktop.

FIGURE 2.30   Creating a shortcut on the desktop

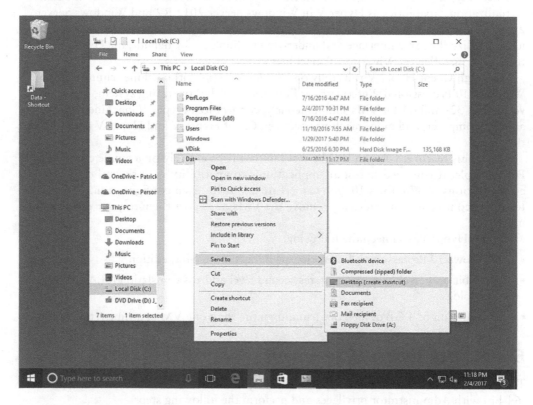

To delete a shortcut icon, follow these steps:

1. Right-click the icon and choose Delete.
2. Click OK. The shortcut is removed and sent to the Recycle Bin.

Configuring Hyper-V

Client Hyper-V enables you to create and manage virtual machines (VMs) using a virtual switch. These VMs can be used to test your applications for compatibility with new operating systems, allow you to run applications written for older versions of Windows, or isolate an application. The physical machine that Hyper-V and the VMs run on is often referred to as the *host*.

The Hyper-V is a *hypervisor*, sometimes called a virtual machine monitor (VMM), and is responsible for managing the computer's physical hardware and creating multiple virtualized hardware environments, called virtual machines.

Client Hyper-V, a Microsoft replacement for Windows Virtual PC, provides the same virtualization capabilities as Hyper-V in Windows Server 2012 R2 and Windows Server 2016. Although it does not include all the advanced features available on the server version, it does utilize the same interface and underlying technology. By default, the Hyper-V feature is not installed on Windows 10 machines.

Although Client Hyper-V runs only on Windows 10 (64-bit) machines running the Windows 10 Professional, Enterprise, or Education (64-bit) operating system, it enables you to run 32- and 64-bit VMs simultaneously, connect to a Hyper-V machine running on another computer, and move machines between Client Hyper-V and Hyper-V running on the server.

Using this feature, you can build a test lab that runs entirely on a single computer. For example, if you need to test an application's compatibility with several different configurations of Windows 10, you can create a VM for each configuration. After your testing is complete, you can easily remove the VMs or export them to your production network.

To run Hyper-V, you need the following:

- Windows 10 Professional, Enterprise, or Education (64-bit) edition
- A 64-bit processor that incorporates second level address translation (SLAT) technology
- A minimum of 4 GB of memory (running more than one VM at a time requires more)

Enable the Hyper-V Feature

To enable the Hyper-V feature, log on to the computer running Windows 10 Enterprise (64-bit) with Administrator privileges and perform the following steps:

1. On LON-CL1, right-click Start and choose Control Panel.
2. In the Search Control Panel text box, type Features. Then from the Results list, click Turn Windows features on or off.
3. Click the + next to the Hyper-V folder, as shown in Figure 2.31.

FIGURE 2.31   Enabling the Hyper-V feature on Windows 10 Enterprise

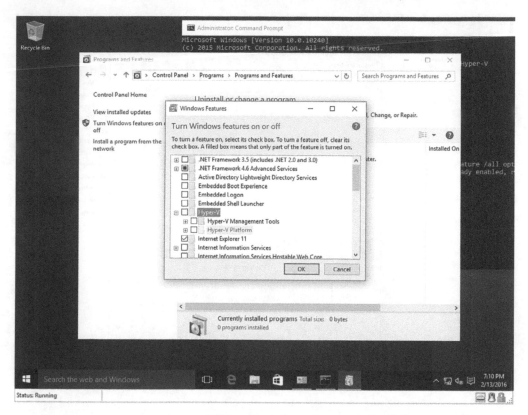

4. Select the Hyper-V check box and click OK.

   Windows searches for the required files and then applies the changes to the computer.

5. Click Close.

6. Restart your computer to complete the installation.

   A restart starts the Windows hypervisor and the Virtual Machine Management service.

   After installing Client Hyper-V, you see two new tiles after logging on with the administrative account:

- *Hyper-V Manager* (see Figure 2.32): This is the management console for creating and managing your VMs and setting up your test network.

- *Hyper-V Virtual Machine Connection*: This is used when working with a single VM that you have already created. It is very similar to the Remote Desktop Connection utility.

FIGURE 2.32   Opening the Hyper-V Manager console

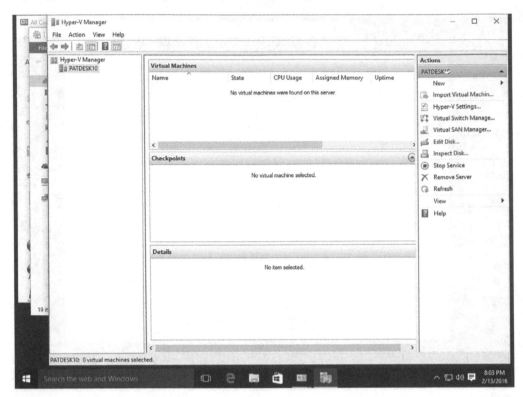

Creating and Configuring Virtual Machines

A *virtual machine (VM)* is a self-contained, isolated unit that can be easily moved from one physical computer to another, runs its own operating system, and includes its own virtual hardware configuration.

Within the Hyper-V Manager console, you can import VMs (Action ➤ Import Virtual Machine) and create virtual hard disks (Action ➤ New ➤ Virtual Machine) to be used by VMs or by the host PC. You can also manage a VM's configuration by modifying the startup order of devices (for example, CD, IDE, network adapter, floppy), allocate memory, determine the number of virtual processors to use, and add hard drives/CD drives to an IDE/SCSI controller.

When you create a virtual machine, you must define the virtual machine's virtual hardware, including:

- The name of the virtual machine
- The location where the virtual machine will be stored

- The VM generation
- How much memory the virtual machine will use
- The virtual switch the virtual machine is connected to
- A virtual hard disk used by the operating system
- The operating system installation options

When you create virtual machines in Hyper-V, you have to choose one of the two virtual machine generations:

- **Generation 1:** Provides the same virtual hardware used in older versions of Hyper-V. Generation 1 VMs support 32-bit and 64-bit guest operating systems.

- **Generation 2:** Provides new functionality on a virtual machine, including PXE boot by using a standard network adapter, boot from a SCSI virtual hard disk or DVD, Secure Boot, and UEFI firmware support. Generation 2 VMs only support 64-bit guest operating systems.

Once a virtual machine has been created, you cannot change its generation.

When creating and configuring a virtual machine, you can specify how much memory is assigned to a virtual machine. The *startup RAM* specifies the amount of memory that you want to allocate to the VM when it starts. When you are using Dynamic Memory, this value can be the minimum amount of memory needed to boot the system.

In Windows 10, Dynamic Memory is enabled by default. *Dynamic Memory* reallocates memory automatically to the VM from a shared memory pool as its demands change. If a virtualized server needs more memory, Hyper-V can increase the memory allocated to the system, and then reduce it when the traffic subsides.

Create a Virtual Machine

To create a virtual machine in Hyper-V running on Windows 10, perform the following steps:

1. On LON-CL1, right-click Start and choose Control Panel.

2. In the Search Control Panel text box, type **Administrative Tools**. Then from the search results, click Administrative Tools.

3. In the Administrative Tools window, double-click Hyper-V Manager. If you are prompted to confirm if you want to allow this app to make changes to your PC, click Yes.

4. Right-click the host and choose New ➤ Virtual Machine.

5. In the New Virtual Machine Wizard, on the Before You Begin page, click Next.

6. On the Specify Name and Location page (as shown in Figure 2.33), in the Name text box, type the name of the virtual machine.

FIGURE 2.33   Creating a virtual machine

7. The default location to store the VM is `C:\ProgramData\Microsoft\Windows\Hyper-V\` folder. Click Next.

8. On the Specify Generation page, Generation 1 is already selected. Click Next.

9. On the Assign Memory page, the default startup memory is 1024. In the Startup memory box, type **2048**. Click Next.

10. Normally, you would select a virtual switch. However, because a virtual switch is not configured yet, on the Configuring Networking page, click Next.

11. On the Connect Virtual Hard Disk page (as shown in Figure 2.34), change the size to 50 GB. Click Next.

12. On the Installation Options page, click "Install an operating system from a bootable CD/DVD-ROM," as shown in Figure 2.35.

FIGURE 2.34   Creating a virtual hard disk

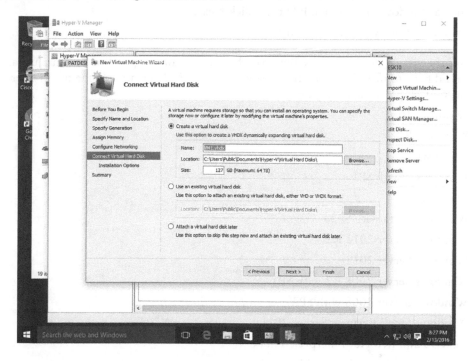

FIGURE 2.35   Specifying Installation Options

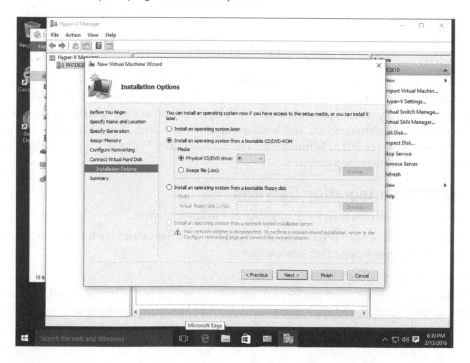

13. Click Image file (.iso) and click Browse. In the Open dialog box, browse to and double-click a Windows installation ISO file. Click Next.

14. On the Summary page, click Finish.

After the virtual machine is installed, you have to install an operating system, just as you would have to install an operating system on a physical machine. Some of the operating systems that Hyper-V supports are:

- Windows 10
- Windows 8.1
- Windows 8
- Windows 7 with SP1
- Windows 7
- Windows Vista with SP2
- Windows Server 2012 R2
- Windows Server 2012
- Windows Server 2008 R2 with SP1
- Windows Server 2008 with SP2
- Windows Small Business Server 2011
- CentOS and Red Hat Enterprise Linux
- Debian virtual machines on Hyper-V
- SUSE
- Oracle Linux
- Ubuntu
- FreeBSD

In some cases, the Hyper-V guest operating system does not function properly using the default drivers that are installed. For these operating systems, you can install guest integration services, which includes drivers for Hyper-V. It also supports operating system shutdown, time synchronization, and backup support. However, Windows 10, Windows 8/8.1, Windows Server 2012, Windows Server 2012 R2, and Windows Server 2016 already include the guest integration services.

Install Guest Integration Services

To install guest integration services, perform the following steps:

1. On LON-CL1, in the Server Manager window, click Tools and click Hyper-V Manager. The Hyper-V Manager console opens.

2. In the left pane, click a Hyper-V server.

3. In the Actions pane, start the virtual machine on which you want to install the guest integration services and click Connect. A Virtual Machine Connection window opens.

4. In the Virtual Machine Connection window, click Action and click Insert Integration Services Setup Disk. Hyper-V mounts an image of the guest integration services disk to a virtual disk drive and displays an Autoplay window.

5. Click Install Hyper-V Integration Services. A message box appears, prompting you to upgrade the existing installation.

6. Click OK. The system installs the package and prompts you to restart the computer.

7. Click Yes to restart the computer.

Creating and Managing Virtual Switches

To set up a test network that includes multiple systems, you need to configure a virtual switch using the Virtual Switch Manager. This enables your VMs to communicate with each other and access your physical network for Internet access.

Hyper-V includes three types of virtual switches:

- **External:** Creates a virtual switch that binds to the physical network adapter. This enables your VMs to access your physical network.

- **Internal:** Creates a virtual switch that is used only by the VMs that run on the physical computer and between the VMs and the physical host computer.

- **Private:** Creates a VM that can only be used by the VMs running on the computer.

To create a virtual switch, in the Actions pane, click Virtual Switch Manager. In the Virtual Switch Manager dialog box, click the type of switch to use and click Create Virtual Switch. If you select the external switch type, you need to specify the physical network adapter (on the host) to connect the switch to.

Create a Virtual Switch

To create a virtual switch in Hyper-V running on Windows 10, perform the following steps:

1. On LON-CL1, right-click Start and choose Control Panel.

2. In the Search Control Panel text box, type **Administrative Tools**. Then from the search results, click Administrative Tools.

3. In the Administrative Tools window, double-click Hyper-V Manager. If you are prompted to confirm if you want to allow this app to make changes to your PC, click Yes.

4. In the Actions pane, click Virtual Switch Manager. The Virtual Switch Manager dialog box opens, as shown in Figure 2.36.

5. Click the type of switch that you want to create and click Create Virtual Switch.

6. On the New Virtual Switch page (as shown in Figure 2.37), in the Name text box, type a descriptive name for the switch.

7. Click OK to close the Virtual Switch Manager. When you are prompted to apply networking changes, click Yes.

FIGURE 2.36   Selecting the type of virtual switch

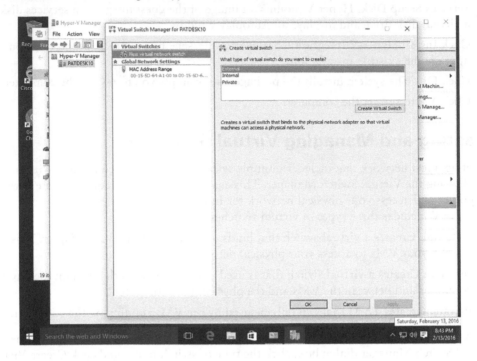

FIGURE 2.37   Configuring a virtual switch

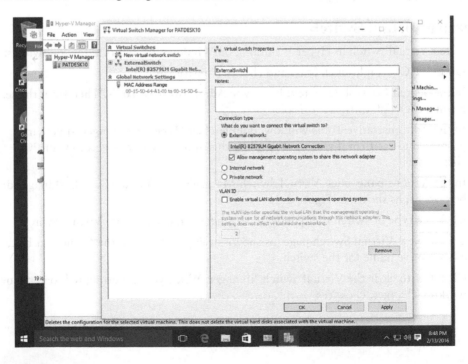

Select a Virtual Switch for a VM

To select a virtual switch for a VM in Hyper-V running on Windows 10, perform the following steps:

1. On LON-CL1, using Hyper-V Manager, right-click the VM and choose Settings.
2. In the Settings dialog box, click Network Adapter, as shown in Figure 2.38.

FIGURE 2.38   Configuring VM settings

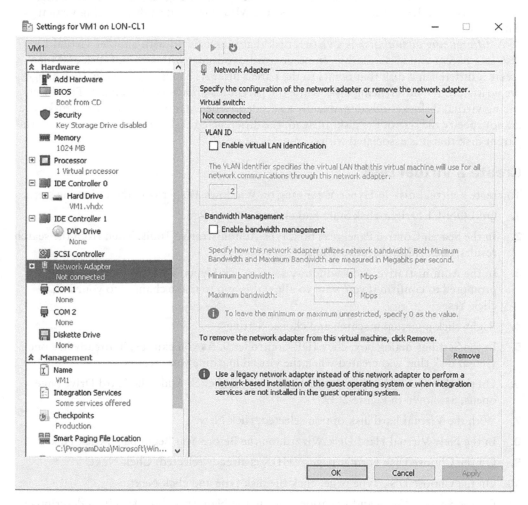

3. On the Network Adapters page, for the Virtual switch, click the new virtual switch.
4. Click OK to close the Settings dialog box.

Creating and Managing Virtual Disks

A *virtual disk* is a file that represents a physical disk drive to a guest operating system running on a virtual machine. The user can install a new operating system onto the virtual disk without repartitioning the physical disk or rebooting the host machine.

The New Virtual Hard Disk Wizard provides you with a simple way to create a virtual hard disk. With the wizard, you have to specify the file format and the type of virtual disk. Besides fixed-size virtual hard disks and dynamically expanding virtual hard disks that were discussed in Lesson 2, you can also use the wizard to create a differencing virtual hard disk.

A *differencing virtual disk* is a virtual disk that is associated with another virtual hard disk in a parent-child relationship. In other words, you start with a parent disk and then create a differencing disk that points to the parent disk. As changes are made, the changes are written to the differencing disk, while the parent disk remains unchanged. The differencing virtual disk expands dynamically as needed. When you use a differencing disk, you do not specify the size of the disk. Instead, the differencing disk grows up to the size of the parent disk that it is associated with.

Create a Virtual Disk

To create a virtual disk in Hyper-V running on Windows 10, perform the following steps:

1. On LON-CL1, right-click Start and choose Control Panel.

2. In the Search Control Panel text box, type **Administrative Tools**. Then from the search results, click Administrative Tools.

3. In the Administrative Tools window, double-click Hyper-V Manager. If you are prompted to confirm if you want to allow this app to make changes to your PC, click Yes.

4. Right-click a virtual machine and choose Settings.

5. In the Settings dialog box, click IDE Controller 0. As you can see, it already has one virtual disk that was created when the virtual machine was created.

6. On the IDE Controller page, click Hard Drive and click Add. The Hard Drive page opens, as shown in Figure 2.39.

7. With the Virtual hard disk option selected, click New.

8. In the New Virtual Hard Disk Wizard, on the Before You Begin page, click Next.

9. On the Choose Disk Format page, VHDX is already selected. Click Next.

10. On the Choose Disk Type page, click the disk type and click Next.

11. On the Specify Name and Location page, in the Name text box, specify a descriptive name for the disk. Click Next.

12. On the Create a New Blank Virtual Hard Disk page, specify the size of the disk, such as **10 GB**. Click Next.

13. On the Summary page, click Finish.

14. Click OK to close the Settings dialog box.

FIGURE 2.39   Creating a virtual disk

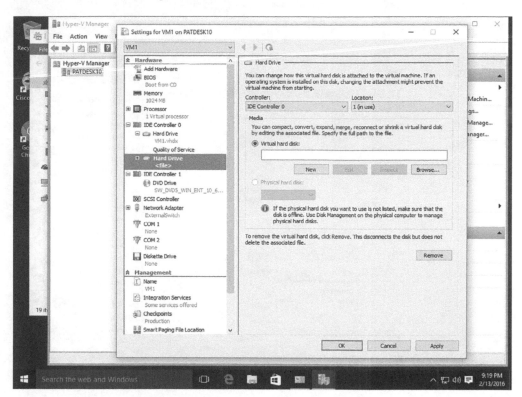

Creating and Managing Checkpoints

In Hyper-V, a *checkpoint* is a captured image of the state, data, and hardware configuration of a VM at a particular moment in time.

When you are testing an application and want to troubleshoot compatibility issues or test a new application update before rolling it out to production machines, you can use the Hyper-V snapshot feature (right-click the machine and choose Checkpoint, as shown in Figure 2.40). By creating a checkpoint, you can return to a known state on the VM (for example, the state before you installed the application).

Although checkpoints are a useful tool for you when implementing a test environment in Hyper-V, this tool is not recommended for heavy use in production environments. Apart from consuming disk space, the presence of snapshots can reduce the overall performance of a VM's disk subsystem.

To revert to the previous state, right-click the checkpoint and choose Apply. When you no longer need the checkpoint, right-click the checkpoint and choose Delete Checkpoint.

FIGURE 2.40   Creating a checkpoint in Hyper-V Manager

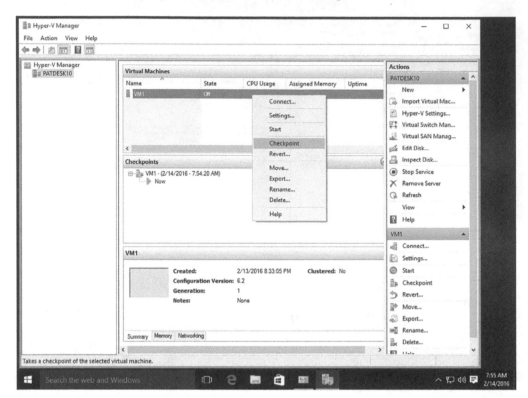

Skill Summary

In this lesson, you learned:

- The desktop is the main screen area that you see when you first start the computer and log on to Windows. Like the top of an actual desktop, it is where you perform your work by opening and running one or more applications. It also includes the Recycle Bin, which is used to recover files that have been previously deleted.

- In Windows 10, many of the Windows configuration is done within Settings. Settings can be accessed by clicking Start ➤ Settings.

- With versions of Windows prior to Windows 10, Control Panel was the primary graphical utility to configure the Windows environment and hardware devices. In Windows 10, it can be accessed by right-clicking Start and choosing Control Panel.

- File Explorer, previously known as Windows Explorer, is the file manager that is included with Windows operating systems. It provides a graphical user interface to access and manage the file system including opening files, moving and copying files, and deleting files.

- In Windows 10, a library is a virtual folder that can display content from different locations (folders, for example) on your computer or from an external drive. A library looks like an ordinary folder but simply points to files and folders that are located elsewhere.

- In Windows 10, simple power management settings can be accessed by opening Settings and clicking System ➤ Power & Sleep. The screen settings allow you to specify how long the screen will remain on if you are not actively using your computer when the computer is using battery power or when it is using AC power (plugged in). The sleep settings will specify how long the computer will operate before going into sleep mode when the computer is using battery power or when it is using AC power.

- Microsoft has built many features into Windows 10 that work with assistive technologies or as stand-alone features that make the user experience better for the visually and hearing impaired. Most accessibility features can be configured in the Ease of Access Center.

- Client Hyper-V enables you to create and manage virtual machines (VMs) using a virtual switch. These VMs can be used to test your applications for compatibility with new operating systems, allow you to run applications written for older versions of Windows, or isolate an application. The physical machine that Hyper-V and the virtual machines run on is often referred to as the host.

Knowledge Assessment

You can find the answers to the following sections in the Appendix.

Multiple Choice

1. Which of the following is *not* an account type in Windows 10?
   A. Guest
   B. Limited user
   C. Standard user
   D. Administrator

2. Which power mode first goes into a low-power mode for computers, and then to Hibernate mode when the system is almost out of power?
   A. Balanced mode
   B. Power mode
   C. Zip mode
   D. Hybrid mode

3. Which of the following actions is most likely to trigger a User Account Control dialog box?
   A. Uninstalling a program
   B. Creating a shortcut
   C. Changing resolution
   D. Adding a gadget

4. Which of the following can be used to directly access Event Viewer?
   A. Gadgets window
   B. Programs applet in Control Panel
   C. Administrative Tools
   D. User Account Control dialog box

5. Which of the following is not a UAC notification level?
   A. Always notify me
   B. Notify me only when users try to access my files
   C. Notify me only when programs try to make changes to my computer
   D. Never notify me of installations or changes

6. Which feature allows you to quickly minimize all open windows except the active one?
   A. Shake
   B. Snap
   C. Peek
   D. Show Desktop

7. Which of the following settings is not configurable from the Screen Resolution window?

   A. Orientation

   B. Font size

   C. Display

   D. Windows theme

8. Which of the following allows you to manage programs that run when Windows starts or when you log on?

   A. Task Scheduler

   B. Performance Monitor

   C. Programs applet in Control Panel

   D. System Configuration

9. Which versions of Windows 10 support Windows XP Mode? (Choose all that apply.)

   A. Mobile

   B. Professional

   C. Education

   D. Enterprise

10. Which of the following correctly explains the abbreviation VHD?

    A. Variable Hex Determinant

    B. Virtual Home Directory

    C. Virtual Hard Disk

    D. Virtual Hard Drive

Fill in the Blank

1. A _____ is a collection of information that defines the actions you can take on a computer and which files and folders you can access.

2. The _____ account type is best for everyday use.

3. _____ is used to prevent unauthorized changes to your system without your knowledge.

4. To configure accessibility options, open the _____.

5. To minimize all open windows at once, click the _____ button.

6. _____ includes several applets, including System and Security, Programs, User Accounts, and Ease of Access.

7. Use _____ to troubleshoot and resolve computer problems, and to keep your system running optimally.

8. The Windows 10 _____ window allows you to configure several display-related settings.

9. _____ can be used to run older applications made for Windows XP, for example, on a computer running Windows 10.

10. _____ is used to manage files and folders on a drive.

True/False

1. A User Account Control dialog box opens when you open your data files.

2. You cannot change the desktop resolution setting because it's a fixed value.

3. Deleting a shortcut does not delete the resource it represents.

4. A user account and a user profile are the same thing.

5. Windows 10 Settings replaced Windows Control Panel.

Case Scenarios

You can find the answers to the following sections in the Appendix.

Scenario 2-1: Getting Administrative-Level Privileges

As an IT technician, you need to perform some maintenance tasks on an employee's computer that will require elevated privileges. When you go to the Manage Accounts window in Control Panel on that employee's computer, you see only the employee's standard user account. Describe how to log on as a user with administrative-level privileges.

Scenario 2-2: Configuring Accessibility Features

Alexandra, an employee at your company, is visually impaired. Which features can be configured in Windows 10 to help her perform her work more efficiently?

Scenario 2-3: Running a Legacy Application

Oscar is the warehouse manager for The OEM Connection, an auto parts business. Although the business is standardized on Windows 10 Professional, Oscar needs to run a legacy parts lookup program that does not run in Windows 10. You provide technical support to The OEM Connection. Describe your recommended solution.

Scenario 2-4: Creating a Better User Experience

Oscar at The OEM Connection would like to use his Windows 10 Professional computer more efficiently. He would also like to be able to quickly launch Microsoft Excel each time he logs on to his computer, and he does not want the Windows Media Player to be present on the taskbar. Describe your recommended solution.

Lesson 3

Understanding Native Applications, Tools, Mobility, and Remote Management and Assistance

Objective Domain Matrix

Technology Skill	Objective Domain Description	Objective Domain Number
Configuring SmartScreen Filter	Configure applications	3.1
Configuring Microsoft Edge	Configure native applications and tools	1.3
Configuring Cortana	Configure native applications and tools	1.3
Supporting Mobile Access and Data Synchronization	Configure mobility settings	1.4
	Understand offline files	4.4
Accessing a Computer Remotely	Configure and use management tools	1.5
	Configure native applications and tools	1.3

Key Terms

ActiveX controls

ActiveX Filtering

add-ons

cmdlets

Common Information Model (CIM)

Compatibility View

Component Object Model (COM)

Computer Management

cookie

dynamic security

Favorites

InPrivate Browsing

Internet Explorer

Microsoft Edge

Network Address Translation (NAT)

one-way sync

phishing

Pop-up Blocker

PowerShell Remoting

proxy server

Remote Assistance

Remote Desktop Connection (RDC)

Remote Desktop Protocol (RDP)

Remote Desktop Services (RDS)

screen shot

Secure Sockets Layer (SSL)

security zones

SmartScreen Filter

snap-ins

Snip & Sketch (formerly the Snipping Tool)

Sync Center

sync conflict

Tracking Protection

two-way sync

Web Services for Management

Windows Management Instrumentation (WMI)

Windows Media Player 12

Windows Mobility Center

Windows PowerShell

Windows PowerShell Integrated Scripting Environment (ISE)

Windows Remote Management (WinRM)

WinRS.exe

Configuring Internet Explorer

Windows 10 includes two browsers, Internet Explorer and Microsoft Edge. *Internet Explorer* is the traditional Microsoft browser that offers a number of features to protect your security and privacy while you browse the Web, including phishing filters, Protected Mode, Pop-up Blocker, Add-On Manager, download files or software notification, and the use of digital signatures and 128-bit secure (SSL) connections when using secure websites.

Microsoft still offers Internet Explorer with Windows 10, but Microsoft's preferred method of browsing is by using Microsoft Edge. Both are covered in this chapter, since Microsoft still offers Internet Explorer.

Internet Explorer has changed significantly over the years. As a result, it has a lot of features and functionality. Some features are simple, such as the Zoom feature (Tools (gear) button ➤ Zoom). Because you use the web browser to access information from throughout the world over the Internet, your computer or private information might be at risk of being accessed by others.

Managing Cookies and Privacy Settings

Your web browser can reveal plenty of information about your personality and interests. Therefore, you need to take steps to ensure that this information cannot be read or used without your knowledge.

A *cookie* is text stored by a user's web browser. It can be used for a wide range of functions, including identifying you as a user, authenticating you as a user, and storing your site preferences and shopping cart contents. Cookies can provide a website with a lot of helpful information that can make your browsing experience easier and faster, but they also can be used by spyware programs and websites to track your online behavior. Unfortunately, some websites will not operate without cookies.

Delete Cookies and Temporary Internet Files

To delete cookies and temporary Internet files, perform the following steps:

1. Open Internet Explorer.

2. Click the Tools (gear) button and then click Internet Options.

3. On the General tab, under Browsing History, click Delete. The Delete Browsing History dialog box opens (see Figure 3.1).

4. Ensure that the "Cookies and website data" check box and the "Temporary Internet files and website files" check box are selected. Click Delete.

FIGURE 3.1   Deleting cookies and temporary files

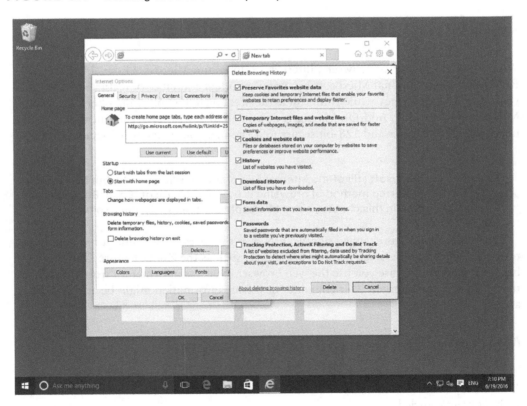

Being aware of how your private information is used when browsing the Web is important to help prevent targeted advertising, fraud, and identity theft.

View Privacy Settings

To view privacy settings, perform the following steps:

1. Open Internet Explorer.

2. Click Tools ➢ Internet Options.

3. Click the Privacy tab (see Figure 3.2).

FIGURE 3.2   Configuring privacy settings

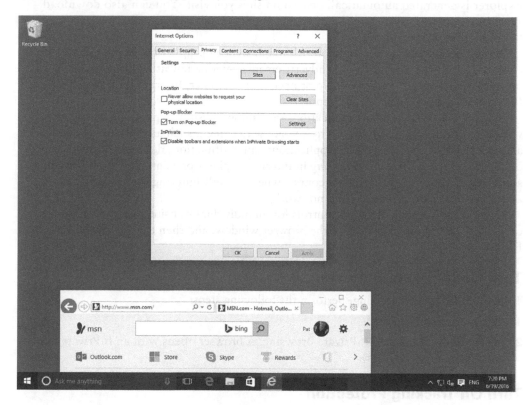

When you click the Advanced button, you can change settings that affect how cookies are handled and when you click the Sites button, you can allow or block cookies from individual websites.

To prevent Internet Explorer from storing data about your browsing session, Internet Explorer 11 includes *InPrivate Browsing*. This helps prevent anyone who might be using your computer from seeing where you visited and what you looked at on the Web.

When you start InPrivate Browsing, Internet Explorer opens a new window. The protection that InPrivate Browsing provides is only in effect during the time that you use that window. You can open as many tabs as you want in that window, and they will all be protected by InPrivate Browsing. However, if you open another browser window, that window will not be protected by InPrivate Browsing unless you configure that window to also use InPrivate Browsing. To end your InPrivate Browsing session, close the browser window.

Some websites can be used to gather information about which pages you visit on the Internet. *Tracking Protection* blocks this content from websites that appear on Tracking Protection Lists. A Personalized Tracking Protection List included with Internet Explorer is generated automatically based on sites you visit. You can also download Tracking Protection Lists and then Internet Explorer will periodically check for updates to the lists.

Pop-up windows are very common. Although some pop-up windows are useful website controls, most are simply annoying advertisements—with a few attempting to load spyware or other malicious programs. To help protect your computer, Internet Explorer's *Pop-up Blocker* can suppress some or all pop-ups.

ActiveX controls are small applications that allow websites to provide content such as videos and games and to allow you to interact with content such as those used in toolbars and stock tickers. However, these applications can malfunction, deliver unwanted content, or contain malware. *ActiveX Filtering* in Internet Explorer prevents sites from installing and using ActiveX applications. Of course, when ActiveX Filtering is on, videos, games, and other interactive content might not work.

If you want to enable ActiveX controls for an individual website, visit the website, click the Filter button at the top of the browser window, and then click Turn off ActiveX Filtering.

Turn On InPrivate Browsing

To turn on InPrivate Browsing, perform the following steps:

1. Open Internet Explorer.
2. Click Tools ➤ Safety ➤ InPrivate Browsing. A browser opens with an InPrivate button at the top of the window.

Turn On Tracking Protection

To turn on Tracking Protection, perform the following steps:

1. Open Internet Explorer.
2. Click Tools ➤ Safety ➤ Turn on Tracking Protection.
3. In the Manage Add-ons dialog box, with Tracking Protection selected, double-click Your Personalized List.
4. In the Personalized Tracking Protection List, click Automatically Block (as shown in Figure 3.3) and then click OK.
5. Click Close.

FIGURE 3.3   Turning on Tracking Protection

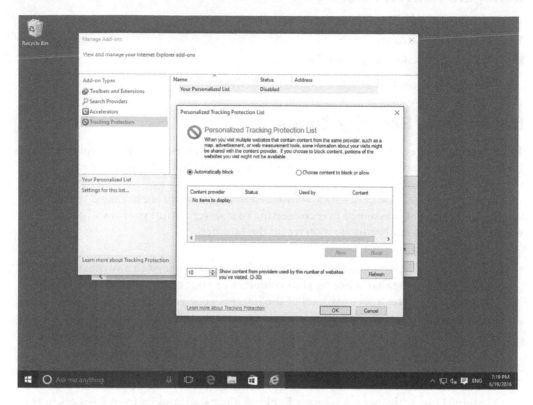

Configure the Pop-Up Blocker

To configure the Pop-up Blocker, perform the following steps:

1. Open Internet Explorer.
2. Click Tools ➤ Internet options.
3. Click the Privacy tab.
4. Click Settings. The Pop-up Blocker Settings dialog box opens.
5. To allow pop-ups from a specific website, in the Address of website to allow text box, type the URL of the site and click Add.

    Repeat the process to add additional sites to the Allowed sites list.
6. Adjust the Blocking level drop-down list to one of the following settings:

    - **High:** Blocks all pop-ups
    - **Medium:** Blocks most automatic pop-ups
    - **Low:** Allows pop-ups from secure sites

7. Click Close to close the Pop-Up Blocker Settings dialog box.
8. Click OK to close the Internet Properties dialog box.

Configure ActiveX Filtering

To configure ActiveX Filtering, perform the following steps:

1. Open Internet Explorer.

2. Click Tools ➤ Safety ➤ ActiveX Filtering.

   There should now be a check mark next to ActiveX Filtering.

Configuring Security Zones

To help manage Internet Explorer security when visiting websites, Internet Explorer divides your network connection into *security zones* based on four content types. For each zone, a security level is assigned.

The security for each security zone is assigned based on dangers associated with that zone. For example, it is assumed that connecting to a server within your own corporation would be safer than connecting to a server on the Internet.

The four default content types are:

- **Internet Zone:** This zone includes anything that is not assigned to any other zone as well as anything that is not on your computer or your organization's network (intranet). The default security level of the Internet zone is Medium-High.

- **Local Intranet Zone:** This zone applies to computers that are part of the organization's network (intranet) that do not require a proxy server, as defined by the system administrator. These include sites specified on the Connections tab, network, paths (such as \\computername\foldername), and local intranet sites (such as http://internal). You can add sites to this zone. The default security level for the Local Intranet zone is Medium-Low, which means Internet Explorer allows all cookies from websites in this zone to be saved on your computer and read by the website that created them. Lastly, if the website requires NT LAN Manager (NTLM) or integrated authentication, it automatically uses your user name and password.

- **Trusted Sites Zone:** This zone includes trusted sites that you believe you can download or run files from without damaging your computer. This also includes sites from which you believe you can download data or sites that you don't consider to be a security risk. You can assign sites to this zone. The default security level for the Trusted Sites zone is Medium, which means Internet Explorer allows all cookies from websites in this zone to be saved on your computer and read by the website that created them.

- **Restricted Sites Zone:** This zone includes sites that you do not trust; downloading or running files from these sites might damage your computer. You can assign sites to this zone. The default security level for the Restricted Sites zone is High, which means Internet Explorer blocks all cookies from websites in this zone.

To determine which zones the current web page falls into, press Alt to show the menu and click File ➤ Properties.

Modify the Security Level for a Web Content Zone

To modify the security level for a web content zone, perform the following steps:

1. Open Internet Explorer.

2. Click Tools ➢ Internet options.

3. In the Internet Options dialog box, click the Security tab.

4. Click the zone on which you want to set the security level (as shown in Figure 3.4). Drag the slider to set the security level to High, Medium-High, or Low. Internet Explorer describes each option to help you decide which level to choose. You are prompted to confirm any reduction in security level.

FIGURE 3.4   Configuring the security content zones

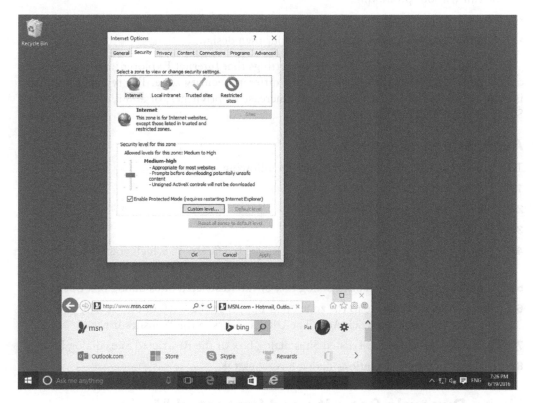

5. To customize individual settings, click the Custom Level button to open the Security Settings dialog box for the selected zone.

6. Click radio buttons for the individual settings in each security category. The radio buttons typically make it possible to enable a setting, disable it, or prompt the user before enabling it.

7.　To close the Security Settings dialog box, click OK.

8.　To close the Internet Options dialog box, click OK.

For each web content zone, there is a default security level. The security levels available in Internet Explorer are:

- **High:** Excludes any content that can damage your computer by maximizing safeguards and disabling less secure features.

- **Medium-High:** Appropriate for most websites; prompts before downloading potentially unsafe content.

- **Medium:** Warns you before running potentially damaging content.

- **Medium-Low:** Appropriate for local network\intranet websites; allows most content to be run without prompting.

- **Low:** Does not warn you before running potentially damaging content.

- **Custom:** Creates a security setting of your own design.

The easiest way to modify the security settings that Internet Explorer imposes on a specific website is to manually add the site to a different security zone. The typical procedure is to add a site to the Trusted Sites zone to increase its privileges, or add it to the Restricted Sites zone to reduce its privileges.

Add a Site to a Security Zone

To add a site to a security zone, perform the following steps:

1.　Open Internet Explorer.

2.　Click Tools ➤ Internet Options.

3.　Click the Security tab.

4.　Click the zone—either Trusted Sites or Restricted Sites—to which you want to add a site.

5.　Click Sites. The Trusted Sites dialog box or the Restricted Sites dialog box opens.

6.　In the "Add this website to the zone" text box, type the URL of the website you want to add to the zone and click Add. The URL appears in the Websites list.

7.　Click Close to close the Trusted Sites dialog box or the Restricted Sites dialog box.

8.　To close the Internet Options dialog box, click OK.

Using Dynamic Security and Protected Mode

Internet Explorer offers multiple security features to defend against malware and data theft, including dynamic security and Protected Mode. *Dynamic security* is a set of tools and technology that protects your computer as you browse the Internet with Internet Explorer. It includes ActiveX opt-in, Security Status Bar, Phishing Filter, Address Bar Protection, and Protected Mode.

The Security Status Bar keeps you notified of the website security and privacy settings by using color-coded notifications next to the address bar. Some of these features include:

- The address bar turns green to indicate websites bearing new High Assurance certificates, indicating the site owner has completed extensive identity verification checks.

- Phishing Filter notifications, certificate names, and the gold padlock icon are now also adjacent to the address bar for better visibility.

- Certificate and privacy detail information can easily be displayed with a single click on the Security Status Bar.

- The address bar is displayed to the user for every window, whether it's a pop-up or a standard window, which helps to block malicious sites from emulating trusted sites.

- To help protect you against phishing sites, Internet Explorer warns you when you're visiting potential or known fraudulent sites and blocks them if appropriate. The opt-in filter is updated several times per hour with the latest security information from Microsoft and several industry partners.

- International Domain Name Anti-Spoofing notifies you when visually similar characters in the URL are not expressed in the same language.

If Internet Explorer is still using its original settings, you'll see the Information bar in the following circumstances:

- When a website tries to install an ActiveX control on your computer or run an ActiveX control in an unsafe manner

- When a website tries to open a pop-up window

- When a website tries to download a file to your computer

- When a website tries to run active content on your computer

- When your security settings are below recommended levels

- When you access an intranet web page, but have not turned on intranet address checking

- When you start Internet Explorer with add-ons disabled

- When you need to install an updated ActiveX control or add-on program

- When the website address can be displayed with native language letters or symbols but you don't have the language installed

To help protect your computer, Internet Explorer Protected Mode runs as a low-integrity procedure, which means that Internet Explorer writes to only low-integrity disk locations, such as the Temporary Internet Files folder and the standard Internet Explorer storage areas, including the History, Cookies, and Favorites folders. As a result, Protected Mode is a feature that makes it more difficult for malicious software to be installed on your computer.

Protected Mode is not a complete defense against malware. Therefore, it is recommended to use an up-to-date antivirus package with antispyware capability and to keep your system up to date with Windows and Internet Explorer security updates and patches.

Enable Protected Mode

Before Protected Mode can be enabled, you must ensure that UAC is enabled. To enable Protected Mode perform the following steps.

1. Open Internet Explorer.
2. Click Tools ➤ Internet Options.
3. Click the Security tab.
4. Click to select Enable Protected Mode.
5. Close the Internet Options dialog box by clicking OK.
6. Close Internet Explorer and then restart Internet Explorer.

Configuring the SmartScreen Filter and Phishing

Phishing is a fraudulent technique based on social engineering. With phishing, users are enticed (usually through email or other websites) to go to illegitimate websites that look similar to legitimate websites in an effort to persuade users to supply personal information, such as passwords and account numbers.

Certification Ready

Which Windows 10 browser technology is used to protect against phishing activity when visiting websites? Objective 3.1

To help protect against phishing, Internet Explorer 11 includes *SmartScreen Filter*, which examines traffic for evidence of phishing activity and displays a warning to the user if it finds any. It also sends the address back to the Microsoft SmartScreen service to be compared against lists of known phishing and malware sites. If SmartScreen Filter discovers that a website you're visiting is on the list of known malware or phishing sites, Internet Explorer displays a blocking web page and the address bar is shown in red. From the blocking page, you can choose to bypass the blocked website and go to your home page instead, or you can continue to the blocked website, though this is not recommended. If you continue to the blocked website, the address bar continues to appear in red.

To protect your privacy, information that is submitted to the SmartScreen web service is transmitted in encrypted format over HTTPS. This information is not stored with your IP address or other personally identifiable information and will not be used to identify, contact, or provide advertising to you.

You can set up the browser by using express settings or by configuring settings individually. The express settings option enables the SmartScreen Filter, but you can disable it at any time by clicking the Safety button on the toolbar and clicking SmartScreen Filter ➤ Turn Off SmartScreen Filter (which opens the Microsoft SmartScreen Filter dialog box).

Even without SmartScreen Filter turned on, you can remain safe from phishing attempts as long as you obey the following unofficial rules of web surfing:

- Don't trust hyperlinks.

- Never supply a password or any other confidential information to a website unless you type the URL yourself and you are sure that it is correct.

Managing Add-Ons

To make Internet Explorer more flexible, Internet Explorer allows you to add *add-ons* to your browser, such as extra toolbars, animated mouse pointers, stock tickers, and pop-up blockers. Add-ons are downloaded from the Internet and installed as an executable program.

The four basic types of add-ons supported by Internet Explorer are as follows:

- **Toolbars and Extensions:** Enable the browser to open and manipulate websites or file types that Internet Explorer does not support natively. Some applications add their own toolbars to Internet Explorer, enabling you to work with their documents within an Internet Explorer session.

- **Search Providers:** Enable the user to perform searches directly from the Internet Explorer interface using search engines on the Internet or the local network.

- **Accelerators:** Enable users to send text or other media they select in an Internet Explorer browser window to another application, such as an email client or an Internet resource (such as a blog).

- **Tracking Protection:** Enables you to import and export XML files containing InPrivate filters.

View Your Current Add-Ons

To view your current add-ons, perform the following steps:

1. Open Internet Explorer.
2. Click Tools ➤ Manage Add-ons.
3. Under Toolbars And Extensions (see Figure 3.5), under Show, you can select one of the following views of your add-ons:
   - To display a complete list of the add-ons that reside on your computer, click All Add-ons.
   - To display only those add-ons that were needed for the current web page or a recently viewed web page, click Currently Loaded Add-ons.

- To display add-ons that were preapproved by Microsoft, your computer manufacturer, or a service provider, click Run Without Permission.
- To display only 32-bit ActiveX controls, click Downloaded Controls.

4. Click Close.

FIGURE 3.5   Managing add-ons

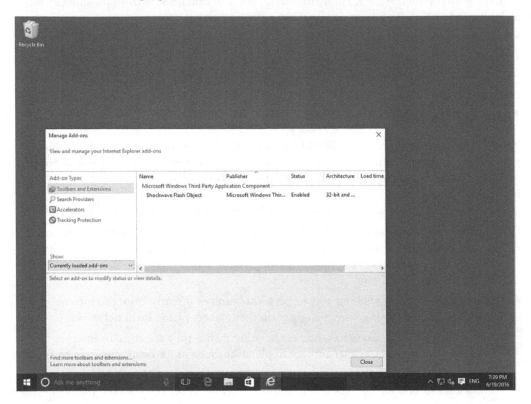

Delete ActiveX Controls

To delete ActiveX controls you have installed, perform the following steps:

1. Open Internet Explorer.
2. Click Tools ➢ Manage Add-ons.
3. Under Show, click Downloaded Controls to display all downloaded ActiveX controls.

4. Click the ActiveX control you want to delete and click More Information.

5. In the More Information dialog box, click Remove. If you are prompted for an administrator password or confirmation, type the password or provide confirmation.

Disable Add-Ons

To permanently disable add-ons, perform the following steps.

1. Open Internet Explorer.

2. Click Tools ➤ Manage Add-ons.

3. Under Show, click All Add-ons.

4. Click the add-on you want to disable and click Disable.

Configuring Compatibility Mode

Through the years, web pages have changed quite a bit. Unfortunately, as newer technology is implemented on websites, sometimes websites don't look like you expect them to. Images might not appear, menus might be out of place, and text could be jumbled together. In these situations, you can try to run the site in compatibility mode.

Once you turn on Compatibility View, Internet Explorer automatically shows that site in Compatibility View each time you visit. You can turn it off by removing it from your compatibility list.

View Compatibility View

To turn Compatibility View on or off, click the Compatibility View button, or perform the following steps:

1. Open Internet Explorer.

2. Click Tools ➤ Compatibility View Settings.

3. In the Compatibility View Settings dialog box (as shown in Figure 3.6), you can perform the following tasks:

   - **Display intranet sites in Compatibility View:** To include all of your internal corporate websites, make sure the Display Intranet Sites In Compatibility View check box is selected.

   - **Use Microsoft compatibility lists:** Selecting this check box automatically puts sites into Compatibility View if they are on the list compiled by Microsoft.

   - **Add this website:** To run a website in Compatibility View, type the website into the Add This Website text box, and click Add.

4. Click **Close** to close the Compatibility View Settings dialog box.

FIGURE 3.6   Managing Compatibility View settings

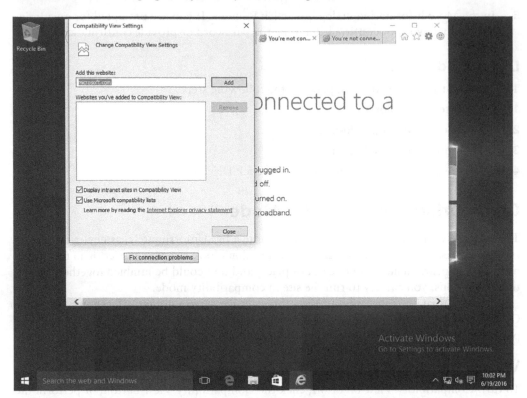

Configuring Secure Sockets Layer (SSL) and Certificates

You might need to transmit private data over the Internet, such as credit card numbers, Social Security numbers, and so on. You should use HTTP over SSL (HTTPS) to encrypt the data sent over the Internet. By convention, URLs that require an SSL connection start with https: (instead of http:).

Secure Sockets Layer (SSL) uses a cryptographic system that uses two keys—one key to encrypt the data and another key to decrypt the data. The public key is known to everyone and a private or secret key is known only to the recipient of the message. The public key is published in a digital certificate, which also confirms the identity of the web server.

When you connect to a site that is secured using SSL, a lock icon appears in the address bar. Clicking the lock icon displays more information about the site (see Figure 3.7), including the identity of the certificate authority (CA) that issued the certificate. For even more information, you can click the View certificates link to open the Certificate dialog box.

FIGURE 3.7   Viewing certificate information

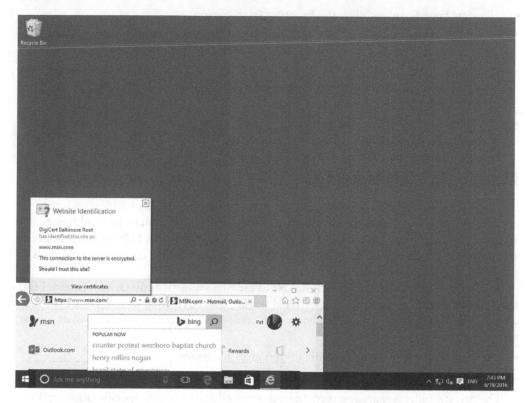

When visiting certain websites, Internet Explorer might find problems with the digital certificate, such as the certificate has expired, it is corrupted, it has been revoked, or it does not match the name of the website. When this happens, Internet Explorer blocks access to the site and displays a warning stating that there is a problem with the certificate. You then have a chance to close the browser window or ignore the warning and continue on to the site. Of course, if you choose to ignore the warning, make sure you trust the website and you believe that you are communicating with the correct server.

Managing Favorites

Favorites allow you to keep track of websites that you visit frequently so that you can visit them quickly in the future. If you're on a site that you want to make a favorite, click the Favorites (star) button and click Add to favorites. You can also save a favorite by pressing Ctrl+D. You will then be prompted to name the favorite and identify which folder the favorite will be stored in. The favorites are stored in the user's profile folder (c:\Users\<Username>\Favorites).

Some of the popular tasks related to favorites are:

- To view your favorites, click the Favorites (star) button.

- To organize your favorites, click the Favorites (star) button, click the small down arrow next to the Add to favorites button, and then click Organize favorites.

- To export the favorites to an HTML file, which can be imported into another machine, click the small down arrow next to the Add to favorites button, click Import and export, and then click Export to a file.

- To import the favorites from an HTML file, click the small down arrow next to the Add to favorites button, click Import and export, and then click Import from a file.

Managing LAN Settings

Although Classless Inter-Domain Routing (CIDR) helped use the IPv4 addresses more efficiently, additional steps were necessary to prevent the exhaustion of IPv4 addresses. *Network Address Translation (NAT)* is used with masquerading to hide an entire address space behind a single IP address. In other words, it allows multiple computers on a network to connect to the Internet through a single IP address.

NAT enables a local area network (LAN) to use one set of IP addresses for internal traffic and a second set of addresses for external traffic. The NAT computer or device is usually a router (including routers made for home and small-office Internet connections) or a proxy server. As a result, you can:

- Provide a type of firewall by hiding internal IP addresses.

- Enable multiple internal computers to share a single external public IP address.

The private addresses are reserved addresses not allocated to any specific organization. Because these private addresses cannot be assigned to global addresses used on the Internet and are not routable on the Internet, you must use a NAT gateway or proxy server to convert between private and public addresses. The private network addresses are expressed in RFC 1918 as:

- 10.0.0.0–10.255.255.255

- 172.16.0.0–172.31.255.255

- 192.168.0.0–192.168.255.255

NAT obscures an internal network's structure by making all traffic appear to originate from the NAT device or proxy server. A *proxy server* is a server that acts as an intermediary for clients seeking resources outside their networks. Medium and large organizations typically use a proxy server. In addition, these organizations require their clients to use the proxy server when accessing the Internet. By using the proxy server, organizations can monitor traffic and provide better security. For organizations that use proxy servers, users need to use the proxy server to access Office 365, Microsoft Intune, and Microsoft Azure, because client traffic has to go through the proxy server to connect to the Internet.

Configure a Client to Use a Proxy Server

To configure a client to use a proxy server, perform the following steps:

1. Open Internet Explorer.

2. Click Tools ➤ Internet Options.

3. Click the Connections tab.

4. Click LAN Settings.

5. In the Local Area Network (LAN) Settings dialog box (see Figure 3.8), deselect the Automatically Detect Settings check box.

FIGURE 3.8   Configuring proxy settings

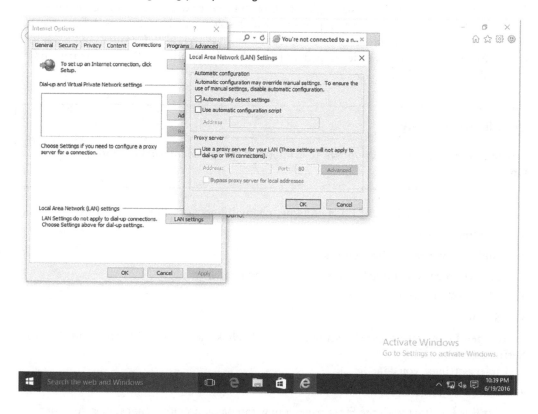

6. Select the Use a proxy server for your LAN check box.

7. In the Address text box, type the host name or IP address of the proxy server. In the Port text box, type the port used by the proxy server, such as 80 or 8080.

8. If you do not want to use proxy servers to access local resources, select the "Bypass proxy server for local addresses" check box.

9. Alternatively, you can click the Advanced button. In the Proxy Settings dialog box, you can specify individual proxy settings for HTTP, Secure, FTP, and Socks. You can also specify exceptions for sites in which you do not want to use the proxy server. Click OK.

10. Click OK to close the Local Area Network (LAN) Settings dialog box.

11. Click OK to close the Internet Options dialog box.

Configuring Microsoft Edge

Microsoft Edge is a new Microsoft lightweight web browser with a layout engine built around web standards designed to replace Internet Explorer as the default web browser. It integrates with Cortana, annotation tools, Adobe Flash Player, a PDF reader, and a reading mode. Extension support was developed and added to the Windows 10 Anniversary Update in July 2016.

Certification Ready

Which browser included in Windows 10 is intended to replace Internet Explorer?
Objective 1.3

At the top of the Microsoft Edge window, you will find the following buttons:

▪ Reading view

▪ Add to Favorites or Reading List

▪ Hub (Favorites, reading list, history, and downloads)

▪ Make a Web Note

▪ Settings

To open Edge Settings (as shown in Figure 3.9), click the More (...) button and click the Settings option.

Under Settings, you can:

▪ Enable or disable the favorites bar.

▪ Set Edge to start with the Start page, a new tab page, previous pages, or a specified web page.

▪ Set whether new tabs will be top sites and suggested content, top sites, or a blank page.

▪ Set your search engine to Bing, Google, or any search engine of your choice by clicking the View advanced settings button.

▪ Clear browsing history and delete media licenses, pop-up exceptions, and location permissions.

▪ Set the Reading view style to Default, Light, Medium, or Dark, along with the Reading font size.

FIGURE 3.9   Configuring Microsoft Edge

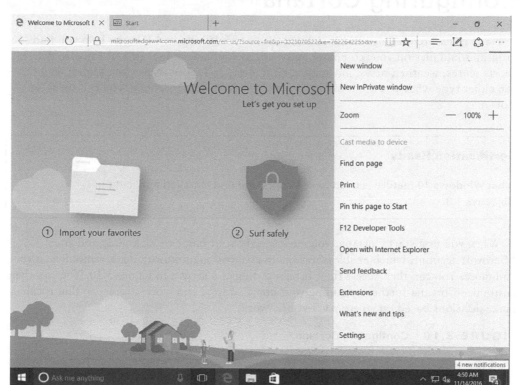

When you click the View advanced settings option, you can:

- Enable or disable Adobe Flash Player.
- Set privacy options.
- Manage saved passwords.
- Opt to save form entries.
- Choose to block pop-ups and cookies.
- Manage protected media licenses.
- Send Do Not Track requests.
- Enable or disable page prediction.
- Enable or disable SmartScreen Filter.
- Turn on or off Cortana integration.
- Set your search engine to Bing, Google, or a search engine of your choice.

Configuring Cortana

Cortana is a search feature and personal assistant for Windows 10. It can help you find programs and files on your computer and manage your calendar events. It can also deliver sports scores, weather, news, navigation, reminders, and more. When you search, you can either type what you are looking for, or if you have a microphone, you can speak to Cortana.

Certification Ready

What Windows 10 feature is used to search for and find installed applications?
Objective 1.3

When you first start Cortana, you must specify your name or nickname and your Microsoft account, which enables Cortana to give you suggestions, ideas, reminders, alerts, and more. You can then access the Cortana settings, as shown in Figure 3.10. You can then customize Cortana further by adding your home address and work address so that it can make decisions based on where you live and work.

FIGURE 3.10   Configuring Cortana

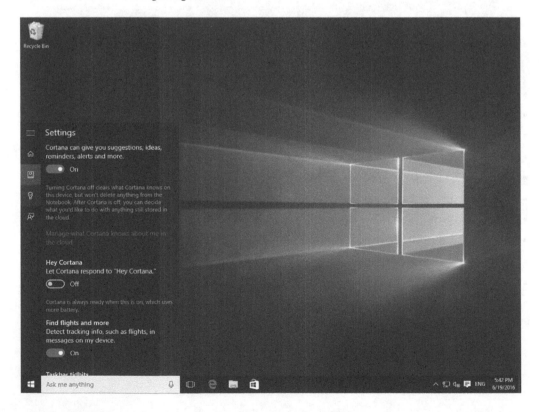

When you click Cortana, you will see four small icons:

- **Home:** Displays news and personalized items that Cortana thinks you will be interested in at the moment.
- **Notebook:** Specifies what appears in the Home view and in search results as a whole. You can also add additional accounts (Connected Accounts).
- **Reminders:** Shows reminders that Cortana has gathered. For the Reminders option to be available, you must be signed into Cortana with a Microsoft account.
- **Feedback:** Sends feedback to Microsoft.

Introducing Accessory Programs

Windows 10 comes bundled with many useful accessory programs (as shown in Table 3.1), such as Calculator, Notepad, Paint, Snip & Sketch, Windows Media Player 12, WordPad, and many more. The programs allow you to be productive in Windows without purchasing third-party programs.

To access these programs, click Start, navigate to and click the application or type the name of the program, and then press Enter.

TABLE 3.1   Windows 10 Accessory Programs

Program	Description
Calculator	Performs basic mathematical functions such as addition, subtraction, multiplication, and division. Also includes scientific, programmer, and statistics functions, along with unit conversions, date calculations, and worksheets to determine mortgage payments, vehicle lease payments, and fuel economy.
Command Prompt	Opens a window in which you run MS-DOS and other computer commands.
Math Input Panel	Allows you to write and correct freehand math equations using your mouse or other pointing device.
Notepad	Serves as a simple text editor.
Paint	Allows you to perform basic image editing.
Remote Desktop Connection	Connects two computers over a network or the Internet, allowing one computer to see and use the other computer's desktop. Remote Desktop Connection is covered later in this lesson.

TABLE 3.1   Windows 10 Accessory Programs *(continued)*

Program	Description
Run	Allows you to run commands from the Start menu. Some commands require elevated or administrative privileges; to run these commands, use the **Run as administrator** command.
Snip & Sketch	Allows you to capture, annotate, and save screen shots. Snip & Sketch is covered later in this lesson.
Sound Recorder	Allows you to record sound from different audio devices, such as a microphone that's plugged into the sound card on your computer.
Sticky Notes	Allows you to keep notes on the desktop to help you remember important items. Available in different colors.
Sync Center	Allows you to sync any folder in your computer with a folder on an external drive connected to your computer or a network drive.
File Explorer	Allows you to access files and folders on your computer, copy and move items, search for items, and more. This graphical file management system is built in to many versions of Windows.
Windows Mobility Center	Allows you to control many different computer settings, such as screen brightness, volume, power/battery, Wi-Fi, Bluetooth, sound, and so on.
WordPad	Serves as a word processor, with many more features than Notepad.
Ease of Access	Allows you to open the Ease of Access Center to configure accessibility options and gives you access to the speech recognition feature. See Lesson 2.
Tablet PC	Gives you access to tools to use a tablet PC's input device.
Windows Media Player 12	Enables you to play audio and video and display images; rip music from and copy music to compact disks; and burn recordable discs in Audio CD format or as a data disk.
Windows PowerShell	Opens a command window useful for IT professionals. Windows PowerShell is covered later in this lesson.

Using Snip & Sketch

Home and business users alike need to capture screen shots occasionally for many different reasons. Windows 10 includes the Snip & Sketch, an easy-to-use screen capture program with a few editing features.

A *screen shot*, also referred to as a snip or screen grab, is a snapshot of whatever is displayed on the computer screen. You might take a screen shot of an error message to help troubleshoot a computer problem, you might capture screen shots of a process in a program to create a how-to guide, or you might capture a screen shot to save as an image to use in a report or other document.

Certification Ready

What is the Snip & Sketch used for? Objective 1.3

In June 2019, Microsoft introduced Screen Sketch as a new Windows 10 screen capture tool as a replacement for the Snipping Tool. The name was then changed to Snip & Sketch. Snip & Sketch provides methods of capturing the screen, including taking instantaneous snips from the New menu, and delayed snips of up 3–10 seconds.

Features with Snip & Sketch:

- Create new screen snip or open image file.
- Mark up images with pen, pencil, or highlighter.
- The drawing canvas supports inking in the margins.
- Save, copy to clipboard, or share your creation.

FIGURE 3.11   Microsoft Snip & Sketch

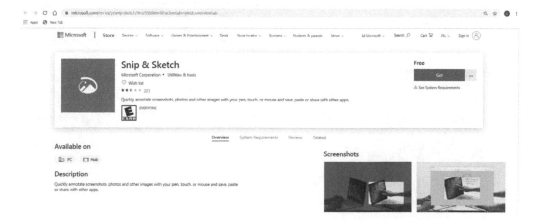

Snip & Sketch is an accessory program that comes with Windows 10 that allows you to take screen shots, annotate them, and save them. When using Snip & Sketch, you can capture the entire screen, a window, a rectangular portion of the screen, or a free-form image. The free-form capture allows you to use your mouse pointer or other pointing device to draw around a non-rectangular object on the screen.

You can save images in GIF, JPG, PNG, or HTML format, then use Snip & Sketch to add freehand annotations, highlight or erase part of the image, or send it to a recipient via email. If you select the HTML format, Snip & Sketch saves the screen shot as a web archive file in MHT format, which you can open in a web browser such as Internet Explorer.

Use Snip & Sketch to Capture a Screen Shot

To capture a screen shot with Snip & Sketch and save it as a graphics file, perform the following steps:

1. Open Start.

2. Search for Snip & Sketch, click the top result to open the experience.

3. Click the New button in the top-left corner. (See Figure 3.12)

FIGURE 3.12   Create a New Screen Shot with Snip & Sketch

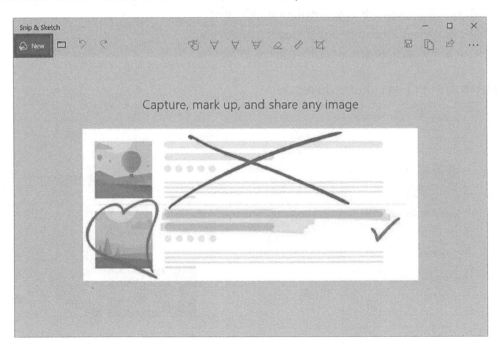

4. Select the type of snip you want to use, including:

   - Rectangular Clip.
   - Freeform Clip.
   - Fullscreen Clip.

5. Take the screenshot.

 You can turn off the Snip & Sketch overlay. Click Options, deselect the "Show screen overlay when Snip & Sketch is active" check box, and then click OK.

FIGURE 3.13 The captured image

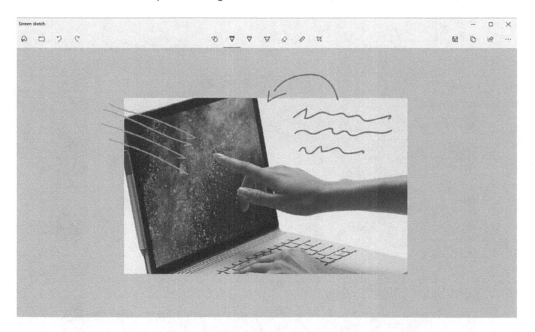

6. On the far-right corner, are the options to save the snip as a PNG file. Can also use the copy button to copy the image to the clipboard, so you can then paste on a document. Also, a feature that allows you to share by using the share button. The share button allows you to send the screen shot to another person using email, nearby sharing, or another supported applications. (See Figure 3.12).

GIF files support 256 colors and are used primarily for websites. JPG is the most common picture file format, and it supports over 16 million colors. PNG files are an improvement to the GIF format and support "lossless compression," which means you can enlarge a PNG file to a certain extent without losing clarity and crispness.

Use Snip & Sketch to Annotate an Image

To annotate an image using Snip & Sketch, perform the following steps:

1.   In the Snip & Sketch editing window, click the Pen button on the toolbar. Click a pen color in the list.

2.   Write or draw on the image (see Figure 3.14).

FIGURE 3.14   Annotating an image

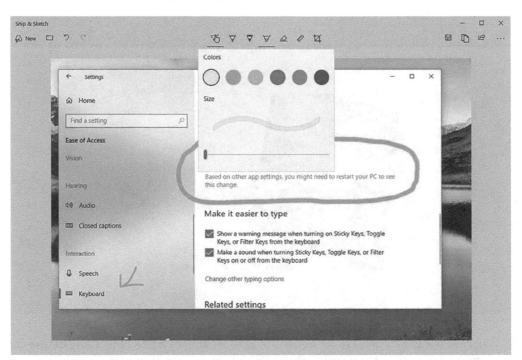

3.   Click Save Snip to save the annotated image under the current file name or a new file name.

Remember, you can open an image saved with Snip & Sketch in any graphics program (including Paint) to make detailed edits.

Using Windows Media Player 12

Windows Media Player has been around in various forms for many years. It used to be the default Windows media player, however, with Windows 10 it needs to be installed before it is available.

If you need to simply play back almost any type of multimedia file, Windows Media Player should be the program you use. It has media burning and ripping features, along with the ability to stream multimedia to other networked computers, which makes it a great choice at home and at work.

Windows Media Player 12 is a program that allows you to play back music and video files and view photos. Files stored in your Music, Pictures, and Videos libraries appear in the Windows Media Player file list by default. If you're connected to a network, you can stream digital media files—audio, video, or photos—for playback or viewing from another computer or a server that hosts Windows media files.

The quickest way to see if you have Windows Media Player 12 installed and enabled is to open the Start menu and search for it.

Windows Media Player 12 comes as an "optional feature" for most Windows 10 versions. But it is disabled by default. There are a number of apps available if you do not wish to use Windows Media Player 12; these include the Movies & TV app and the Groove Music app. The Microsoft Store offers a wide variety of audio and video playback.

The main window in Windows Media Player is called the Player Library (see Figure 3.15).

FIGURE 3.15   Windows Media Player main window—the Player Library

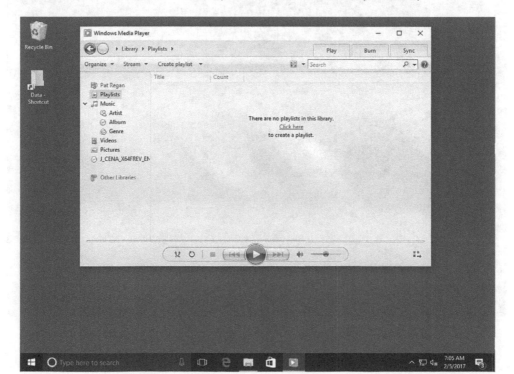

Certification Ready

What is the name of the main window of Windows Media Player? Objective 1.3

 Windows Media Player 12 supports the 3GP, AAC, AVCHD, MPEG-4, WMV, and WMA audio and video formats. It also supports most AVI, DivX, MOV, and Xvid files.

Whether playing digital files on your computer or from a CD or DVD, Windows Media Player includes common playback controls, such as Play, Shuffle, Repeat, Stop, Next, Previous, and a volume slider. You can switch to a smaller window, referred to as Now Playing mode, by clicking the Switch To Now Playing button in the lower-right corner. The Now Playing mode window appears (see Figure 3.16). To return to your library, click Go to Library.

FIGURE 3.16   Windows Media Player—Now Playing mode

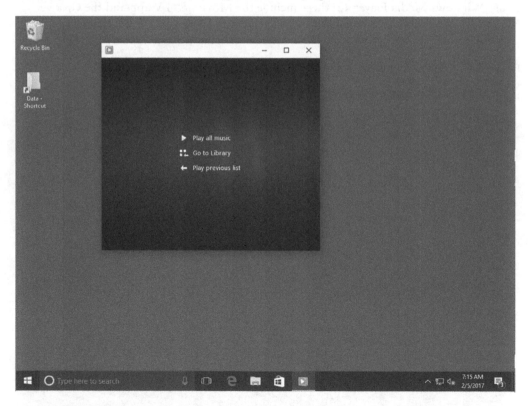

With Windows Media Player, you can do the following as well:

Create Playlists   Organize your music files into playlists, which are simply lists of music composed of songs from different albums, and may even be located on different areas of your computer or attached devices. Whatever appears in the library may be included in a playlist.

- **Rip Music from CDs to Your Computer:** Insert a CD and, when a list of its tracks appears in the Windows Media Player window, click Rip CD. Windows Media Player rips the tracks on the CD to your Music library.

- **Burn CDs:** If you have a recordable optical drive on your computer, you can use Windows Media Player to burn a collection of your favorite songs to a CD.

- **Create Slide Shows:** Use Windows Media Player to create slide shows with playback controls in just a few clicks.

- **Share Media across a Network:** You can use the Play to command to share multimedia files across a network with a homegroup (a personal network, usually set up at home) or across the Internet.

If you pin Windows Media Player 12 to the Windows 10 taskbar, you can take advantage of Jump Lists for previously accessed files. The Jump List also includes playback controls at the bottom of the Jump List window to play music or a video or view photos without having to open Windows Media Player first.

Play Back Media Files

To listen to music files, watch videos, or view photos in Windows Media Player, perform the following steps.

To listen to music files in Windows Media Player:

1. Open Windows Media Player by clicking Start, typing **Media Player,** and then selecting Windows Media Player.

2. Click the Music library in the navigation pane, click the file you want to hear in the file list, and then click Play at the bottom of the window.

   Another option is to click the Play tab in the upper-right corner of the Windows Media Player window, drag the songs you want to hear to the Play tab, and then click the Play button.

3. After the file has finished playing, Windows Media Player automatically plays the next file in the list.

To watch a video in Windows Media Player:

1. Click the Videos library in the navigation pane and double-click the file you want to view in the file list. Windows Media Player launches a special viewing window and plays back the video.

2. Place your mouse pointer over the window to display playback controls.

To view photos in Windows Media Player:

1. Click the Pictures library in the navigation pane. Thumbnails of the photos in your Pictures library appear.

2. To view all of the photos as a slide show, click Play. Windows starts the slide show in its own window (see Figure 3.17).

FIGURE 3.17 A slide show in Windows Media Player

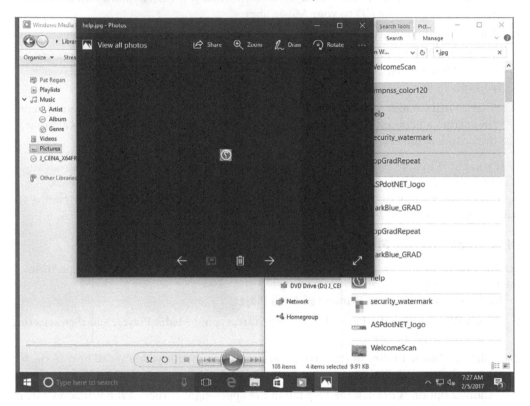

To stop any playback feature, click Stop in the playback controls and click Go To Library.

Create a Playlist

To create a playlist of music, perform the following steps:

1. In Windows Media Player, in the Player Library, click Playlists.

2. To create a playlist, click the Click Here link.

3. With the title in Edit mode (as shown in Figure 3.18), type a name for the new playlist that appears in the Navigation pane.

4. Drag and drop songs from the file list to the new playlist.

FIGURE 3.18   Creating a playlist in Windows Media Player

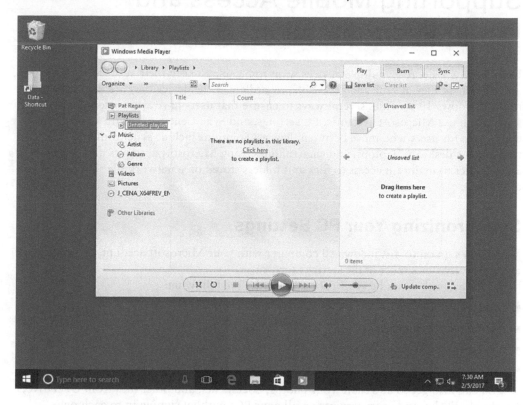

An auto playlist gives you more control and options. To create an auto playlist, click the down arrow on the Create Playlist button, click Create Auto Playlist, and then follow the prompts.

Burn a Music CD

To burn a music CD, perform the following steps:

1. Insert a blank CD or DVD into your computer's recordable media drive.

2. In Windows Media Player, in the Player Library, click the Music library to display the file list.

3. Click the Burn tab.

4. Drag individual songs, playlists, or entire albums to the burn list on the right.

5. Click Start burn.

The CD ejects when the burning process completes. The burn process works similarly for other types of media files.

Supporting Mobile Access and Data Synchronization

Users who work across multiple devices want to be able to keep their address books, music, and document files in sync and accessible, regardless of the device they are using at the time. Windows 10 provides several ways to ensure that users have a consistent experience.

You can use Microsoft accounts, PC settings, and Sync Center to ensure a consistent experience for users who move between devices. Solutions include synchronizing PC settings across desktops, laptops, and smartphones using Microsoft accounts and configuring Sync Center to maintain access to files and folders stored on a network file share when you are offline.

Synchronizing Your PC Settings

When you sign on to a Windows 10 computer with your Microsoft account, the system automatically syncs most of the settings for you.

Information that can be synchronized includes the following:

- Start screen layout, chosen colors, and themes
- Language preferences
- Browser history and favorites
- Windows Store app settings

You can also get to and share your photos, documents, and other files from OneDrive, Facebook, Flickr, and other services on all your PCs without signing in to each one.

Sync Your PC Settings

To sync your PC Settings, log on to a Windows 10 computer using your Microsoft account and perform the following steps:

1. Click Start ➢ Settings.
2. In the Settings window, click Accounts.
3. On the Accounts page, click Sync Your Settings.
4. For Sync settings, drag the slider bar all the way to the right to turn on sync for each item that you want to synchronize between your devices, as shown in Figure 3.19.
5. Close the Settings window.

FIGURE 3.19   Synchronizing via PC Settings

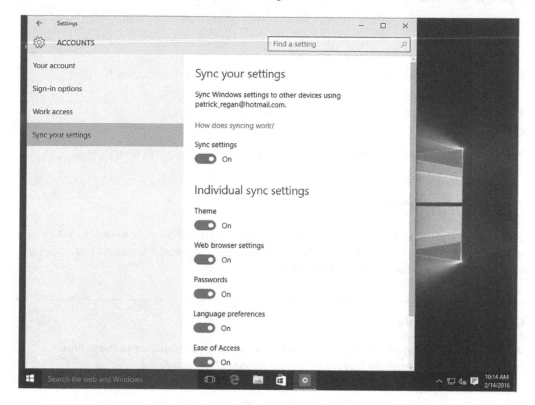

Using Sync Center

Sync Center enables you to sync certain mobile devices as well as files stored in folders on network servers (offline files).

Sync Center offers two ways to sync your data:

- *One-way sync*: Data kept in a primary location is synchronized with data in another location. For example, if you have a portable MP3 device, you can configure a one-way sync so that you maintain the music files on your computer and the MP3 player holds only a copy of the files. When it comes time to sync, only data on the computer will be transferred to the MP3 player, not vice versa.

- *Two-way sync*: Data is transferred in both directions. This works well when you want to make sure key files you work with on the network and on your device are always in sync. As a result, you can still work with those files when you are not connected to the network where the files are stored (offline files).

When working with mobile devices, Microsoft recommends using the software that comes with your device (mobile phone, music device, and so on) to perform synchronization. If your device is compatible with Sync Center, you can perform the next exercise to sync your device.

Sync a Device

If your device is compatible with Sync Center, sync your device by performing the following steps:

1. Right-click Start and choose Control Panel.
2. In the Search Control Panel text box, type Sync Center. From the results, click Sync Center.
3. Open Sync Center and click "Set up new sync partnerships."
4. Click Set Up.
5. Configure the settings and schedule for how and when you want to sync with the device.

Configuring Offline Files

Sync Center's primary purpose is to synchronize files available on your network. When you set up an offline files sync partnership with a folder, any time you disconnect from the network, you can continue to work on the files.

Certification Ready

What can you do to sync files from a shared folder so that you can access those files when you are not connected to your corporate network? Objective 4.4

Changes you make to the files while offline will be made to the files in the network folder when you reconnect. Sync Center tracks the version number for a file. If the file has changed, it copies the updated version to the other location to keep both locations in sync. In case of conflicts, Sync Center notifies you and you can choose to address the conflict.

If offline files are enabled, when you click the Manage offline files link within Sync Center, the Offline Files dialog box opens (see Figure 3.20), displaying the following tabs:

- **General:** Configures how offline files are used and synced.
  - **Disable Offline Files:** Enables and disables the Offline Files feature.
  - **Open Sync Center:** Opens Sync Center and checks for conflicts.
  - **View Your Offline Files:** Provides access to your offline files.
- **Disk Usage:** Provides information on how much disk space is currently used and is available for storing offline files; enables you to change the maximum amount of space offline files and temporary files can use on your computer.
- **Encryption:** Enables you to encrypt and unencrypt your offline files.
- **Network:** Enables you to determine how often the computer will check for a slow connection; by default, it is set to 5 minutes.

FIGURE 3.20   Reviewing Offline Files property settings

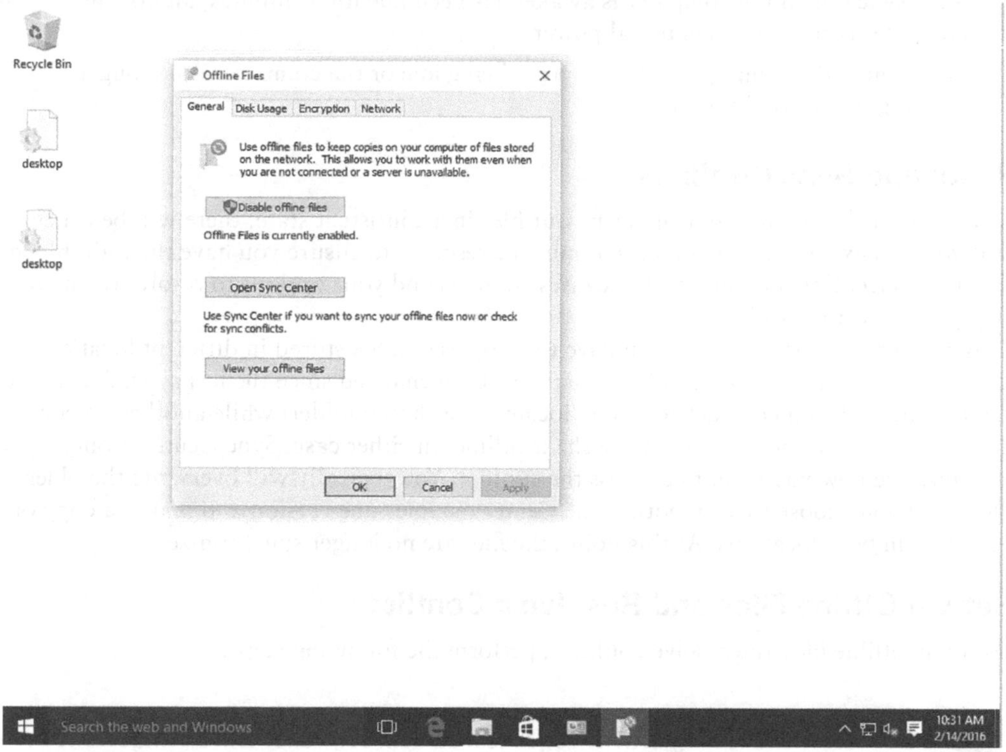

Scheduling for Offline Files

To set a schedule for the items you want to synchronize along with the date/time or the event that triggers the synchronization, simply right-click the Offline Files icon and choose Schedule for Offline Files. The options are as follows:

- **At a Scheduled Time:** This option enables you to set a start date and time, and determine the frequency you want to repeat the schedule (minutes, hours, days, weeks, or months).

- **When an Event Occurs:** This option configures synchronization to occur when one of the following events occurs:

  - You log on to your computer.

  - Your computer is idle for x minutes/hours.

  - You lock Windows.

  - You unlock Windows.

Additional start-and-stop scheduling options include the following:

- Start sync only if the computer is awake, has been idle for x minutes, and/or the computer is running on external power.

- Stop sync if the computer wakes up from being idle or the computer is no longer running on external power.

Resolving Sync Conflicts

Although synchronizing can help keep your files in a consistent state, there will be times that you will experience a conflict that must be resolved to ensure you have the right file in the right place. Understanding what causes conflicts and your options to resolve them will help you protect your files.

A *sync conflict* occurs when you have two copies of a file stored in different locations (e.g., locally and in a network folder) that have both changed since the last sync. A conflict can also occur if someone deletes a file (located in a shared folder) while another person makes a change to the same file while she is offline. In either case, Sync Center prompts you to determine how you want to address the conflict. You typically will overwrite the older file, but if you choose to keep both, Sync Center renames one version and makes a copy of both files in both locations. At this point, the files are no longer synchronized.

Set Up Offline Files and Resolve a Conflict

To set up offline files and resolve conflicts, perform the following steps.

 The following activity requires a domain controller and a Windows 10 client computer connected to the domain.

First, from your Windows server, create a folder, share it, and then create a file called MyFile.txt in the folder.

1. Log on to LON-DC1 as **adatum\administrator** with the password of **Pa$$w0rd**.
2. On the taskbar, click File Explorer.
3. Click the C: drive on your computer to open it.
4. Right-click the C: drive, choose New ➤ Folder, and then type **Data**.
5. Right-click the Data folder and choose Properties.
6. In the Properties dialog box, click the Sharing tab.
7. Click the Advanced Sharing button.
8. Select the Share This Folder option.
9. Click the Permissions button.
10. In the Permissions dialog box, select the Allow Full Control check box.
11. Click OK to close the Permissions dialog box.

12. Click OK to close the Advanced Sharing dialog box.

13. Click Close to close the Properties dialog box.

14. Double-click the Data folder.

15. Right-click the Data folder and choose New ➤ Text Document.

16. Type **MyFile** for the name and press Enter.

Now, from a Windows 10 client computer, connect to the shared folder on the domain controller.

1. Log on to the Windows 10 client computer with a regular domain user account.

2. On the taskbar, click File Explorer.

3. In the Address text box, type **\\rwdc01\data** and then press Enter.

4. Double-click MyFile.txt to open it and type **Connected over network**.

5. Click File ➤ Save and then close Notepad.

6. Right-click the file and choose Always Available Offline. Notice the icon changes to show that the file is available offline.

7. Right-click the Network icon on the taskbar and choose Open Network And Sharing Center.

8. Click Change Adapter Settings.

9. In the Network Connections window, right-click your Ethernet adapter and choose Disable. Your Ethernet adapter is now disabled, which simulates an offline environment for this computer.

From LON-DC1, delete the file while the Windows 10 client computer is disconnected from the network. This creates a conflict that you will need to resolve later.

1. From LON-DC1, on the taskbar, click File Explorer.

2. Click the C: drive on your computer.

3. Double-click the Data folder on your computer.

4. Right-click MyFile and choose Delete.

From the Windows 10 client computer, make a change to the file while you are still offline.

1. From the Windows 10 client computer, with the \\rwdc01\data folder open, double-click MyFile.txt to open it and then type **Changes made while offline**.

2. Click File ➤ Save.

3. Close Notepad.

From the Windows 10 client computer, enable your Ethernet adapter and reconnect to the network.

1. From the Windows 10 machine, with the Network Connection window open, right-click your Ethernet adapter and choose Enable.

2. Once your Ethernet adapter has reconnected to the network, close the Network Connections dialog box.

3. Right-click MyFile.txt and choose Sync ≻ Sync Selected Offline Files.

4. In the Resolve Conflict dialog box, click "Keep this version and copy it to the other location."

5. Close the dialog box.

The file has now been restored on RWDC01.

Using Windows Mobility Center

Rather than using different tools to adjust your laptop's screen brightness, wireless settings, and more, just open the Windows Mobility Center, which displays groups of settings all in one interface.

Certification Ready

What set of tools are only found on mobile computers that help manage mobile features?
Objective 1.4

Windows Mobility Center is a control panel of sorts that gives you access to several laptop settings, from volume to screen brightness to power options to Wi-Fi and Bluetooth settings—all in one place. Although the settings can be accessed from various icons and commands within Windows, you can make adjustments from a single window in Windows Mobility Center. Figure 3.21 shows the Windows Mobility Center window.

 Windows Mobility Center is only available on laptops.

Windows Mobility Center displays settings in boxes, or tiles. The tiles that are displayed depend on your hardware and laptop manufacturer. In addition, a setting that is turned off or disabled might not display, or it might display with a red X—such as when you turn off your Wi-Fi antenna by pressing a Fn key, such as F4 or F10.

Table 3.2 describes common Windows Mobility Center settings. Not all settings are available on all laptops, so a few settings in the table are not displayed in Figure 3.21.

FIGURE 3.21   The Windows Mobility Center window

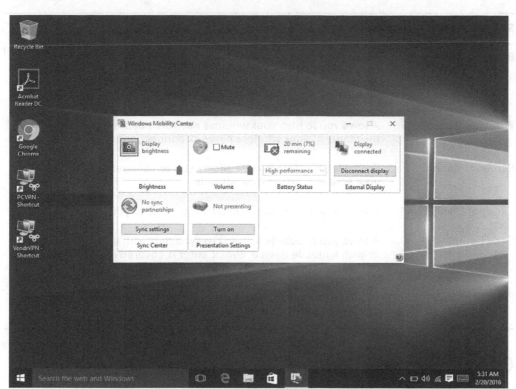

Certification Ready

Which settings can be adjusted by using the Windows Mobility Center? Objective 1.4

TABLE 3.2   Typical Window Mobility Center Settings

Setting	Description
Brightness	Allows you to adjust the brightness of your laptop display. Move the slider to the left to decrease brightness or to the right to increase brightness. Display brightness is related to the power plan for your laptop; those settings are adjusted in the Battery Status tile.
Volume	Allows you to increase or decrease speaker volume or select the Mute check box to temporarily disable audio.

TABLE 3.2   Typical Window Mobility Center Settings *(continued)*

Setting	Description
Battery Status	Allows you to see how much battery charge remains and adjust the power plan for your laptop. Power plans vary but offer two at a minimum: one for running on battery power and another for running on AC power.
Wireless Network	Allows you to turn your wireless network adapter on or off and see the status of your wireless network connection.
Screen Rotation	For tablet PCs, this feature allows you to change the orientation of your screen (portrait or landscape).
External Display	Allows you to connect an external monitor to your laptop.
Sync Center	Allows you to access settings to sync files with a network location or with a mobile device. Sync Center is covered in more detail in this lesson.
Presentation Settings	Provides you with access to settings for connecting your laptop to a projector for presentations.

Change Mobility Center Settings

To adjust settings in Windows Mobility Center, perform the following steps:

1. Open Windows Mobility Center by clicking Start, typing **windows mobility,** and then clicking Windows Mobility Center in the results list.

2. Adjust the screen brightness by dragging the Brightness slider left or right.

3. Click the Battery Status drop-down list and click another power plan, such as Power Saver. Notice how the screen brightness changes again.

4. Click the Battery Status drop-down list again and click the original power plan.

Click the drop-down lists in other tiles of Windows Mobility Center to see which options are available.

Accessing a Computer Remotely

These days, large organizations may be located throughout the country (or the world), have a mobile work force, and offer work-from-home capability. As an administrator, you need a way to access these systems remotely. Microsoft includes multiple tools within Windows that allow you to access clients and servers remotely.

These tools include the following:

- Remote Desktop Connection
- Remote Assistance
- Microsoft Management Console (MMC)
- Remote PowerShell

Configuring Remote Desktop

The *Remote Desktop Protocol (RDP)* is a proprietary protocol that was developed by Microsoft to connect to another computer over a network connection using the same graphical interface that you would use if you were sitting in front of the physical server. RDP uses TCP port 3389. Typically, you would access computers remotely using the *Remote Desktop Connection (RDC)*, which would allow you to connect to a Remote Desktop Session Host or to a Remote Application.

Certification Ready

Which Windows 10 tool allows you to remotely connect to Windows servers and provides a remote desktop and taskbar? Objective 1.4

Remote Desktop Services (RDS) allows users to access a remote computer just as if they were sitting in front of the computer. Within a Window, the user has a Start button, desktop, applications, and folders as well as access to local resources such as the user's local drive and mapped drives. Users could use RDS to run applications that they can't run on their own machines. You could go one step further and use multiple servers to create an entire RDS infrastructure to provide a robust, resilient service for your users.

By default, Windows Server 2012 R2 and Windows Server 2016 can support up to two remote sessions at once, while Windows 10 only supports one remote connection. For servers, if you need additional users to access the server, you have to install a Remote Desktop Licensing server, and then add licenses based on either the number of devices that can connect to the RDS server or the number of concurrent users.

 Remote Desktop is included with all editions of Windows 10; however, you can only connect to computers running the Professional, Enterprise, or Education editions.

When planning for remote access, you must deliver a consistent experience to your users whether they connect over the local network or across low-bandwidth networks when working from remote locations. For users to be productive while working remotely, they must have access to their remote resources at all times. As part of your remote access design, review your current topology and ensure that you have redundancy built in not only to your devices (routers and switches), but also to your network links.

You need to ensure that the firewalls do not block access to the remote servers when access is needed. You typically would not make the remote access available through the RDP from the Internet unless the client was connected over a VPN tunnel or was using the Remote Desktop Services Gateway.

Although the RDP uses compression and caching mechanisms to limit the amount of traffic transmitted over network links, consider the different types of traffic that will traverse the network links. For example, if you are using virtualization for your operating systems and applications to support your remote users, expect to see large bursts of data when the operating system and applications are sent to the remote client. Make sure your core infrastructure is capable of providing the bandwidth needed by your users.

If you are concerned about protecting sensitive data sent between remote users and your servers, configure group policies to require the use of a specific security layer to secure communications during RDP connections. RDP connections can be configured to support 128-bit encryption (the maximum level of encryption supported by the client) or 52-bit encryption mechanisms. The option you choose for your design depends on the capabilities of your remote clients and the level of encryption needed to meet your specific data protection needs. In general, your design should use the strongest encryption supported by your remote clients.

RDP 10 is integrated with Windows Server 2016 and Windows 10. With RDP 10, you can deploy remote clients (laptops, desktops, and/or VMs hosted in a data center) as part of your remote access strategy.

To connect to a computer, use the Remote Desktop Connections (mstsc.exe) program, which is found in the Windows Accessories folder. In the Remote Desktop Connection dialog box (see Figure 3.22), specify a server name or IP address, and click Connect.

FIGURE 3.22   Opening the Remote Desktop Connection program

Connect to a Remote Computer using Remote Desktop Connection

To connect to a remote computer using RDC, perform the following steps:

1. Log on to a Windows 10 computer.

2. Click Start and type **remote desktop**. From the search results, click Remote Desktop Connection.

3. In the Computer text box, type the computer name or IP address of the computer (such as **LON-DC1** or **192.168.1.68**) and click Connect.

4. If you are prompted to confirm that you want to trust this remote connection, click Connect again.

On occasion, you might need to use the `mstsc.exe /admin` command to connect to a server with the administrative session. This becomes particularly useful when the terminal server or RDS has exceeded the maximum number of allowed connections or when you get a black screen after you RDP to a system, assuming the system has not crashed.

When you open RDC, click Show Options to display additional options (as shown in Figure 3.23). These options are arranged in the following tabs:

- **General:** Allows you to specify the remote computer and user name to connect to. At the bottom of the tab, you can save the current connection settings to an RDP file or open a saved RDP file.

- **Display:** Controls how the remote desktop appears on the client computer, including the size of the remote desktop in pixels (including the full screen option), use of all monitors for the remote session, and the number of colors.

- **Local Resources:** Allows you to control which client resources are available to the remote session.

- **Experience:** Specifies which display options are available for a remote connection. If you select LAN (10 Mbps or higher), all options are selected. However, if you select a faster option than what the network actually is, your remote session may be slow or have a choppy display.

- **Advanced:** Allows you to specify server authentication options and a Remote Desktop Gateway.

On the Display tab (see Figure 3.24), you can specify the size of the remote desktop as it appears on the client computer. By default, the Remote Desktop size slider is set to Full Screen, which causes the client to occupy the client computer's entire display, using the computer's configured display resolution.

FIGURE 3.23   Remote Desktop options

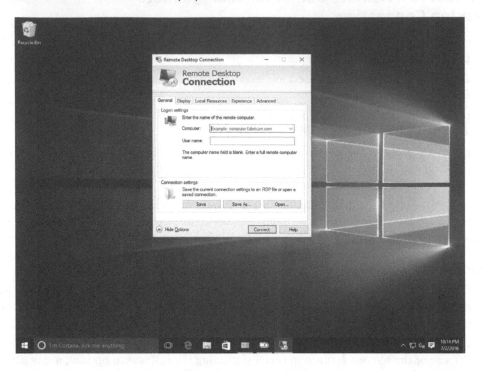

FIGURE 3.24   Remote Desktop Display tab

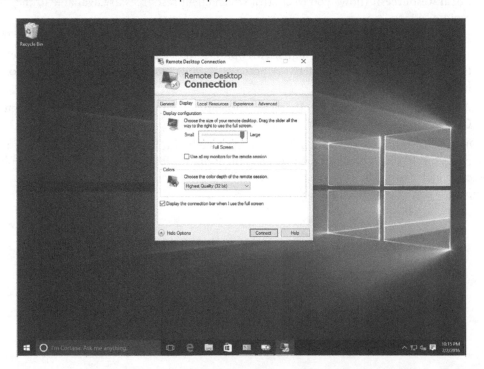

To avoid confusion when displaying multiple desktops on a system (the local desktop and one or more multiple remote desktops), the "Display the connection bar when I use the full screen" check box is selected, which will display a title bar at the top of each remote desktop session.

In addition to the desktop size, you can use the Colors drop-down list to adjust the color depth of the RDC display. The settings available in this drop-down list depend on the capabilities of the video display adapter installed on the client computer.

One of the new features implemented in RDP 6.*x* is support for 32-bit color, which enables clients to run graphic-intensive applications, such as image editors, with a full color palette. However, the trade-off for this capability is the increased network bandwidth required to transmit the display information from the terminal server to the client.

For example, when you configure RDC to use 32-bit color, the client and the terminal server open a special RDP channel just for that color information. This enables the client to assign a lower priority to the extra color information so that it does not interfere with the basic functionality of the client. However, 32-bit color increases the overall bandwidth consumed by the connection substantially. As a general rule, you should set the Colors parameter to the High Color (16-bit) setting unless the client will be running terminal server applications that can benefit from the additional color information.

On the Local Resources tab, shown in Figure 3.25, you configure how the RDC client should reconcile the resources on the Remote Desktop server with those on the client computer. You can click the Settings button to specify whether audio playback is played on the local computer or the remote computer and whether remote audio recordings are recorded from the local computer.

FIGURE 3.25   Remote Desktop Local Resources tab

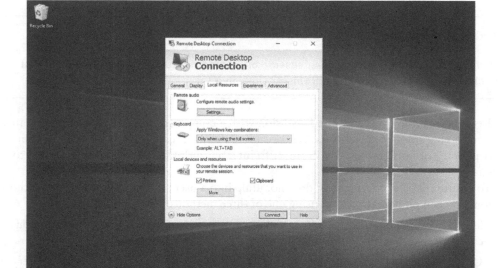

To make the remote connection more flexible, Remote Desktop allows you to redirect many of the local resources, such as local printers and disk drives (including local mapped drives). When you log on to the remote computer, you can open a document on the remote computer and print the document to your local printer. In addition, you can open a document on your local hard drive on the remote computer.

By default, the Printers and Clipboard check boxes are already selected. By redirecting the Clipboard, you can cut and paste to and from the remote computer. If you click the More button, you can specify ports, drives, and other supported Plug and Play (PnP) devices.

With Windows 10, you can select USB devices for redirection and swap them between the remote computer and the local computer. To redirect USB devices, you must enable the RemoteFX USB redirection feature in a Group Policy Object (GPO). Navigate to the Computer Configuration\Policies\Administrative Templates\Windows Components\Remote Desktop Services\Remote Desktop Connection Client\RemoteFX USB Device Redirection\ Allow RDP redirection of other supported RemoteFX USB devices from this computer, enable the policy, and specify whether you want to allow all users or only administrators to redirect devices. When RemoteFX USB Redirection is enabled, click the new Devices icon on the connection bar to choose which devices you want to redirect.

Configuring Remote Assistance

Remote Assistance is a Windows 10 feature that enables an administrator, trainer, or support person to connect to a remote user's computer, chat with the user, and either view all of the user's activities or take complete control of the system. Similar to Remote Desktop, it also uses TCP port 3389.

Certification Ready

Which tool allows you to view a user session on a computer running Windows 10 so that you can assist the user through a problem? Objective 1.5

Remote Desktop is used to open a session with a computer, whereas Remote Assistance is used to view and interact with a user session remotely. It can be used by technical support people, administrators, and trainers to interact with the user without traveling to the user.

To ensure that a support person does not jump into a user session without proper authorization, you can send an invitation using one of three methods:

▪ **Save This Invitation as a File:** Use this option to save the invitation as a file that you can send to a user via an attachment, copy to a disk, or send over the network.

▪ **Use Email to Send an Invitation:** Use this option to send the invitation to the sender through email. Of course, you cannot use this option if you do not have a configured email program, such as Microsoft Outlook.

- **Use Easy Connect:** If the local network uses the Peer Name Resolution Protocol (PNRP), which requires IPv6, you can use Easy Connect. The Windows 10 system will start listening for incoming connections without an invitation. Instead, you only need to share the unique password.

Create an Invitation

To create an invitation, perform the following steps:

1. Log on to a Windows 10 computer.

2. Right-click Start and choose Control Panel.

3. In Control Panel, click System And Security. Under System, click Launch Remote Assistance.

4. In the Windows Remote Assistance dialog box (as shown in Figure 3.26), click "Invite someone you trust to help you."

FIGURE 3.26 The Windows Remote Assistance "Do you want to ask for or offer help?" page

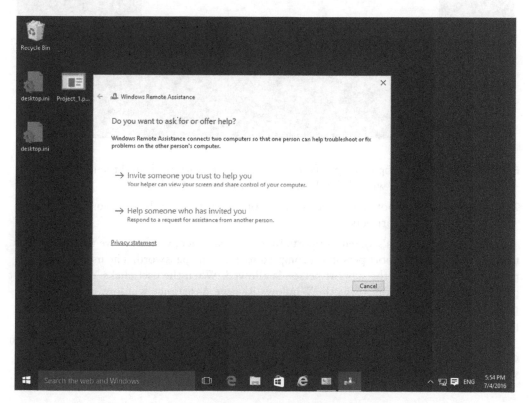

5. The "How do you want to invite your trusted helper?" page appears, as shown in Figure 3.27. Click "Save this invitation as a file."

FIGURE 3.27   The Windows Remote Assistance "How do you want to invite your trusted helper?" page

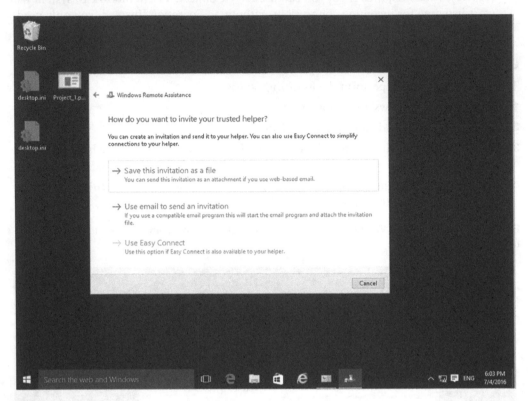

6. In the Save As dialog box, specify a name for the invitation file and the location of the folder in which the wizard should create the invitation. Click Save.

7. The Windows Remote Assistance window opens, displaying the password you must supply to the support person.

If the support person's system supports Remote Assistance, you just have to double-click the invitation. The support person is prompted to enter the password. The user is then prompted to confirm if the support person is allowed. When the user clicks Yes, the support person can see the session. Using the Windows Remote Assistance window, the support person and user can send messages back and forth, as shown in Figure 3.28. For the support person to take control, he or she has to click the Request control button.

In the following exercise, you will use Remote Assistance Easy Connect. However, if you do not have Peer Name Resolution Protocol (PNRP) and IPv6, the Easy Connect options will be greyed out.

FIGURE 3.28   Interacting with a user via Remote Assistance

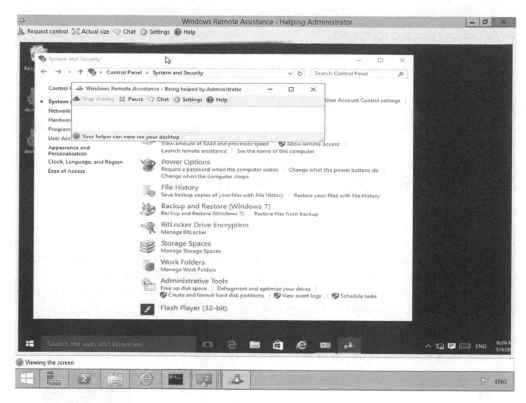

Use Easy Connect

To use Easy Connect to remotely connect to a computer, perform the following steps:

1. Log on to a Windows 10 computer that needs help.

2. Right-click Start and choose Control Panel.

3. In Control Panel, click System And Security. Under System, click Launch Remote Assistance.

4. In the Windows Remote Assistance dialog box, click "Invite someone you trust to help you."

5. The Windows Remote Assistance Wizard opens, displaying the "How do you want to invite your trusted helper?" page.

6. Click Use Easy Connect. If you get a "Can't connect to global peer-to-peer network" error message, you probably do not have PNRP installed on your network.

7. In the Windows Remote Assistance window, record the unique password that you will provide to the user who is trying to help you.

8. Log on to the remote Windows 10 computer.

9. Right-click Start and choose Control Panel.

10. In Control Panel, click System And Security. Under System, click Launch Remote Assistance.

11. In the Windows Remote Assistance dialog box, click "Help someone who has invited you."

12. In the Windows Remote Assistance dialog box, click Use Easy Connect.

13. In the Remote Assistance dialog box, type the Easy Connect 12-character password and click OK.

Configuring Remote Management Settings

As mentioned in the previous two sections, the two methods to connect to another computer are Remote Desktop and Remote Assistance. However, before you can use Remote Desktop or Remote Assistance, you have to use the System Properties to enable these two technologies. In addition, you have to make sure the Windows Firewall (or whatever firewall you are using) will allow Remote Desktop and/or Remote Assistance traffic.

To enable either or both of these technologies, open the System Properties (open Control Panel, click System and Security ➢ System, and then click Remote settings), as shown in Figure 3.29. By default, Remote Assistance is enabled and Remote Desktop is not.

FIGURE 3.29 Enabling Remote Desktop and Remote Assistance

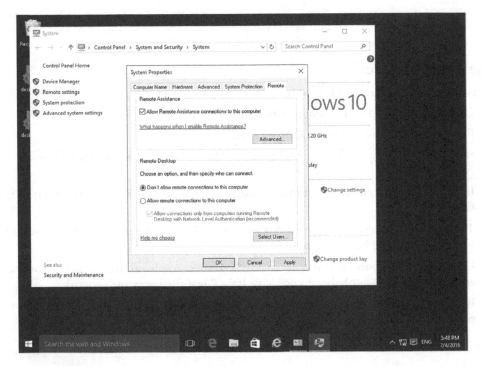

Click the Advanced button in the Remote Assistance section to specify the maximum amount of time an invitation can remain open (the default is 6 hours) and whether the computer can be controlled remotely or not. You can also specify whether you can create invitations that can only be used from computers running Windows Vista or later, which will encrypt the IP address, which, in turn, cannot be read by Windows XP.

For Remote Desktop, the "Allow connections only from computers running Remote Desktop with Network Level Authentication (recommended)" option is used to require the user to be authenticated before the session is created, which helps protect the remote computer from malicious users and software. To use Network Level Authentication, the client computer must be using at least Remote Desktop Connection 6.0 and an operating system such as Windows XP with Service Pack 3 or Windows Vista or newer.

The Select Users button is used to specify which users can connect to the system using the RDP. These users are added to the local computer Remote Desktop Users group. The Administrators group already has access even though they are not listed in the Remote Desktop Users list.

Configure Remote Management Settings

To configure remote management settings, perform the following steps:

1. Log on to LON-CL1 as **adatum\administrator** with the password of **Pa$$w0rd**.
2. Right-click Start and choose System.
3. In the Control Panel System window, click Remote Settings.
4. In the System Properties dialog box, the Remote tab is selected. To enable Remote Assistance, make sure the "Allow Remote Assistance connections to this computer" check box is selected.
5. In the Remote Assistance section, click the Advanced button.
6. In the Remote Assistance Settings dialog box, select the "Create invitations that can only be used from computers running Windows Vista or later" check box to tighten security.
7. To close the Remote Assistance Settings dialog box, click OK.
8. In the System Properties dialog box, in the Remote Desktop section, click the "Allow remote connection to this computer" option to enable remote connections.
9. Click the Select Users button.
10. In the Remote Desktop Users dialog box, click Add to add a user or group.
11. In the Select Users Or Groups dialog box, in the "Enter the object names to select" text box, type the name of the user group, and click OK.
12. To close the Remote Desktop Users dialog box, click OK.
13. To close the System Properties dialog box, click OK.

Using the Microsoft Management Console to Manage Systems Remotely

When assisting users with computer problems or maintaining systems, a support person often needs to check computer events, look at computer resource usage, or examine a disk's partition, among other tasks. You may use Microsoft Management Console (MMC) tools and utilities for this purpose.

Certification Ready

What are the Windows 10 Administrative Tools built on? Objective 1.3

The MMC is a collection of administrative tools called *snap-ins*. An MMC snap-in is a utility provided by Microsoft or a third party that's accessible through a common interface. Administrators use MMC tools for managing hardware, software, and network components on a computer. Administrative Tools is a popular collection of tools that use the MMC.

Computer Management, shown in Figure 3.30, is a popular snap-in that includes several tools such as Disk Management, which is used to configure hard disks and their partitions, and Event Viewer, which allows you to view computer event information, such as program starting and stopping (including program crashes) and security problems. You can manage system performance and resources using Performance Monitor, which is under Performance ➤ Monitoring Tools.

FIGURE 3.30   The Computer Management window

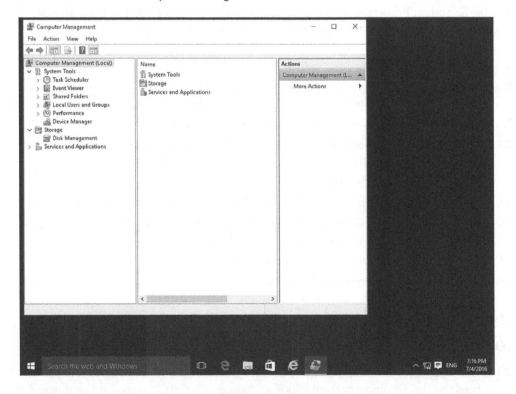

Some administrators and power users create custom MMCs that include only tools they use regularly—creating a toolkit of sorts.

Create a Custom MMC and Modify Settings Remotely

To create a custom MMC and then modify settings remotely, perform the following steps:

1. Right-click Start, click Run, and then type **mmc** in the Run dialog box. Click Yes to open the MMC Console.

2. In the MMC Console window, click File ➤ Add/Remove Snap-in. The Add or Remove Snap-ins dialog box opens (as shown in Figure 3.31).

FIGURE 3.31   Selecting snap-ins for a custom MMC

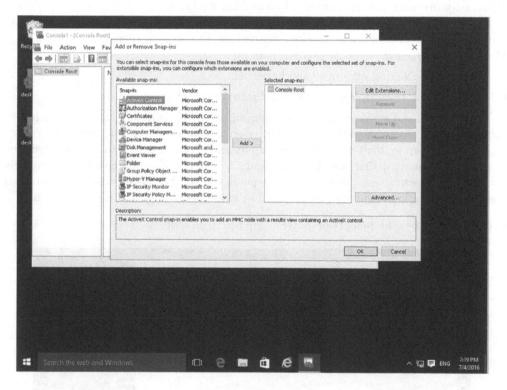

3. In the Available snap-ins list on the left, click a snap-in of your choice, such as Computer Management. In the middle of the dialog box, click Add. In the dialog box that opens, leave Local Computer selected (unless the computer you want to manage is one other than the current computer).

4. Click Finish. The snap-in is added to the Selected snap-ins pane on the right.

5. You can then repeat Steps 3 and 4 for each snap-in you want to include in the custom MMC.

6. When you have finished adding snap-ins, click OK.

7. Click File ➤ Save As. In the File Name text box, type a name for the custom MMC and click Save.

8. If you loaded the Computer Management MMC, expand System Tools ➤ Event Viewer ➤ Windows Logs and click System.

9. View the logs on the remote computer.

10. Expand the Services And Applications node and click Services.

11. Right-click the Computer Browser service and choose Restart.

12. Close the MMC console.

To avoid exposing a computer to malicious attacks, Microsoft recommends that you use MMC snap-ins when you are not logged on as Administrator.

Many of the snap-ins supplied with Windows 10 enable you to manage other Windows computers on the network as well. There are two ways to access a remote computer using a Microsoft Management Console (MMC) snap-in:

▪ Redirect an existing snap-in to another system

▪ Create a custom console with snap-ins directed to other systems

To connect to and manage another system using an MMC snap-in, you must launch the console with an account that has administrative credentials on the remote computer. You then click the snap-in, then right-click the snap-in, and choose Connect to another computer. The Select Computer dialog box shown in Figure 3.32 opens. If your credentials do not provide the proper permissions on the target computer, you will be able to load the snap-in, but you will not be able to read information from or modify settings on the target computer.

FIGURE 3.32   The Select Computer dialog box in an MMC console

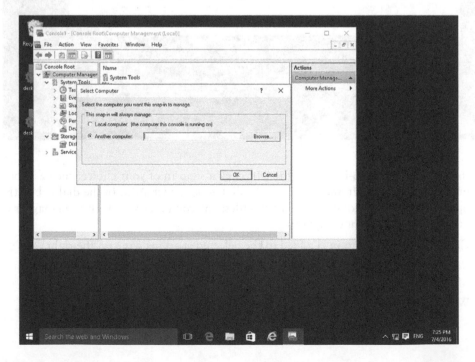

Not every snap-in has the capability to connect to a remote computer because some do not need it. For example, the Active Directory Domain Services consoles automatically locate a domain controller for the current domain and access the directory service from there. There is no need to specify a computer name. However, you will find Change Domain and Change Domain Controller commands in the Action menu in these consoles, which enable you to manage a different domain or select a specific domain controller in the present domain.

The other factor that can affect the ability of an MMC snap-in to connect to a remote computer is the existence of Windows Firewall rules that block the necessary network traffic between the computers. The traffic that an individual snap-in requires and whether the default Windows Firewall rules restrict it depends on the functions that the snap-in performs.

Connecting to a remote computer by redirecting an existing console is convenient for impromptu management tasks, but it is limited by the fact that you can only access one computer at a time. You also have to open the console and redirect it every time you want to access the remote system. A more permanent solution is to create a custom console with snap-ins that are already directed at other computers.

When you add a snap-in to a custom console, you select the computer you want to manage with that snap-in. You can also add multiple copies of the same snap-in to a custom console, with each one pointed at a different computer. This adds a whole new dimension to MMC's functionality. Not only can you create custom consoles containing a variety of tools, but you can also create consoles containing tools for a variety of computers. For example, you can create a single console containing multiple instances of the Event Viewer snap-in, with each one pointing to a different computer. This enables you to monitor the event logs for computers all over the network from a single console.

Using Windows Remote Management

Using Windows Remote Management, administrators can execute programs from the command line on remote computers without having to open a Remote Desktop session.

Windows Remote Management (WinRM) is a Windows 10 service that enables administrators to execute commands on remote computers using Windows PowerShell or the Windows Remote Shell (WinRS.exe) command-line program. However, Windows 10 does not start the service by default or configure the computer to allow remote management communications.

WinRM is responsible for routing the packets to the right location, while *Web Services for Management* structures the packets and requires a port to be made accessible via your firewall. To enable remote management for a target computer, you can do one of the following:

- Open a command prompt and execute the `winrm quickconfig` command.
- Open Windows PowerShell on the computer, and then type Enable-PSRemoting.

The following tasks are performed when you run `winrm quickconfig` or Enable-PSRemoting:

- Start or restart (if already started) the WinRM service.
- Set the WinRM service startup type to automatic.
- Create a listener to accept requests on any IP address.
- Enable Windows Firewall inbound rule exceptions for WS-Management traffic (for http only). This inbound rule is listed as Windows Remote Management via WS-Management (TCP port 5985) in the inbound rules of your Windows Firewall.

Configure Remote Management with the WinRM Command

Log on to Windows 10 using an account with administrative privileges and then perform the following steps:

1. Open a Command Prompt with Administrator privileges. If the User Account Control dialog box opens, click Yes.

2. Execute the following command:

   `winrm quickconfig`

3. When the command responds, indicating that it will start the WinRM service and set it to delayed auto start, type **y**, and press Enter.

4. When you are prompted to create a WinRM listener, enable the WinRM firewall exception, type **y**, and then press Enter.

5. Close the Administrator: Command Prompt window.

The WinRM.exe program will fail to configure the required firewall exception if the computer's network location is set to Public. The computer must use either the Private or Domain location settings for the remote management configuration process to succeed.

Alternatively, you can use the Windows PowerShell Set-WSManQuickConfig cmdlet to configure the Remote Management.

WinRM can be enabled for all computers within a domain via a Group Policy Object. To help keep the use of WinRM secure, you can enable the Computer Configuration\ Policies\Administrative Templates\Windows Components\Windows Remote Management (WinRM)\WinRM Service\Allow remote server management through WinRM setting, and specify the IP Address ranges that the service will accept connections from.

Using WinRS.exe

After you have configured the Remote Management service, you can execute commands on other computers that have been similarly configured. To execute a command from the Windows 10 command prompt, you must use the WinRS.exe program.

To use WinRS.exe, frame the command you want to execute on the remote computer as follows:

```
winrs -r:computer [-u:user] [-p:password] command
```

- –r:*computer*: Specifies the name of the computer on which you want to execute the command, using a NetBIOS name or a fully qualified domain name (FQDN).

- -u:*user*: Specifies the account on the remote computer that you want to use to execute the command.

- -p:*password*: Specifies the password associated with the account specified in the –u parameter. If you do not specify a password on the command line, WinRS.exe prompts you for one before executing the command.

- command: Specifies the command (with arguments) that you want to execute on the remote computer.

Introducing Windows PowerShell

Windows PowerShell is a command-line interface used mainly by IT professionals to run cmdlets (pronounced command-lets), complete background jobs (processes or programs that run in the background without a user interface), and run scripts to perform administrative tasks.

The Windows PowerShell environment is built on the .NET Framework, which allows administrators to use many more tools and commands than the MS-DOS command window environment. PowerShell and the MS-DOS command environment are compatible. For example, you can run Windows command-line programs in Windows PowerShell and also start Windows programs like Calculator and Notepad at the Windows PowerShell prompt. Windows PowerShell providers enable you to access other data stores, such as the registry and the digital signature certificate stores, as easily as you access the filesystem. PowerShell also provides full access to COM and WMI, which enables administrators to perform tasks on both local and remote Windows systems and with some remote Linux systems.

Component Object Model (COM) provides a platform-independent, distributed, object-oriented system for creating software components. Software can call these components at will. For example, File Explorer is an empty shell that links to multiple COM interfaces that allow you to navigate and display the file structure, and related objects such as This PC/My Computer, drives, folders, and files. Other programs such as Microsoft Office can call up the same COM objects so that you can browse, store, and access documents on disks.

Windows Management Instrumentation (WMI) is the Microsoft implementation of Web-Based Enterprise Management (WBEM) that allows accessing management information in an enterprise environment. WMI uses the *Common Information Model (CIM)* industry standard to represent systems, applications, networks, devices, and other managed components. With WMI, you can retrieve the status of local and remote computers and their components. You can configure security settings, configure system properties, change permissions of users and groups, manage processes, and view and configure error logging.

Cmdlets (pronounced *command-lets*) are native commands available in Windows PowerShell. Cmdlets follow a Verb-Noun naming pattern, such as get-process, get-service, get-help, set-date, or stop-process. Common verbs include:

- **Add:** Add a resource to a container, or attach an item to another item.
- **Get:** Retrieve data from a resource.
- **New:** Create a new resource.
- **Remove:** Delete a resource from a container.
- **Set:** Modify a resource, such as data or system parameters.
- **Start:** Begin an operation such as a process or program.

Knowing the legal verbs and remembering the singular noun rule is helpful when guessing cmdlet names.

Windows PowerShell includes more than 100 basic core cmdlets, and additional cmdlets will be added when you install additional software components such as Microsoft Exchange. You can even write your own cmdlets and share them with other users.

To get help on a cmdlet, you can use the get-help cmdlet. For example, to get help for the ps cmdlet, you would type the following command:

```
Get-Help ps
```

To get more detailed help, add a -full at the end of the command.

Run a Cmdlet in Windows PowerShell

To run a cmdlet in Windows PowerShell, perform the following steps:

1. Click Start and type **PowerShell**. From the results, click Windows PowerShell.

2. A commonly used command is ps (or get-process). The ps command lists the currently running processes and their details, such as the process ID, process name, and percentage of processor usage (CPU). Type **ps** and press Enter, as shown in Figure 3.33.

3. To get help with the ps command, execute **get-help ps**.

4. To view running services, execute **get-service**. A list of services displays along with their status (Running or Stopped).

5. To exit the Windows PowerShell window, execute **exit**.

FIGURE 3.33   Running the ps command in Windows PowerShell

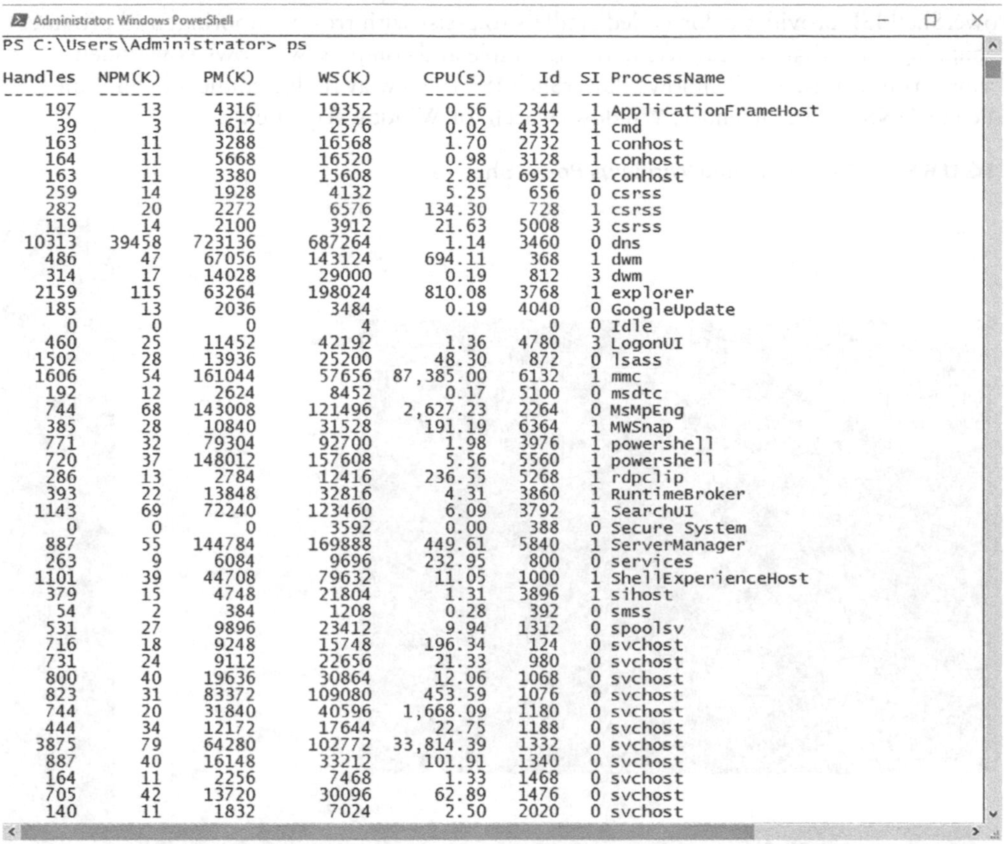

```
Administrator: Windows PowerShell                                      —   □   ×
PS C:\Users\Administrator> ps

Handles  NPM(K)    PM(K)    WS(K)    CPU(s)     Id  SI ProcessName
-------  ------    -----    -----    ------     --  -- -----------
    197      13     4316    19352      0.56   2344   1 ApplicationFrameHost
     39       3     1612     2576      0.02   4332   1 cmd
    163      11     3288    16568      1.70   2732   1 conhost
    164      11     5668    16520      0.98   3128   1 conhost
    163      11     3380    15608      2.81   6952   1 conhost
    259      14     1928     4132      5.25    656   0 csrss
    282      20     2272     6576    134.30    728   1 csrss
    119      14     2100     3912     21.63   5008   3 csrss
  10313   39458   723136   687264     1.14   3460   0 dns
    486      47    67056   143124    694.11    368   1 dwm
    314      17    14028    29000      0.19    812   3 dwm
   2159     115    63264   198024    810.08   3768   1 explorer
    185      13     2036     3484      0.19   4040   0 GoogleUpdate
      0       0        0        4                 0   0 Idle
    460      25    11452    42192      1.36   4780   3 LogonUI
   1502      28    13936    25200     48.30    872   0 lsass
   1606      54   161044    57656  87,385.00  6132   1 mmc
    192      12     2624     8452      0.17   5100   0 msdtc
    744      68   143008   121496  2,627.23   2264   0 MsMpEng
    385      28    10840    31528    191.19   6364   1 MWSnap
    771      32    79304    92700      1.98   3976   1 powershell
    720      37   148012   157608      5.56   5560   1 powershell
    286      13     2784    12416    236.55   5268   1 rdpclip
    393      22    13848    32816      4.31   3860   1 RuntimeBroker
   1143      69    72240   123460      6.09   3792   1 SearchUI
      0       0        0     3592      0.00    388   0 Secure System
    887      55   144784   169888    449.61   5840   1 ServerManager
    263       9     6084     9696    232.95    800   0 services
   1101      39    44708    79632     11.05   1000   1 ShellExperienceHost
    379      15     4748    21804      1.31   3896   1 sihost
     54       2      384     1208      0.28    392   0 smss
    531      27     9896    23412      9.94   1312   0 spoolsv
    716      18     9248    15748    196.34    124   0 svchost
    731      24     9112    22656     21.33    980   0 svchost
    800      40    19636    30864     12.06   1068   0 svchost
    823      31    83372   109080    453.59   1076   0 svchost
    744      20    31840    40596  1,668.09   1180   0 svchost
    444      34    12172    17644     22.75   1188   0 svchost
   3875      79    64280   102772  33,814.39  1332   0 svchost
    887      40    16148    33212    101.91   1340   0 svchost
    164      11     2256     7468      1.33   1468   0 svchost
    705      42    13720    30096     62.89   1476   0 svchost
    140      11     1832     7024      2.50   2020   0 svchost
```

Because most cmdlets have multiple parameters, Windows PowerShell commands can get very complicated by combining cmdlets. A pipe (|) will use the output of one command as the input to another command. For example, Get-VM will list VMs on a Hyper-V host. Get-vmmemory server01 will display the memory settings of one VM called server01. However, if you combine the two with a pipe:

```
Get-vm | Get-vmmemory
```

you will get the memory settings for all of the servers in a list.

Windows 10 includes the *Windows PowerShell Integrated Scripting Environment (ISE)* that helps you create Windows PowerShell scripts. If you need the scripts to be executed on a regular basis, you can execute the scripts using Task Scheduler.

ISE provides command-completion functionality, and enables you to see all available commands and the parameters that you can use with those commands. While you can use a text editor to create a PowerShell script, the Windows PowerShell ISE makes it easier, since you can view cmdlet parameters, and it can help you create syntactically correct Windows PowerShell commands.

After you open Windows PowerShell ISE (as shown in Figure 3.34), you can use the File menu to create a new script, open saved scripts, save scripts, and run scripts. Windows PowerShell ISE provides color-coded cmdlets to assist with troubleshooting, and provides debugging tools that you can use to debug simple and complex Windows PowerShell scripts. You can use the Windows PowerShell ISE to view available cmdlets by module (such as DNSClient, Defender, WindowsSearch, or WindowsUpdate).

FIGURE 3.34   Opening Windows PowerShell ISE

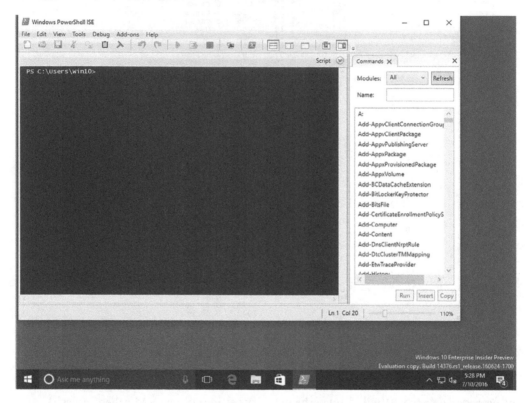

If you need help running a script, such as sending an email to a group of users, use the following command:

```
Send-MailMessage -SmtpServer smtp.adatum.com -From administrator@adatum.com -To
managers@adatum.com --BodyAsHtml "hello world"
```

If you start typing Send-, you will see a list of commands that begin with Send-. If you click Send-MailMessage, you get the syntax of the command, as shown in Figure 3.35.

To create a script using the Windows PowerShell ISE, you would click View ➢ Show Script Pane. Alternatively, you can click the little down arrow next to Script at the top of the main pane. You will then type your commands (as shown in Figure 3.36) and save the script with a .ps1 filename extension. You can execute the script to test it anytime by clicking the Execute button (the right green arrow button). After the script has been thoroughly tested, you can then use Task Scheduler to automatically execute the script.

FIGURE 3.35 Using Windows PowerShell ISE to get help on PowerShell cmdlets

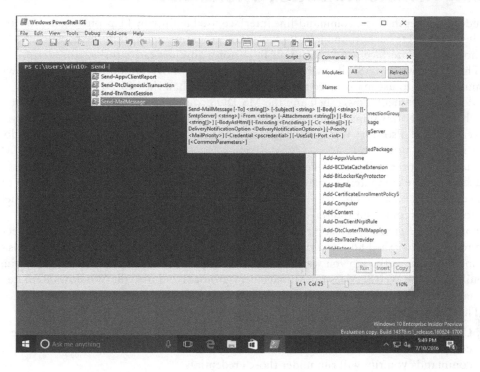

FIGURE 3.36 Creating a script with Windows PowerShell ISE

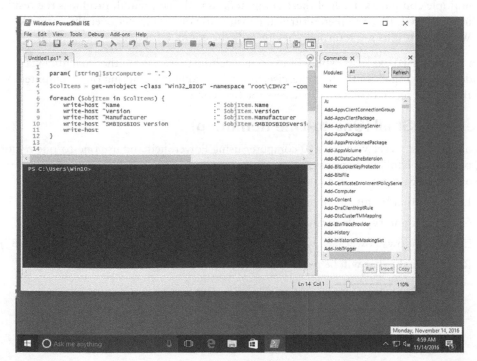

Using Remote Windows PowerShell

Windows PowerShell is a command-line interface used mainly by IT professionals to run cmdlets, complete background jobs (processes or programs that run in the background without a user interface), and run scripts to perform administrative tasks.

The Windows PowerShell environment is built on the .NET Framework, which allows administrators to use many more tools and commands than the MS-DOS command window environment. PowerShell and the MS-DOS command environment are compatible, however. For example, you can run Windows command-line programs in Windows PowerShell and also start Windows programs like Calculator and Notepad at the Windows PowerShell prompt.

Another feature of Windows PowerShell is remoting. Administrators can use cmdlets to access remote computers or they can use the Windows PowerShell Remoting service to run commands on a remote computer or on many remote machines. Windows PowerShell Remoting can require substantial setup, which is not within the scope of this book.

PowerShell Remoting is a server-client application that allows you to securely connect to a remote PowerShell host and run script interactively. It allows you to run commands on a remote system as though you were sitting physically at its console. PowerShell Remoting is built upon the Web Services for Management protocol and uses the Windows Remote Management service to handle the authentication and communication elements.

There are two types of remoting:

- **One-to-One Remoting:** Allows you to bring up the PowerShell prompt on a remote computer. The credentials you use are delegated to the remote computer. Any commands you run will run under those credentials.

- **One-to-Many Remoting:** Allows you to send one or more commands, in parallel, to multiple computers. Each of these computers runs the command, produces the results into an XML file, and then returns the results to your computer over the network. When the results are returned, they include the computer name.

In the next two exercises, you will use one machine to access another machine via Windows PowerShell. In the first exercise, you will enable PSRemoting on a computer. You will then use a second computer to access the first computer.

Use PowerShell (One-to-One Remoting)

To connect to a target Windows 10 computer using PowerShell and use one-to-one remoting, perform the following steps.

To enable PSRemoting on a target computer:

1. Log on with administrative privileges to a computer running Windows 10.
2. Click Start and type **PowerShell**. From the results, click Windows PowerShell.
3. In the Windows PowerShell window, execute **Enable-PSRemoting** (see Figure 3.37).
4. Read the tasks that will be performed, type **A**, and then press Enter.

FIGURE 3.37   Enabling PSRemoting

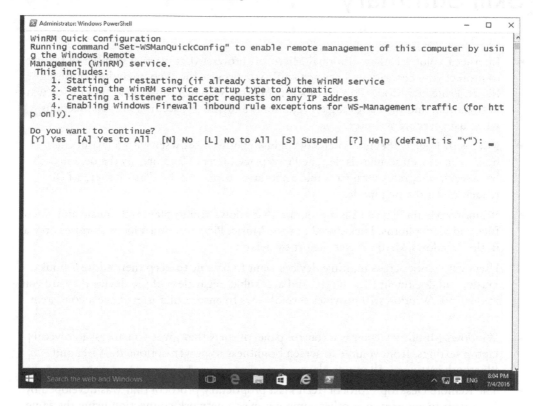

From the source Windows 10 computer, log on with administrative privileges to the domain and perform the following steps:

1. Press Windows logo key+r, type **PowerShell** in the Run box, and then click OK.

2. In the Windows PowerShell window, execute the following command:

   ```
   enter-pssession -ComputerName <computername>
   ```

   Replace <computername> with your domain controller's name. Once connected, the PowerShell prompt should include the name of the computer you are currently connected to remotely.

3. Execute **get-service** to see the services running on the domain controller.

4. Execute **get-process** to see a list of all processes running on the domain controller.

5. Execute **get-acl c:** to see the access control list applied via NTFS for the c: drive.

6. Execute **exit-pssession** to exit PowerShell.

Skill Summary

In this lesson, you learned:

- Internet Explorer is the traditional Microsoft browser that offers a number of features to protect your security and privacy while you browse the Web, including phishing filters, Protected Mode, Pop-up Blocker, Add-on Manager, download files or software notification, and the use of digital signatures and 128-bit secure (SSL) connections when using secure websites.

- Microsoft Edge is the new Microsoft lightweight web browser with a layout engine built around web standards designed to replace Internet Explorer as the default web browser. It integrates with Cortana, annotation tools, Adobe Flash Player, a PDF reader, and a reading mode.

- Windows Media Player 12 is a program that allows you to play back music and video files and view photos. Files stored in your Music, Pictures, and Videos libraries appear in the Windows Media Player file list by default.

- Users who work across multiple devices want to be able to keep their address books, music, and document files in sync and accessible, regardless of the device they are using at the time. Windows 10 provides several ways to ensure that users have a consistent experience.

- Windows Mobility Center is a control panel of sorts that gives you access to several laptop settings, from volume to screen brightness to power options to Wi-Fi and Bluetooth settings—all in one place.

- The Remote Desktop Protocol (RDP) is a proprietary protocol that was developed by Microsoft to connect to another computer over a network connection using the same graphical interface that you would use if you were sitting in front of the physical server. RDP uses TCP port 3389. Typically, you would access computers remotely using the Remote Desktop Connection (RDC), which would allow you to connect to a Remote Desktop Session Host or to a Remote Application.

- Remote Assistance is a Windows 10 feature that enables an administrator, trainer, or support person to connect to a remote user's computer, chat with the user, and either view all of the user's activities or take complete control of the system. Similar to Remote Desktop, it also uses TCP port 3389.

- Windows PowerShell is a command-line interface used mainly by IT professionals to run cmdlets (pronounced command-lets), complete background jobs (processes or programs that run in the background without a user interface), and run scripts to perform administrative tasks.

Knowledge Assessment

You can find the answers to the following sections in the Appendix.

Multiple Choice

1. Which of the following tools are available in Administrative Tools? (Choose all that apply.)
    A. Print Management
    B. System Information
    C. Computer Management
    D. Event Viewer

2. Which of the following actions can be performed with the Snip & Sketch?
    A. Annotate an image with the pen tool
    B. Change the color of a captured image
    C. Add typed callouts
    D. Save in PDF format

3. When you right-click a program you want to run that requires elevated or administrative privileges, which of the following commands can be chosen from the shortcut menu?
    A. Run elevated
    B. Run protected
    C. Run with permission
    D. Run as administrator

4. Which of the following actions can be performed with Windows Media Player 12? (Choose all that apply.)
    A. Stream video files over the Internet
    B. Rip music from a CD
    C. Play a slide show
    D. Create playlists

5. Which of the following locations allows you to configure security zones in Internet Explorer 11?
    A. Internet Options Security tab
    B. Internet Options Privacy tab
    C. Safety menu
    D. Tracking Protection window

6. Which of the following utilities runs the ps cmdlet?
   A. MS-DOS command window
   B. Windows Remote Assistance
   C. Windows PowerShell
   D. Computer Management

7. Which of the following tools are accessible from the Computer Management window? (Choose all that apply.)
   A. Event Viewer
   B. Performance Monitor
   C. Remote Desktop Connection
   D. Disk Management

8. Which of the following tools can be used when you want to access your home computer from work to get a file you worked on last night?
   A. Disk Management
   B. Remote Desktop Connection
   C. Windows Remote Assistance
   D. Sync Center

9. Which Remote Assistance method uses Peer Name Resolution to allow for quick and easy connection?
   A. Invitation via files
   B. Invitations via email
   C. Easy Connection
   D. Auto Connect

10. Which programming environment can be used to create complicated PowerShell scripts?
    A. PowerShell Dev Center
    B. Windows PowerShell Integrated Scripting Environment
    C. Remote PowerShell
    D. Windows Management Instrumentation

Fill in the Blank

1. Microsoft's newest browser is _____.

2. Remote Desktop Connections and Remote Assistance use TCP port _____.

3. _____ helps prevent personal information and browsing history from being stored by Internet Explorer 11.

4. The _____ detects threats on websites, such as phishing attacks and malware downloads, and prevents them from running.

5. _____ is an accessory program included with Windows 10 that allows you to take screen shots, annotate them, and save them.

6. _____ is a feature of Internet Explorer 11 that helps you control which websites can track your online browsing activity.

7. After you synchronize files between your computer and a network location, the files you use on your computer are referred to as _____.

8. _____ allows you to set up a computer for remote access and then connect to that computer wherever you are located.

9. An MMC _____ is a utility provided by Microsoft or a third party that's accessible through a common interface, such as Administrative Tools.

10. _____ is a command-line interface used mainly by IT professionals to run cmdlets, background jobs, and scripts to perform administrative tasks.

True/False

1. Windows Mobility Center is found on all editions of Windows 10 Professional.

2. Remote Desktop Connection and Windows Remote Assistance refer to the same program used in different ways.

3. Windows Remote Assistance sessions are encrypted for safety.

4. Remote Desktop comes with all editions of Windows 10; however, you can only connect to computers running the Professional, Enterprise, or Education editions.

5. Windows Mobility Center includes access to power plans and screen brightness.

Case Scenarios

You can find the answers to the following sections in the Appendix.

Scenario 3-1: Securing Internet Explorer 11

Your co-worker is finalizing a big project for a medical client and has many sensitive client files on her computer. She asks you to help her make her computer as safe as possible while accessing the Internet. Describe your recommended solution.

Scenario 3-2: Offering Remote Assistance

The sales staff travels extensively and often needs technical assistance with configuration settings on their Windows 10 laptops. Which feature or program is used to provide remote support for these employees?

Scenario 3-3: Viewing Logs Remotely

Joe has been having problems with his system and you have been assigned a ticket to investigate those problems. However, Joe is a very busy person who always needs to use his machine. Therefore, you don't have access to the machine to look through the system logs. Describe how you can look at the Event Viewer logs without interrupting Joe.

Scenario 3-4: Creating a Playlist

You provide technical support to a small dental practice. The office manager hands you several company-owned music CDs. She wants the music piped to the lobby area where patients wait to be seen for their appointments. The computer used at the receptionist's desk is running Windows 10 and has wireless speakers that can be set up in the waiting area. Describe how you can provide the requested music without investing in further resources.

Lesson 4

Managing Applications, Services, and Disks

Objective Domain Matrix

Technology Skill	Objective Domain Description	Objective Domain Number
Configuring Applications	Configure applications	3.1
Managing Windows Store Apps	Configure applications	3.1
Understanding Services	Understand services	3.4
Using MSConfig (System Configuration Utility)	Configure native applications and tools	1.3
Managing Processes and Applications with Task Manager	Configure native applications and tools	1.3
Understanding Storage	Understand storage	5.2
	Understand file systems	4.1
Encrypting and Compressing Files and Folders	Understand encryption	4.3

Key Terms

Configuring Applications

A *software program* (also known as an *app*) is a sequence of instructions written to perform a specified task for a computer. Today, most of these programs are installed as desktop apps or Windows Store apps.

Desktop apps are traditional apps, such as Microsoft Office or Adobe Acrobat. The applications are installed using an .exe or .msi installer file, which is obtained from a DVD, over a network from a shared folder, or over the Internet from the vendors' websites.

Configuring Desktop Apps

One of the advantages of any modern operating system is that you can use it to run a wide range of applications. Because each application is unique, each program has its own settings. To determine the settings for a desktop application, you will have to refer to the documentation that is included with the desktop application.

Because those applications are running in the Windows 10 desktop environment, there are centralized settings that you can configure for each application. For example, you can specify which files are associated with an application, and you can configure how older applications interact with Windows 10.

To start a desktop application, you:

- Double-click an icon, which is usually a shortcut to the executable file.

- Double-click a data file that is tied to or associated with the application.

- Click the Start button, navigate to the application, and then click the application.

For example, when you install Microsoft Office, .doc and .docx files are associated with Microsoft Word. Therefore, anytime you double-click a .doc or .docx file on a system with Microsoft Office installed, Microsoft Word opens, which then opens the document.

Change the Default Apps

To change the default apps in Windows 10, perform the following steps:

1. Click Start ➢ Settings.

2. In the Settings window, click System.

3. On the System page, click the Default Apps vertical tab. To change the primary web browser from Microsoft Edge to Microsoft Internet Explorer, scroll down (as shown in Figure 4.1) and under Web browser, click Microsoft Edge, and then click Internet Explorer.

FIGURE 4.1   Managing default apps

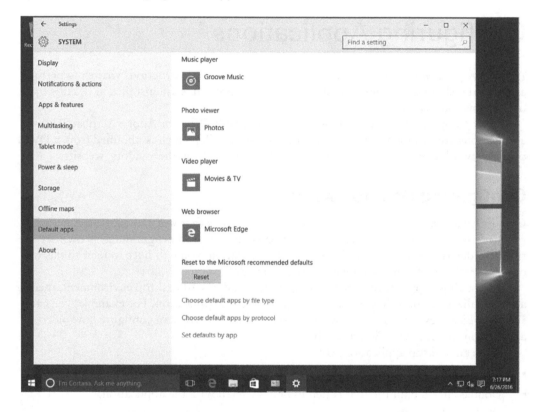

4. To reset to the Microsoft recommended default apps, click the Reset button. After the applications have been reset, a check mark appears next to the Reset button.

5. Click Choose default apps by file type.

6. On the Choose Default Apps By File Type page, scroll down to .gif. The current program to open a .gif file is Photos. To change the default program for .gif files, click Photos and click Paint.

7. Close the Settings window.

Configuring Windows Features

You can also use the Programs and Features to uninstall and change an installed program. Most Windows programs allow you to uninstall a program from your computer if you no longer use it or if you want to free up space on your hard disk.

In Windows 10, you can use Control Panel's Programs and Features to uninstall programs or to change a program's configuration by adding or removing certain options. If the program you want to uninstall isn't listed, it might not have been certified for or registered with Windows. You should check the documentation for the software.

Uninstall or Change a Program

To uninstall a program or change a program in Windows 10, perform the following steps:

1. Right-click Start and choose Programs and Features. Alternatively, open Control Panel and if you are in Category view, click Programs ➤ Programs and Features. If you are in Large Icons view or Small Icons view, click Programs and Features.

2. Click a program such as Microsoft SQL Server 2012 Native Client (see Figure 4.2) and click Uninstall. Click No to not uninstall the app.

3. Close the Control Panel.

FIGURE 4.2   Managing programs with Programs and Features

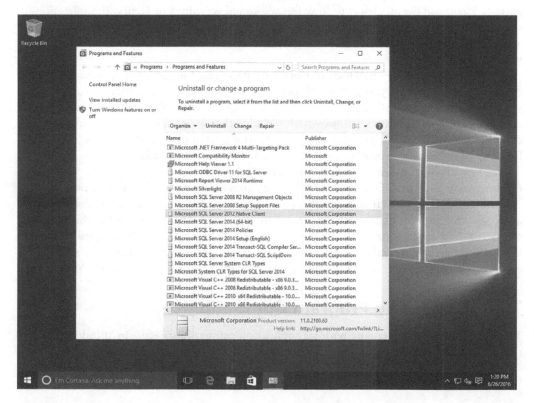

Some programs include the option to repair the program or to change the installed options, but many simply offer the option to uninstall the program. To change the program, click Change or Repair. If you are prompted for an administrator password or confirmation, type the password or provide confirmation.

Supporting Desktop Application Co-Existence

Because Windows 10 follows the same architecture used in Windows Vista, Windows 7, and Windows 8/8.1, most applications written for Windows Vista, Windows 7, and Windows 8/8.1 will run on Windows 10. The few applications that do not run on Windows 10 are usually primarily security-class applications or applications that bypass the Windows application programming interface (API) to communicate with system hardware by performing low-level kernel calls. If an application does not run in Windows 10, not even under the application compatibility mode, you can try to run the application under a Hyper-V virtual machine, a RemoteApp, or App-V.

Before you deploy Windows 10 in an organization, you must thoroughly test each application to make sure that it runs as expected. If it does not, either you need to take additional steps to make the application run on Windows 10, or you need to contact the vendor to get an upgraded version of the application.

Of course, as with any problem, when dealing with application compatibility issues, don't forget to follow basic troubleshooting. First, record any error messages that are displayed. Then, use Event Viewer to look for additional warnings or errors. If applications seem to be slow, you can use Task Manager and other performance monitoring tools such as Performance Monitor. Lastly, be sure to perform research on the Internet and to check vendor websites.

There are several ways in which you can have users run the same application but with different versions. First, you can run Hyper-V on a client machine, so that you create virtual machines that will run other versions of an application. You can also have users connect to remote desktop sessions, which include other versions of the application. You can also access RemoteApps, which are applications hosted on a server running Remote Desktop Services, but appear as applications that are running locally.

Application Virtualization (App-V), which is part of the Microsoft Desktop Optimization Pack (MDOP), is used to mitigate application-to-application incompatibilities or conflicts. To run virtual applications, you use the App-V 5.1 Sequencer, which converts an application into a virtual package. You then deploy the App-V 5.1 client, which runs the virtualized application on the computer. When you run the virtualized application on a local computer, the virtualized application runs in an isolated environment. Therefore, you could run different versions of the same application at the same time by using App-V.

Troubleshooting Program Compatibility

The simplest method of coping with an application compatibility issue in Windows 10 is to run the Program Compatibility Troubleshooter.

The *Program Compatibility Troubleshooter* is a wizard-based solution that users or administrators can use to automatically configure an executable file to use an appropriate Windows 10 compatibility mechanism. Thus, the troubleshooter is not a compatibility mechanism in itself; it is simply a method for applying other mechanisms.

To run the Program Compatibility Troubleshooter, right-click an executable file or a shortcut to an executable file and choose Troubleshoot Compatibility from the shortcut menu. When the troubleshooter launches, it attempts to determine what is preventing the program from running properly. The troubleshooter then gives you two options:

- **Try Recommended Settings:** Implements the compatibility settings that the troubleshooter has determined will resolve the problem and configures the executable to use those settings whenever you run it.

- **Troubleshoot Program:** Displays a What Problems Do You Notice? page, shown in Figure 4.3, on which you can select the problems you have experienced. The troubleshooter then leads you through a series of pages that further identify the problem and configure the executable with specific compatibility settings.

FIGURE 4.3   The What Problems Do You Notice? page in the Program Compatibility Troubleshooter

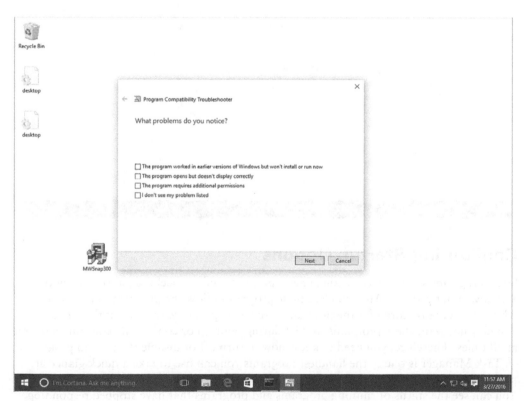

Another way to overcome compatibility issues is to manually configure the compatibility settings for an executable file. To access these settings, right-click an executable file, choose Properties, and then click the Compatibility tab (as shown in Figure 4.4). You can then define the compatibility mode for the application, such as Windows 95, Windows XP (Service Pack 3), Windows 7, or Windows 8. You can also reduce the color mode, run the application in a 640 × 480 screen resolution, or run the program as an administrator.

FIGURE 4.4   Manually configuring program compatibility settings

Configuring Startup Options

Some programs start or have a component (program and service) that starts during the Windows boot process. Also, some of these programs allow the program to run faster, while others are required for the program to function properly. In some of these situations, you may not want these programs to start during boot-up or continually consume resources at all times. Therefore, you need to know how to turn off or disable the startup programs.

Task Manager is one of the handiest programs you can use to take a quick glance at performance to see which programs are using the most system resources on your computer. You can see the status of running programs and programs that have stopped responding, and you can stop a program running in memory. For this lesson, you can also use Task Manager to manage your startup programs and services.

The Startup tab shows the programs that are configured to automatically start when you start Windows, as shown in Figure 4.5. You can disable a startup program by right-clicking an item and choosing Disable. You can also access the properties of the program file for the application, and the location of the program file.

FIGURE 4.5   Managing startup programs

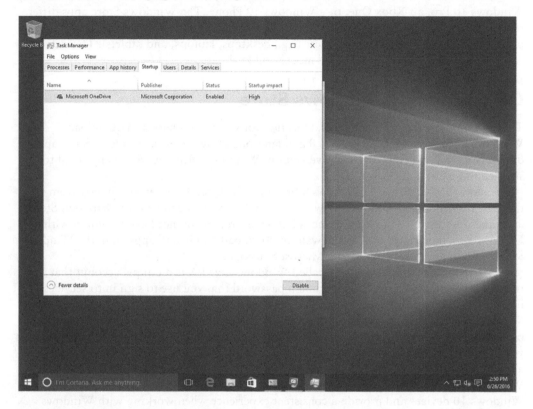

Disable a Startup Program

To disable a startup program in Windows 10, perform the following steps:

1. Right-click the taskbar and click Task Manager.
2. In the Task Manager window, click More details.
3. To view the startup programs, click the Startup tab.
4. To disable a startup program, right-click the program and choose Disable.
5. Close the Task Manager.

Managing Windows Store Apps

Windows Store apps refers to a class of applications for Microsoft Windows devices including PCs, tablets, phones, Xbox One, Microsoft HoloLens, and the Internet of Things. They are typically distributed and updated through the Windows Store.

Universal Windows Platform (UWP) apps are a special type of Windows Store apps that can be installed on multiple hardware platforms, such as an Intel tablet that is running Windows 10 Pro, an Xbox One, or a Windows 10 Phone. The Windows Store apps differ from traditional applications in that they are designed to run in a single, full-window display across multiple form factor devices (e.g., desktops, laptops, and tablets). These devices can be touch-based or use a standard mouse and keyboard.

Configuring the Windows Store

The *Windows Store* provides a central location for you to purchase and download Windows apps that run on Windows 8 and later operating systems. Windows Store apps do not run on Windows 7 or earlier versions of Windows. Windows Store apps tend to be smaller and faster than desktop apps.

Windows 10 includes the Windows Store app, which can be accessed directly from the taskbar. In Windows 10, the Windows Store enables users to deploy both Windows Store apps and desktop apps. To browse the Windows Store, you do not have to sign in with a Microsoft account. However, if you want to download and install apps from the Windows Store, you do have to sign in with a Microsoft account.

A *Microsoft account*, previously called Windows Live ID, is a unique account that is the combination of an email address and a password that you use to sign in to services like Outlook.com, MSN.com, Hotmail.com, OneDrive, Windows Phone, or Xbox Live. When you set up a computer running Windows 10 for the first time, you have the option of creating a Microsoft account using an email address that you provide. The email address you use can come from any provider. After the account is set up, Microsoft will use it, along with your password, to help manage your settings across all of your PCs that run Windows 10. Microsoft accounts enable you to synchronize your desktop across multiple Windows 10 devices and provide a consistent experience when working with Windows Store apps. Purchased apps will be available from each device, feeds you add will be synced across all devices, and state information will be maintained, so you can start a game or read a book and pick it up later on another device. You can create a Microsoft account during the initial installation of the operating system or after the system is running.

When you open the Windows Store, you can click the Sign in icon (the icon next to the Search text box). Also, if you click the Sign up button, you can configure the following:

- **Downloads and Updates:** Allows you to view the current downloads and check for updates for the Windows Store apps.

- **Settings:** Allows you to enable automatic updates, show products on the Live Tile, streamline purchases, and manage your devices that are connected to the Microsoft account. Figure 4.6 shows the Windows Store Settings page.

FIGURE 4.6   Managing Windows Store settings

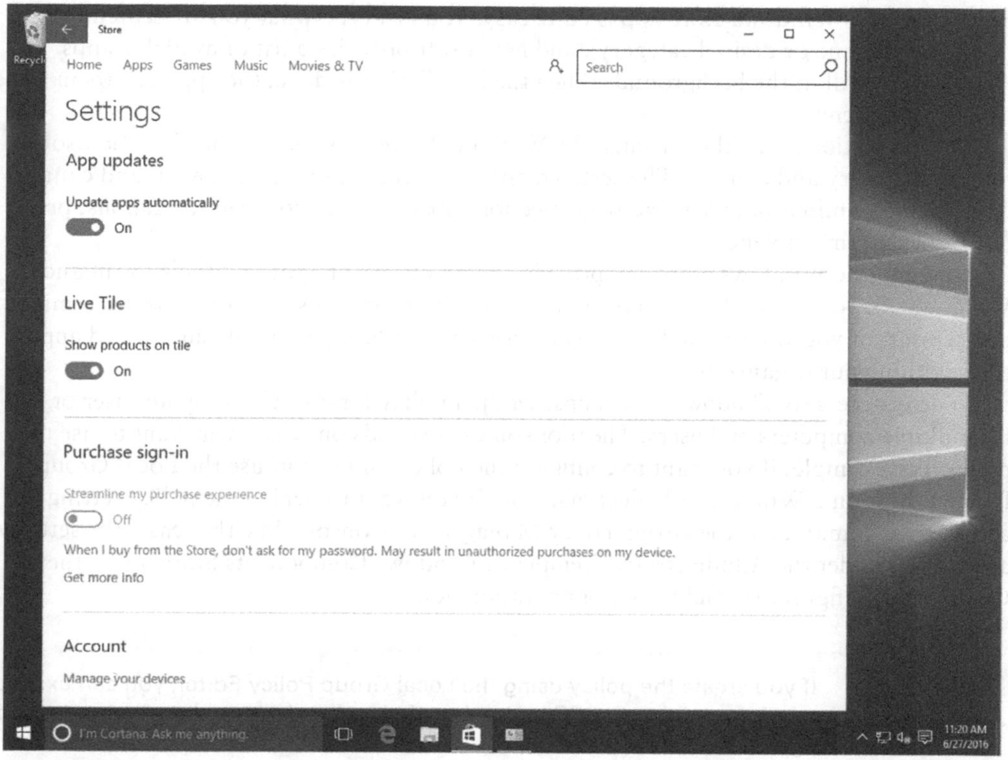

Configure the Windows Store

To configure the Windows Store, perform the following steps:

1. On the taskbar, click the Windows Store button.

2. To sign in to the Windows Store, click the Sign in button and then click Sign in.

3. When you are asked to choose an account, click Microsoft account.

4. Specify the proper credentials in the Email Or Phone dialog box and click Sign in.

5. Click the User icon and click Settings.

6. To update apps automatically, ensure that the Update apps automatically option is set to On.

7. To streamline your purchases so that you will not be asked for a password, ensure that the Streamline my purchase experience is set to On.

8. To view your downloads and updates, click the User icon again and click Downloads and updates.

9. Close the Store window.

Implementing Windows Store Apps

Searching for a Windows Store app is quite easy. You just type what you are searching for (the specific name or desired category), and Microsoft provides a list of available apps. Apps then install in the background. When the installation is done, the app appears in a tile on the Start menu.

The applications available through the Windows Store must be certified by Microsoft for compatibility and content. The certified apps cannot contain adult content and cannot advocate discrimination, illegal activity, alcohol, tobacco products, drugs, weapons, profanity, or extreme violence.

Although the Windows Store can provide a wide variety of apps and tools to enhance Windows 10, you might decide to restrict access to it for your users. This restriction might be necessary if you want to make sure your users are working with only authorized applications within your organization.

To deny access to Windows Store apps, set up a policy for a single computer/user or for multiple computers and users. The tool you use depends on where you want to use the policy. For example, if you want to configure the policy and test it, use the Local Group Policy Editor on a Windows 10 client machine. If you want to deploy the policy settings across your domain, use the Group Policy Management Console. In either case, the settings are located under the Administrative Templates\Windows Components\Store under the Computer Configuration and User Configuration nodes.

> If you create the policy using the Local Group Policy Editor, you can export and import it into a GPO at the domain level. It does not have to be created again.

When configuring the policy using the Local Group Policy Editor for a user (User Configuration\Administrative Templates\Windows Components\Store), there is only one option to set within the policy:

- Turn off the Store application:
  - **Not Configured (default)**: If you select this option, access to the Store is allowed.
  - **Enabled**: If you select this option, access to the Store is denied.
  - **Disabled**: If you select this option, access to the Store application is allowed.

If you set the policy for a computer (Computer Configuration\Administrative Templates\ Windows Components\Store), the following options are available:

- Turn off Automatic Download of updates:
  - **Not Configured (default)**: Download of updates is allowed.
  - **Enabled**: Automatic downloads are turned off.
  - **Disabled**: Automatic downloads of updates are allowed.

- Allow Store to install apps on Windows To Go workspaces:
  - **Not Configured (default)**: Access to the Store is not allowed.
  - **Enabled**: Access to the Store is allowed on the Windows To Go Workspace. Use this option only when the device is used with a single PC.
  - **Disabled**: Access to the Store is denied.
- Turn off the Store application:
  - **Not Configured (default)**: If you select this option, access to the Store is allowed.
  - **Enabled**: If you select this option, access to the Store is denied.
  - **Disabled**: If you select this option, access to the Store application is allowed.

Restrict Access to the Windows Store Using a Local Group Policy

Log on to a Windows 10 computer with administrative credentials. In this activity, you will review the policy settings that control the Windows Store access for both computers and users by performing the following steps:

1. Click Start. Type **gpedit.msc** and press Enter. The Local Group Policy Editor opens.
2. Expand Computer Configuration ➤ Administrative Templates ➤ Windows Components and click Store.
3. Double-click the Turn off the Store application setting. The Turn off the Store application dialog box opens. Click Enabled.
4. Attempt to access the Windows Store. Click the Store tile located on the Windows 10 Start menu. The message Windows Store isn't available on this PC appears.
5. Return to the group policy setting you enabled in Step 3 and click Not Configured to regain access to the Windows Store.

In some situations, you might have a computer in a public area (such as a library or kiosk) that needs to run just a single Windows app. In these situations, you can configure Windows 10 settings to restrict access to a single application.

When you assign access to a single Windows Store app, you restrict the application to a user account. When the user signs into the computer, that user can only access the assigned app.

Restrict a User Account to Run a Single Windows Store App

To restrict a user account to run a single Windows Store app, perform the following steps:

1. Click Start ➤ Settings.
2. Click Accounts and click Family & other people.
3. In the right pane, click Set up assigned access.
4. Click Choose an account and select the account that you want to restrict.
5. Click Choose an app and select the installed app to which you want to restrict the account.
6. Sign out of the computer to make the changes effective.

Understanding Group Policy and Network Application Installation

In a Windows network in a domain environment, administrators can use Group Policy to ease the burden of administering and managing many users and client computers. Group Policy lets you control who can install software and on which computers; it also helps you push software updates and security configurations across the network. Group Policies also exist in Windows 10 and other Windows operating systems. They are referred to as Local Group Policies and affect only the users who log on to a particular computer. This section focuses on Group Policy at the network domain level.

Group Policy is a collection of settings (policies) stored in Active Directory on a Windows network. *Active Directory* is an infrastructure (directory) that stores information and objects. An object can be a file, a printer, a computer, a user account, or other entities. Objects in Active Directory are linked to *Group Policy Objects (GPOs)*, which are used by administrators to control users and computers on a network and to deploy applications, software updates, and security. Group Policy affects users and computers contained in sites, domains, and organizational units.

Certification Ready

How are network applications installed using Group Policy? Objective 3.1

 Group Policy is supported in Windows 10 Professional and Enterprise editions.

Group Policy works well in small to large environments, whether an organization is located in a single area or has multiple offices spread around a state or several states, for example. It's easiest to manage in mostly "heterogeneous environments," in which many of the client computers use the same hardware and users use much of the same software with the same configurations.

If your organization has already deployed Active Directory, such as Microsoft Windows 2016 Active Directory Domain Services (AD DS), using Group Policy to push applications to users or computers is efficient. Using Group Policy, you can *assign* or *publish* an application to all users or computers in a designated site, domain, organizational unit (OU), or to a local, individual user or computer.

For example, let's say you're deploying Microsoft Office for more than 20 users. If you set up Group Policy to assign the software on each *computer*, the software is installed the next time the computer starts and any users with the correct permissions who log on to the computer may run the software. If you use Group Policy to assign the software to *users*, the next time an authorized user clicks the Microsoft Office shortcut or menu item, the software installs on the user's computer and Office opens. If you publish an application to users, the next time a user logs on, he can choose to install the software from a dialog box that opens.

With Group Policy, you can control which users can use the software. If a user logs on who isn't authorized to run the software (considered "out of scope"), the software can be uninstalled automatically.

Once software is installed, you can push updates to the software and even upgrade programs using Group Policy.

Install an Application from a Network Location

Configuring Group Policy in Windows Server is beyond the scope of this book, but this exercise shows you how to install an application from a network location in a domain, from the user's perspective. Perform the following steps:

1. Right-click Start and choose Control Panel. Click Programs ➤ Programs and Features. In the left pane, click Install a program from the network.

2. Browse the list of programs, click a program you want to install, and then click Install.

Follow the prompts to move through the installation. You might be prompted for an administrator password or confirmation during the installation.

These steps work if you set the GPO to install an application to a *user* versus a *computer*.

Understanding Services

Services run in the background on a Windows system to help the operating system run other programs. The Services console is the central management point of services in Windows 10.

Windows uses services to handle requests for print spooling, file indexing, task scheduling, the Windows Firewall, and much more. Services run in the background, essentially helping the operating system work with other programs. Although services do not usually have user interfaces, you can manage services through the Microsoft Management Console (MMC) Services snap-in (see Figure 4.7).

Cross Reference
For more information about MMC, see Lesson 3.

FIGURE 4.7   The Services console in Windows 10

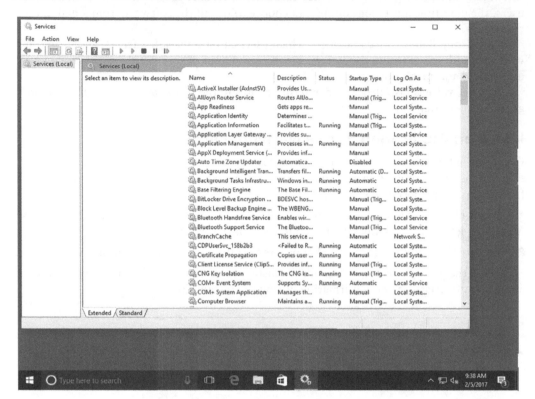

A Windows 10 system can have more than 100 services running at any one time. Each computer can have different services running, depending on the version of Windows in use, the computer manufacturer, and the applications installed, but Windows 10 generally uses many of the same services across its editions.

To use the Services snap-in and configure services, you must be a member of the Account Operators group, the Domain Admins group, or the Enterprise Admins group, or you must have received the appropriate authority. Using the Run as command to open the Services console ensures you have the proper level of authority.

You can access Windows services in many different ways:

- Click Start, type services in the Ask me anything search box, and then click Services or services.msc in the resulting list. (Or right-click Services or services.msc and choose Run as administrator. You must provide an administrative password or confirm to continue.) The Services console opens.

- In Computer Management, expand the Services and Applications node and click Services.

- In Administrative Tools, double-click Services or double-click Component Services and then click Services.

- Open Task Manager and click the Services tab.
- Open MSConfig and click the Services tab. (MSConfig is covered in the next section in this lesson.)

The Extended and Standard tabs (at the bottom of the Services console) both display all of the services in the system; however, the Extended tab provides descriptive information for a selected service in the space to the left of the details pane. Sometimes a link is displayed for you to get more information about a particular service.

The Services console enables you to view all services and their status; add, start, stop, or disable services; select user accounts that might run the service (for security purposes); define how a service recovers from failures; or view a list of service, program, and driver dependencies. To use any of these options, double-click the service to open its Properties dialog box.

You can export service information to a .txt or .csv file.

Understanding Service Startup Types

Certification Ready
What are the four service startup types? Objective 3.4.

The General tab in the service's Properties dialog box (see Figure 4.8) provides options for setting a service's startup type:

- **Automatic (Delayed Start):** The service starts approximately 2 minutes after the system has completed starting the operating system.
- **Automatic:** The service starts as the operating system starts.
- **Manual:** The service must be started manually, by a user, a dependent service, or a program.
- **Disabled:** The service is disabled and will not start.

Be careful when disabling any services. Some services, such as Security Center and Windows Firewall, should not be disabled unless the computer is behind a hardware firewall. Many computer users disable unnecessary services to optimize the speed of their computers. You should create a system restore point (covered in Lesson 8) before disabling services. And although it's time-consuming, disable one service at a time, reboot your computer, and check for side effects of disabling that service before disabling any other services.

FIGURE 4.8   The General tab

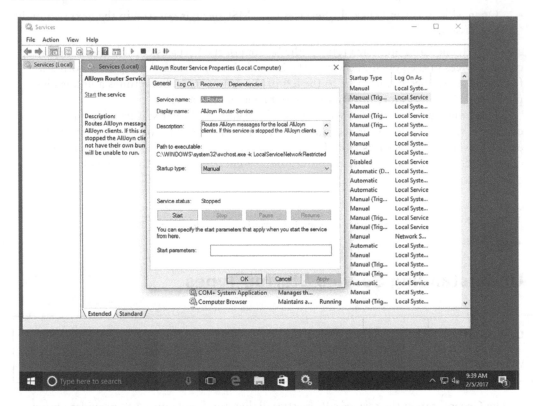

You can also start, stop, pause, or resume a service using the buttons in the Service status section. For example, let's say a printer has several duplicate (unnecessary) print jobs and the queue is not responding. You've restarted the printer a few times but that didn't work. To fix the problem, just restart the Print Spooler service in the Services console to clear the print queues.

 While troubleshooting a service, try pausing the service (if it's an option) and then unpausing it before stopping and restarting the service. By pausing and then continuing, you might be able to resolve the problem without having to reset connections or cancel jobs.

Certification Ready

Which service or user accounts can you specify a service to use? Objective 3.4

The Log On tab (see Figure 4.9) allows you to specify the user account the service can use, which might be different from the logged-on user or the default computer account. Your options are:

- **Local Service Account:** Click This Account and type **NT AUTHORITY\LocalService**. The Local Service account is a built-in account (it's already created in the operating system). It can run services in the background but has limited access to resources and objects, which helps protect the system if individual services are compromised. No password is required.

- **Network Service Account:** Click This Account and type **NT AUTHORITY\NetworkService**. The Network Service is similar to the Local Service account but is geared for networking services. Like the Local Service account, the Network Service account can run services in the background but it helps to protect the computer from compromise.

- **Local System Account:** Click Local System Account. The Local System account is a built-in account that has full control of the operating system.

- **Another Account:** Click This Account, click Browse, browse for a different user account, select it, and then click OK. Type the password for the user account you selected and then click OK.

The service will run in the security context of the account you choose.

FIGURE 4.9   The Log On tab

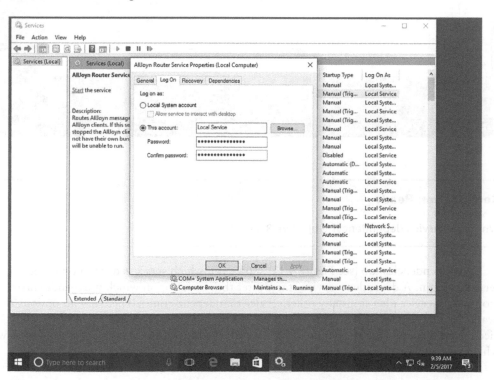

The Recovery tab (see Figure 4.10) lets you choose recovery actions the computer will take if a service fails. For example, if a service fails, the computer might first try restarting the service. If that doesn't work, you can instruct the computer to restart the service again or you can restart the computer to clear memory and refresh connections.

FIGURE 4.10 The Recovery tab

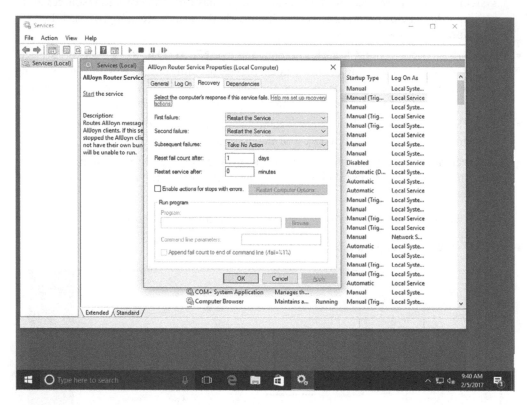

Certification Ready

What is a service dependency? Objective 3.4

The Dependencies tab (see Figure 4.11) shows you which services depend on other services to run. A dependent service starts after the service upon which it depends starts. Stopping a service also stops any other service that depends on it. There are no options available on this tab—it's informational only. However, before you stop or disable a service on the General tab, you should view the information on the Dependences tab to know which other services might be affected by your change.

FIGURE 4.11   The Dependencies tab

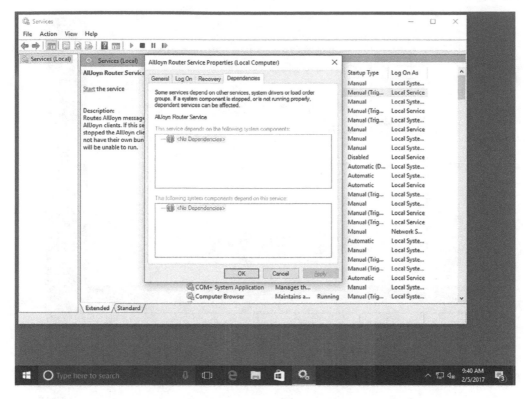

Configure a Service

To configure a service in the Services console, perform the following steps:

1. Click Start and in the Ask me Anything search box, type **services**. Right-click services.msc in the resulting list, choose Run as administrator, and then click Yes to continue (or type a password). Press Enter.

2. In the details pane, double-click the service that you want to configure, such as Print Spooler (see Figure 4.12). The service's Properties dialog box opens.

3. On the General tab, click the Startup type drop-down list (see Figure 4.13). Click Automatic (Delayed Start), Automatic, Manual, or Disabled.

FIGURE 4.12   The Print Spooler service in the Services console

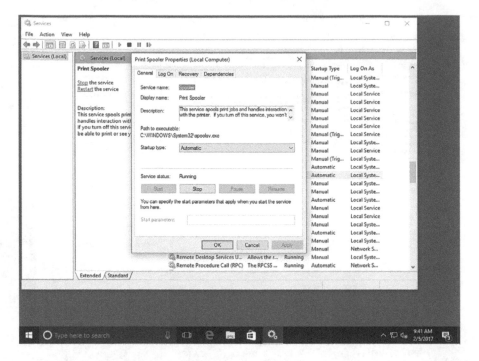

FIGURE 4.13   Selecting a startup type

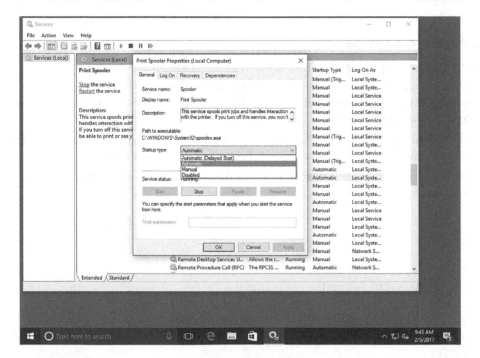

4. Click the Log On tab. To specify the user account that the service can use to log on, perform one of the following steps:

    ▪ To use the Local System account, click Local System account.

    ▪ To use the Local Service account, click This account and then type **NT AUTHORITY\LocalService**.

    ▪ To use the Network Service account, click This account and then type **NT AUTHORITY\NetworkService**.

    ▪ To specify another account, click This account, click the Browse button, and then specify a user account in the Select User dialog box. Click OK to save your changes and close the dialog box.

5. Type the password for the user account in the Password text box and the Confirm password text box and click OK. You do not have to type a password if you selected the Local Service account or the Network Service account.

Using MSConfig (System Configuration Utility)

Use MSConfig, also known as the System Configuration utility, to troubleshoot and diagnose Windows startup problems.

Certification Ready

What is the purpose of MSConfig? Objective 1.3

MSConfig, also known as the *System Configuration utility*, lets you enable or disable startup services, set boot options such as booting into Safe Mode, access tools like Action Center and Event Viewer, and more. You'll use this utility mainly to troubleshoot startup problems with Windows.

To open System Configuration, click Start, type **msconfig** in the Ask me anything search box, and then click msconfig.exe in the resulting list. The System Configuration dialog box opens, showing the General tab (see Figure 4.14). Normal startup is selected by default (unless you've previously changed the startup settings). A normal startup runs all device drivers and services. Other options include the following:

▪ **Diagnostic Startup:** Runs basic devices and services only; equivalent to starting the computer in Safe Mode.

▪ **Selective Startup:** Starts the system with some or all system services and startup items disabled.

FIGURE 4.14   The General tab

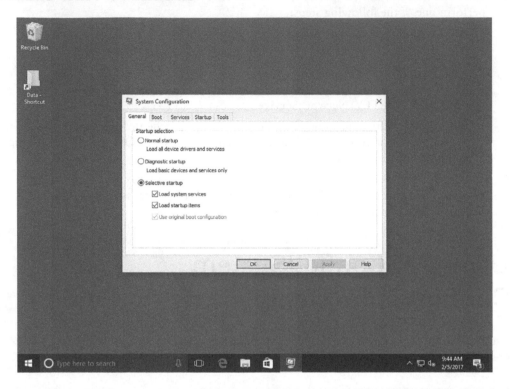

The options on the Boot tab (see Figure 4.15) enable you to adjust boot options, usually for diagnostic purposes. The Boot tab options match the options in the Advanced Boot Configuration menu that displays when you press F8 at startup. To boot the system into Safe Mode, select the Safe Boot check box. When you do this, the Minimal option is selected by default. The other safe boot options are:

- **Alternate Shell:** Boots to the command prompt without network support.

- **Active Directory Repair:** Boots to the Windows GUI and runs critical system services and Active Directory.

- **Network:** Boots into Safe Mode with network services enabled.

    The options in the right column are as follows:

- **No GUI Boot:** Disables the Windows Welcome screen.

- **BootLog:** Creates a boot log of startup activity in a file named ntbtlog.txt.

- **Base Video:** Starts the Windows graphical user interface using standard VGA drivers.

- **OS Boot Information:** Displays driver names as drivers are installed during the startup process.

FIGURE 4.15   The Boot tab

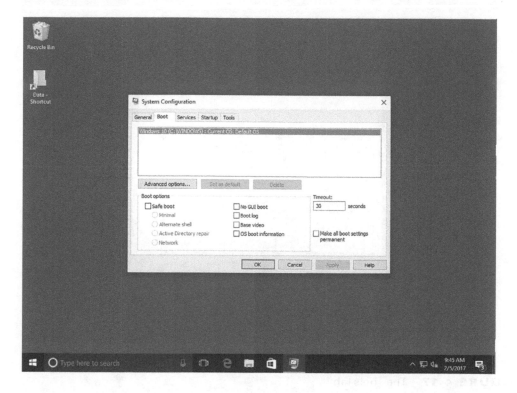

 You can make boot options permanent by selecting the "Make all boot settings permanent" check box, clicking Apply, and then clicking OK. Administrators often do this on test computers that they use to test new programs and updates before rolling them out to ordinary users.

You use the Services tab (see Figure 4.16) to enable or disable Microsoft and third-party services. These are the same services that display in the Services console covered earlier in this lesson.

Finally, the Tools tab (see Figure 4.17) lists many programs you can start for reporting and diagnostic purposes. Some of the tools are Change UAC Settings, Event Viewer, Performance Monitor, and Task Manager.

FIGURE 4.16   The Services tab

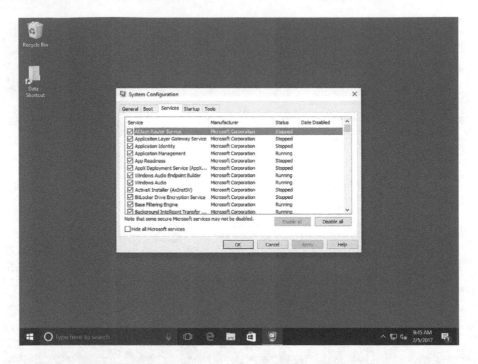

FIGURE 4.17   The Tools tab

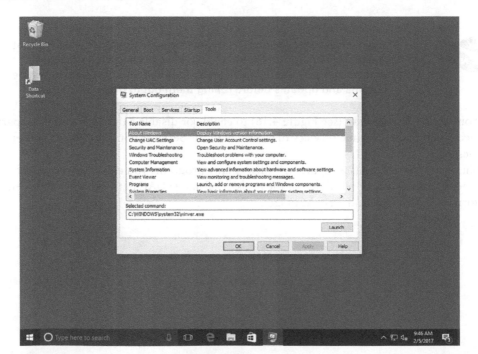

Change System Configuration Settings

To configure settings in the System Configuration utility, perform the following steps:

1. Open the System Configuration utility by clicking Start, typing **msconfig** in the Ask me anything search box, and then clicking msconfig.exe in the resulting list. When prompted, provide an administrative password or confirm to continue.

2. Click the Boot tab, select the Safe boot check box (see Figure 4.18), and then click OK.

FIGURE 4.18   Selecting the Safe boot option on the Boot tab

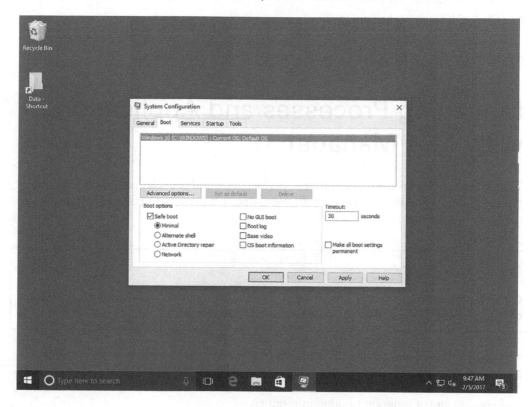

3. Restart your computer. The computer starts in Safe Mode.

4. Open the System Configuration utility, click the Boot tab, deselect the Safe boot check box, and then click OK. Restart your computer and return to the System Configuration utility.

5. Click the Services tab. Browse the list of services and select a service that is not needed on your PC. In this example, we use the LightscribeService Direct Disc Labeling Service because it's seldom used. Deselect the check box to the left of the service name. Click Apply.

Clicking a column heading arranges the entries in alphabetical order.

6. Click the Startup tab. Browse the list of startup items and deselect an item that you don't want to start when your computer starts. In our example, we deselected the Lightscribe program. Click Apply.

7. Click the General tab and notice that Selective startup is now selected (instead of the Normal startup setting).

8. Click OK to close the System Configuration utility.

If you have any problems with your system after disabling a service or startup item, return to the System Configuration utility and enable the service or startup item.

Managing Processes and Applications with Task Manager

Task Manager gives you a quick glance at performance and provides information about programs and processes running on your computer. A *process* is an instance of a program that is being executed.

Certification Ready

Can you describe how to remedy a situation in which a process is consuming 100 percent of the processor utilization for the past 10 minutes? Objective 1.3

Task Manager is one of the handiest programs you can use to take a quick glance at performance to see which programs are using the most system resources on your computer. You can see the status of running programs and programs that have stopped responding, and you can stop a program running in memory.

To start Task Manager, right-click the empty space on the taskbar and choose Task Manager (or you can open the Security menu by pressing the Ctrl+Alt+Del keys and choosing Task Manager). When Task Manager starts, it displays only the running applications (see Figure 4.19).

FIGURE 4.19   Using Task Manager

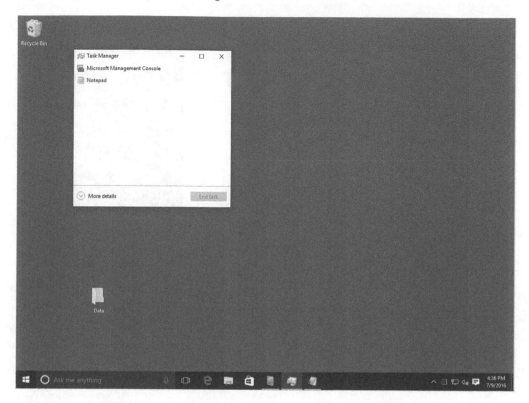

Click the More Details down-arrow to show all the available tabs (see Figure 4.20). When you first start Task Manager on a computer running Windows 10, seven tabs are opened for Task Manager:

- Processes
- Performance
- App history
- Startup
- Users
- Details
- Services

FIGURE 4.20   Viewing the Task Manager tabs

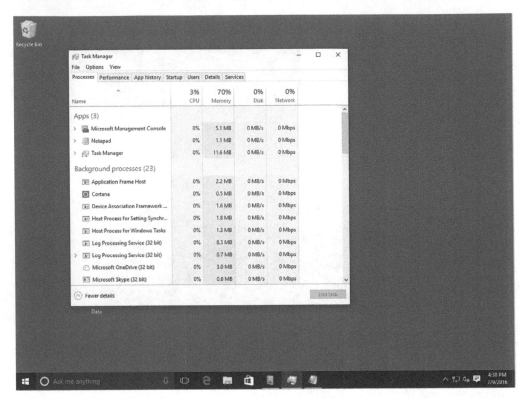

The Processes tab shows all processes running in memory and how much processing and memory each process uses. The processes will display applications (as designated by Apps), Background processes, and Windows processes. On the Processes tab, you can perform the following tasks:

- To see the processes that use the highest percentage of CPU utilization, click the CPU column header.
- To stop a process, right-click the process and choose End task.
- To jump to the Details tab for a particular process, right-click the process and choose Go to details.
- If you want to see the executable that is running the processes, right-click the process and choose Open file location.

To add additional columns, right-click a column header, and select or deselect the desired column such as Process Identification (PID) or Process name.

The Performance tab (as shown in Figure 4.21) displays the amount of CPU usage, physical Memory usage, and Ethernet throughput. For CPU usage, a high percentage indicates the programs or processes are requiring a lot of CPU resources, which can slow your computer. If the percentage seems frozen at or near 100 percent, a program might not be responding.

FIGURE 4.21   Viewing CPU usage

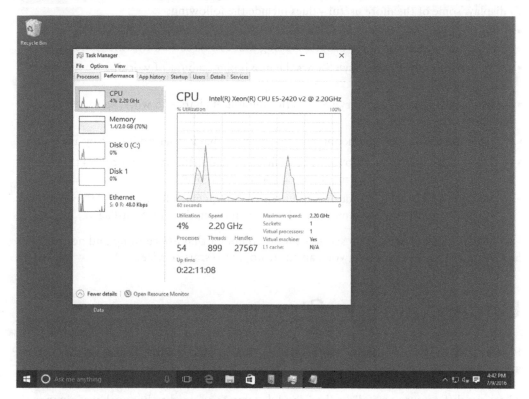

Click Memory to display how much of the paging file is being used (*In use* and *Available*), the amount of Committed and Cached memory, Paged pool, and Non-paged pool. It also shows you the total amount of RAM, the speed of the RAM, and the number of slots used for memory on the motherboard.

The App history tab displays how much resources (including CPU time and network) an application has been using over a period of time. The Startup tab shows the programs that are configured to automatically start when you start Windows. You can disable the startup programs by right-clicking an item and choosing Disable.

The Users tab displays the users who are currently logged on, the amount of CPU and memory usage that each user is using, and the processes the user is running. It also gives you the ability to disconnect them.

The Details tab displays a more detailed look at the processes running on the computer, including the Process Identification (PID). The PID is composed of unique numbers that identify a process while it is running. Similarly, you can stop the process and you can increase or decrease the process priority.

If you are an advanced user, you might want to view other advanced memory values on the Details tab. To do so, right-click the column heading, choose Select columns, and then select or deselect values to be displayed or not displayed. While there are nearly 40 columns to display, some of the more useful values include the following:

- **Working Set (Memory):** Shows the amount of memory in the private working set plus the amount of memory the process is using that can be shared by other processes.

- **Peak Working Set (Memory):** Shows the maximum amount of working set memory used by the process.

- **Working Set Delta (Memory):** Shows the amount of change in working set memory used by the process.

- **Commit Size:** Shows the amount of virtual memory that is reserved for use by a process.

- **Paged Pool:** Shows the amount of committed virtual memory for a process that can be written to another storage medium, such as the hard disk.

- **NP Pool:** Shows the amount of committed virtual memory for a process that can't be written to another storage medium. (NP is an abbreviation for Non-Paged.)

The Services tab displays all services on the computer that are running and not running. Similar to the Services console, you can start, stop, or restart services.

Understanding Storage

Storage in Windows 10 refers to storing data as well as an operating system on disks. There are a number of different types of storage: internal, external, network, and cloud.

When it comes to Windows storage, there's more to it than just saving data on a disk. There are different types of disks (basic and dynamic) you need to know about, along with choices of partition styles such as master boot record (MBR) and GUID partition table (GPT), which determine the number of partitions you are allowed to create along with the size limitations of those partitions.

Understanding Storage Device Types

Windows 10 supports many different types of storage devices in addition to ordinary hard disks. Other storage device types include eSATA, USB, IEEE 1394 (FireWire), and iSCSI.

There are many different types of storage devices supported in Windows 10. This section explains eSATA, USB, IEEE 1394 (FireWire), and iSCSI.

Certification Ready

Which types of storage devices are supported by Windows 10? Objective 5.2

External Serial Advanced Technology Attachment (eSATA)

External Serial Advanced Technology Attachment (eSATA) is an external interface for SATA technologies. eSATA competes with IEEE 1394 (also called FireWire 400) and universal serial bus (USB) 2.0. eSATA is very fast, with read access times of 12.7 milliseconds (ms), read throughput of 93.5 MB/s, and a write throughput of 94 MB/s. In a nutshell, eSATA has a maximum speed of 300 MB/s for 3 Gb/s SATA connections, which is three times faster than either USB 2.0 or FireWire 400. eSATA cables can be up to 6.56 feet or 2 meters in length and are narrow. An eSATA cable is shown in Figure 4.22.

FIGURE 4.22   An eSATA cable

However, there is one negative aspect—eSATA requires its own power connector (USB 2.0 and FireWire 400 do not). The reason eSATA can transfer data so quickly is because it requires no translation between the interface and the computer. This also helps save computer processing resources.

Universal Serial Bus (USB)

Universal serial bus (USB) was a standard developed in the mid-1990s that defines cable connectors and protocols used to connect external devices to a computer. The devices include keyboards, digital cameras, portable media players, and external hard drives, to name a few. Several types of USB cables are shown in Figure 4.23.

USB version 1.0 had data transfer rates of 1.5 megabits per second (Mbps) at low speed and 12 Mbps at full speed.

USB 2.0 increased this speed to 480 Mpbs, which is 40 times faster. USB 2.0 has a read access time of 13.3 milliseconds (ms), a read throughput time of 40.1 megabytes per second (MBps), and a write throughput of 30.9 MBps. USB cables can be up to 16.4 feet (5 meters) in length.

USB 3.0 is the newest version and boasts transfer speeds up to 5 gigabits per second (Gbps). For this reason it has acquired the nickname SuperSpeed. USB 3.0 ports don't need as much power and are backward compatible with USB 2.0 ports.

FIGURE 4.23 USB cables

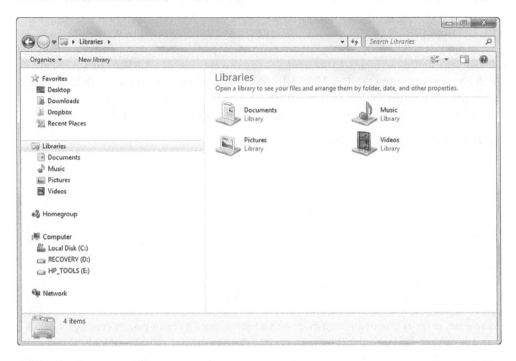

IEEE 1394 (Also Known as FireWire)

IEEE 1394, also known as *FireWire* or i.link, has been around for many years and has undergone several revisions. One of the original reasons behind the creation of IEEE 1394 was to serve as an interface between the computer and a digital video camera so that video could be imported for editing. Today, IEEE 1394 is used for many different types of high-speed data transfers, including video, and serves the same purpose as USB. Several types of IEEE 1394 cables are shown in Figure 4.24.

IEEE 1394 supports plug-and-play technology, hot swapping, multiple speeds on the same bus, *isochronous data transfer* (which means a constant data rate), and it provides power to peripheral devices.

The original standard, FireWire 400 (1394a), provides 400 Mbps throughput and isochronous transfer with read access times of 13.3 ms, read throughput of 40.1 Mbps, and a write throughput of 30.9 Mbps. FireWire 800 (1394b) doubled the throughput to 800 Mbps. IEEE 1394 supports cable lengths up to 14.76 feet (4.5 meters).

FIGURE 4.24 IEEE 1394 cables

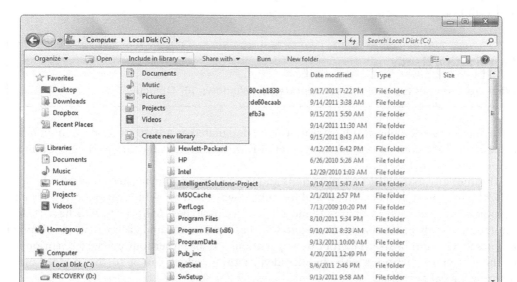

Internet Small Computer System Interface (iSCSI)

While all other storage devices covered in this lesson are mainly for consumer products to connect peripheral devices to laptops and desktop computers, Internet Small Computer System Interface (iSCSI) connects enterprise network storage devices such as a storage area network (SAN). iSCSI is used to transfer data over local area networks (LANs), wide area networks (WANs), and even the Internet.

InfiniBand

InfiniBand is a communications link for the flow of data between processors and I/O devices. InfiniBand offers throughput of up to 2.5 gigabytes per second and can support up to 64,000 addressable devices. InfiniBand is often used as a server connect in high-performance computing (HPC) environments because it is scalable, supports quality of service (QoS), and can provide failover.

InfiniBand uses Internet Protocol Version 6 (IPv6), which enables an almost infinite amount of device expansion.

Understanding Disk and Drive Types

Windows 10 supports two primary types of disks: basic and dynamic. In addition, the operating system supports simple, spanned, striped, and mirrored volumes. Use the Disk

Management tool in the Computer Management snap-in to manage disks, partitions, and volumes.

Certification Ready

What are common types of drives supported by Windows 10? Objective 5.2

In Windows 10, a physical hard drive can be designated as a basic disk or a dynamic disk. *Basic disks* contain only simple volumes. *Dynamic disks* can contain simple, spanned, striped, and mirrored volumes.

Traditionally, basic disks use *partitions* and logical drives. The master boot record (MBR) partition style has been around for quite a while and all Windows operating systems support MBR partitions. But as with most legacy technologies, MBR partitions have their limitations. MBR partitions are limited to four basic partitions and each partition is limited to 2 terabytes (TB) in size. The four basic partitions can be either four primary partitions or three primary partitions with one extended partition, which can be further divided into multiple logical partitions.

A GPT partition style allows for more partitions and larger volume sizes. A disk initialized as a GPT partition style may contain up to 128 primary partitions and each can be larger than 2 TB, in fact, they can be as large as 9.4 zettabytes (ZB).

 One zettabyte is equal to one billion terabytes.

With dynamic disks, free space on a hard drive is divided into *volumes* instead of partitions. Dynamic disks are not limited by partition styles as are basic disks. You can configure dynamic disk volumes as simple, spanned, mirrored, striped, or RAID-5:

- **Simple Volume:** This type of volume uses free space available on a single disk.

- **Spanned Volume:** This type of volume extends a simple volume across multiple disks, up to a maximum of 32.

- **Mirrored Volume:** This type of volume duplicates data from one disk to a second disk for redundancy and fault tolerance; if one disk fails, data can be accessed from the second disk. You cannot span a mirrored volume; a mirrored volume must reside on a single disk. Mirroring is also referred to as RAID-1.

- **Striped Volume:** This type of volume stores data across two or more physical disks. Data on a striped volume is written evenly to each of the physical disks in the volume. You cannot mirror or span a striped volume. Striping is often referred to as RAID-0.

- **RAID-5 Volume:** This type of volume is a type of striped volume that also provides fault tolerance. Data is written to three or more disks; if one disk fails, the remaining drives re-create the data.

You can typically convert a basic disk to a dynamic disk without losing any data, but it's a best practice to back up all data before attempting the conversion. You might need to convert a hard disk from dynamic to basic at some point. For example, a user's computer runs Windows 7 and the single hard disk is configured as a dynamic disk.

Virtual Hard Disk (VHD)

A virtual hard disk (VHD) is a disk image file format for storing the complete contents of a hard drive. The disk image, also called a virtual machine, copies an existing hard drive including all data and structural components.

VHDs can be fixed-size or dynamically expanding. Fixed-size VHDs will take up the specified amount of physical disk space allotted on the host computer's file system, where dynamically expanding disks will allocate space only as needed.

A VHD acts like a normal physical hard disk, having all the capabilities to create disk sectors, files, and folders, run an operating system, and install and execute other applications.

Understanding File Systems

The three primary types of file systems for Windows are FAT32, NTFS, and ReFS. It's best to use NTFS-formatted disks for Windows Vista through Windows 10 because NTFS handles small to very large hard disks, provides better security, and is the most reliable.

A *file system* is the overall structure your computer uses to name, store, and organize files and folders on a hard disk or partition. The file system provides a map of the clusters (the basic units of logical storage on a hard disk) that a file has been stored in. When you install a hard disk in a computer, you must format it with a file system. Today, the primary file system choices for a computer that will run Windows are NTFS, FAT32, and ReFS. In Windows 10, you can view file systems in use on your computer from the Disk Management MMC snap-in.

Certification Ready

What are the differences between FAT32, NTFS, and ReFS? Objective 4.1

FAT32 and *FAT* (which is seldom used today) were popular in earlier versions of Windows (such as Windows 95, Windows 98, Windows Millennium Edition, Windows NT, and Windows 2000). The limitations of FAT32 make it less desirable than NTFS:

- A FAT32 partition is limited to a maximum size of 32 gigabytes (GB).
- The maximum size of a file that can be stored on a FAT32 volume is 4 GB.

So why use FAT32? Many universal serial bus (USB) flash drives come formatted as FAT32 to be compatible with a large variety of operating systems. If you plan to configure your computer for *multi-booting*, where you choose at startup which operating system you want to load, you might need to format a partition with FAT32 if that partition will run Windows 95, Windows 98, or Windows Millennium Edition.

NTFS is the preferred file system that supports much larger hard disks and a higher level of reliability than FAT-based file systems. In addition, NTFS offers better security through permissions and encryption.

You can view all available disks or volumes that have been formatted with a file system in the This PC folder in the Devices And Drives section of File Explorer.

Resilient File System (ReFS) was introduced as an enhanced NTFS file system by offering larger volume sizes and files. ReFS also offers greater resiliency, meaning better data verification, error correction, and scalability. It is recommended that you should use ReFS for very large volumes and file shares. However, you cannot use ReFS for the boot volume. For maximum file name length, NTFS only supports 256 characters, while ReFS supports up to 32,000 characters.

Because ReFS uses a subset of NTFS features, it maintains backward compatibility with NTFS that can be accessed directly by Windows Server 2012 or higher, or Windows 8.1 or higher. Different from NTFS, ReFS has a fixed allocation unit size of 64 KB, and ReFS does not support Encrypted File System (EFS) for files.

When deciding on which file system to use, you should always consider NTFS or ReFS. It is recommended to use ReFS for the following situations:

- **Microsoft Hyper-V Workloads:** ReFS has performance advantages when using both .vhd and .vhdx files.

- **Storage Spaces Direct When Using Shared Direct Attached Storage:** ReFS supports larger volumes and improved throughput.

- **Data Archival That You Want to Retain for Long Periods:** Archive data can benefit from ReFS resiliency.

Table 4.1 compares attributes of the available Windows 10 file systems.

TABLE 4.1   Comparing File Systems

File System	Maximum Partition Size	Maximum File Size
FAT32	32 GB	4 GB
NTFS	256 TB *	Limited by the size of the volume on which it resides
ReFS	1 Yobibyte (2^{80} bytes)	16 exbibytes (2^{64} bytes)
exFAT	128 Pebibtye (2^{50} bytes)	Limited by the size of the volume on which it resides

* with 64 KB clusters

Another file system worth mentioning is the *Extended File Allocation Table (exFAT)*, which is a Microsoft file system optimized for flash drives. It is typically used where the NTFS file system is not ideal because of the data structure overhead. exFAT supports a larger volume than FAT or FAT32 supports. exFAT has been adopted by the SD Card Association as the default file system for SDXC cards larger than 32 GB.

Using Disk Management to Configure Disks, Volumes, and File Systems

When you add a new hard drive to a computer, there are a few steps you need to take to introduce a new drive to the operating system. You need to initialize the disk and then choose a drive type and a partition style (for basic disks). You can perform all of these steps in the Disk Management tool, which is part of the Computer Management MMC snap-in.

To open Computer Management, click Start, type **computer,** and then click Computer Management in the resulting list. Alternatively, you can right-click Start and choose Computer Management. Figure 4.25 shows the tools in the Computer Management snap-in, with the Disk Management tool selected.

FIGURE 4.25   The Disk Management snap-in

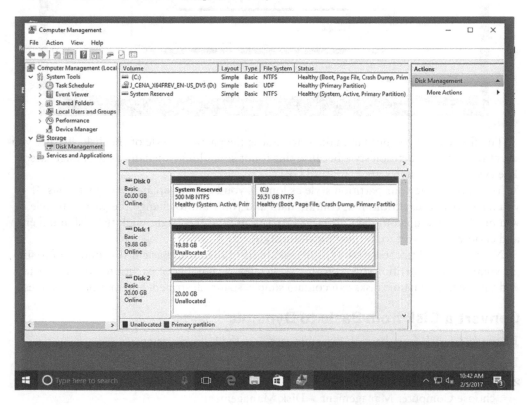

If you just installed a new hard disk and the disk is not initialized, in Disk Management, right-click the disk (such as Disk 1 or Disk 2) and choose Initialize Disk. In the Initialize Disk window, you are prompted to select a partition style, as shown in Figure 4.26.

FIGURE 4.26   The Initialize Disk dialog box

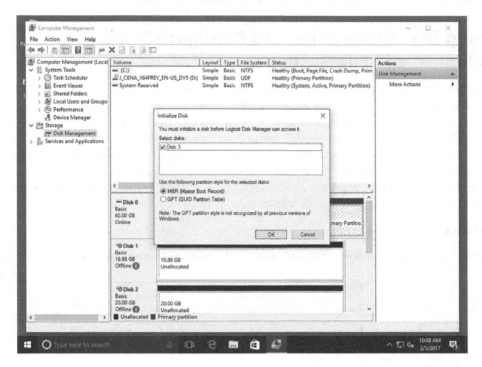

The first choice you need to make is to choose the partition style of the disk. Be sure you select the correct partition style because this is not something you can easily change later. The two partition styles are MBR and GPT.

You can change your partition style as long as you have not created any partitions. If you have created partitions that contain data and you want to change the partition style, you need to back up your data, delete all partitions, and then right-click the disk number and choose to convert to the new partition style.

Next, you need to choose the type of disk: basic or dynamic. Basic disks contain only simple volumes. The partition style you choose dictates the number of partitions you can create and their sizes. Dynamic disks can contain simple, spanned, striped, and mirrored volumes.

Convert a Disk from Basic to Dynamic

To convert a disk from basic to dynamic, perform the following steps:

1. Back up all data on the disk you want to convert.

2. In the Computer Management console, open Disk Management: Right-click Start and choose Computer Management ➢ Disk Management.

3. Right-click the disk (such as Disk 1 or Disk 2) you want to convert and choose Convert to Dynamic Disk.

4. If the disk is currently MBR, the Convert to GPT Disk option appears. If the disk is GPT, the Convert to MBR Disk option appears. Click the appropriate option.

After you convert the partition style, you can create partitions again and restore the data that you previously backed up.

 The conversion from basic to dynamic can occur automatically based on the type of volume you create. You'll see this in action in the step-by-step exercise named "Create a Spanned Volume."

In the next example, a second disk is added to the computer, so two disks have been initialized as MBR. However, you will create a simple volume on only one of the dynamic disks. Spanning, striping, and mirroring, which you will do in subsequent step-by-step exercises, involve two or more disks.

Create a Simple Volume

To create a simple volume, perform the following steps:

1. In the Computer Management console, open Disk Management: Right-click Start and choose Computer Management ➤ Disk Management.

2. Right-click an empty area (unallocated space) of a dynamic disk. In the New Volume menu, choose New Simple Volume (see Figure 4.27).

FIGURE 4.27   The New Volume menu

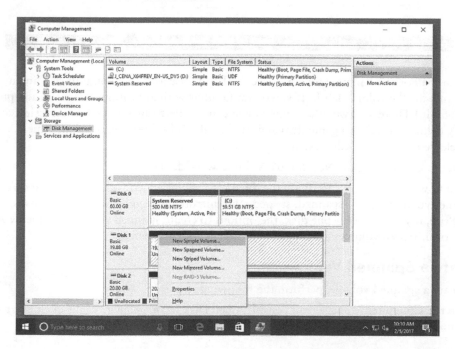

3. The New Simple Volume Wizard starts. Click **Next** on the Welcome screen. Click **Next** to accept the default volume size.

4. On the Assign Drive Letter or Path screen, assign a drive letter or path, click Next, and then on the Format Partition screen (as shown in Figure 4.28), click a file system such as FAT, FAT32, or NTFS.

FIGURE 4.28 Formatting a partition

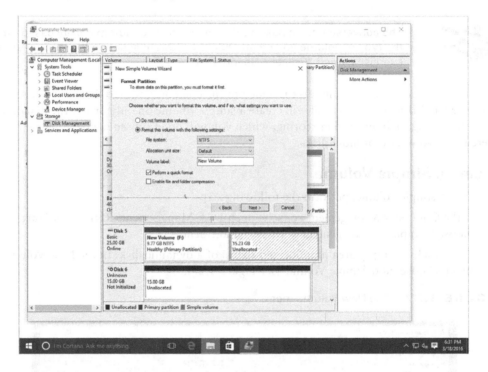

5. On the Format Partition screen, you can also choose an allocation unit size and a name for the volume label. (If you're not familiar with allocation unit sizes, accept the default.) There are two other options you can set: Perform a quick format (selected by default, which is a good idea) and Enable file and folder compression, which is not selected by default. Click Next.

6. In the Completing the New Simple Volume Wizard, click Finish.

You now have a new partition on the dynamic disk on which you can store data. All the other volume types—spanned, striped, and mirrored—require two or more disks. Therefore, if you have only one disk, the options to create spanned volumes, striped volumes, or mirrored volumes are grayed out and cannot be selected.

Create a Spanned Volume

To create a spanned volume, perform the following steps:

1. In the Computer Management console, open Disk Management: Right-click Start and choose Computer Management ➢ Disk Management.

2. Right-click an empty area of a dynamic disk and choose New Spanned Volume.

3. Click Next on the Welcome to the New Spanned Volume Wizard screen.

4. Click the desired disk in the Available box and click Add (see Figure 4.29). You can also double-click the Available disk to add it to the Selected box.

FIGURE 4.29   The Select Disks page

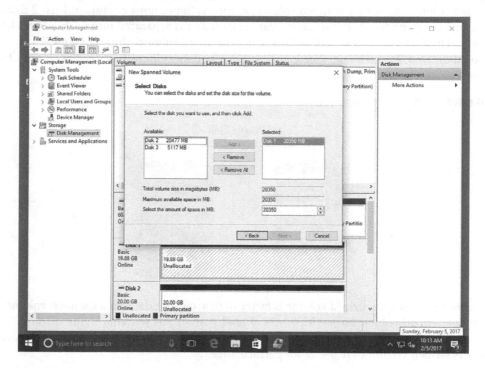

5. When you add disks to the Selected box, the "Total volume size in megabytes (MB)" box displays the combined sizes of all disks, yet when you click one of the disks in the Selected box, the "Maximum available space in MB" box and the "Select the amount of space in MB" box show what you have selected from that specific disk. You can select a different amount of space from each disk you add. You can continue to add as many disks as you would like to include in your spanned volume. After you have selected the disks, click Next.

6. On the Assign Drive Letter or Path screen, click a drive letter and click Next.

7. The Format Volume screen is the same as the screen for creating a simple volume. Set your format volume options and click Next.

8. On the Completing the New Spanned Volume Wizard page, click Finish.

9. A warning message appears, letting you know that in order to create a spanned volume, the basic disk will be converted to a dynamic disk. If you convert the disk to dynamic, you will not be able to start installed operating systems from any volume on the disk. Click Yes to continue or No to cancel the operation.

Do not plan to use spanned volumes for fault tolerance. If one disk in the spanned volume fails, all data in the spanned volume is lost unless you have a backup.

Striped Volumes

Creating a *striped volume* is similar to creating a spanned volume in that almost all the steps are the same. However, the way data is stored on a striped volume is different than a spanned volume. As with a spanned volume, striped volumes must contain at least 2 disks and can contain up to 32. But when the data is stored, it is separated into 64-kilobyte (KB) chunks. The first 64 KB is stored on Disk 1 in the striped volume, the second 64 KB chunk is stored on Disk 2, and so on. (See Figure 4.30.) The data is literally striped across multiple drives.

FIGURE 4.30   A striped volume

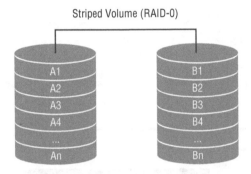

Accessing data on a striped volume is faster than accessing data on a spanned volume because a striped volume has multiple sets of read/write heads working simultaneously when reading and writing data. In this regard, spanned volumes are good for high capacity, whereas striped volumes are better for performance.

Create a Striped Volume

To create a striped volume, perform the following steps:

1. In Disk Management, right-click an empty disk and choose New Striped Volume. On the Welcome to the New Striped Volume Wizard screen, click Next.

2. Click the second disk in the Available box (refer to Figure 4.29) and click Add.

    When you add disks to the Selected box, the "Total volume size in megabytes (MB)" box displays the combined sizes of all disks. This is where one of the big differences between spanned volumes and striped volumes takes place. On spanned volumes, you could take different amounts of hard drive space from each disk—you cannot do this with striped volumes. Striped volumes must use the same amount of disk space from each disk you take to the striped volume. So after you add two or more disks to the Selected box, if you change the "Select the amount of space in MB" setting (regardless of which disk is highlighted in the Selected box), the size difference will be reflected on both (or all) disks that you had added. Both disks have 40957 MB of space but we have changed the Select the amount of space in MB to 39975.

3. After you have selected the disks, click Next.

4. On the Assign Drive Letter or Path screen, select your drive letter and click Next. The Format Volume screen appears. Set your format volume options and click Next. Click Finish.

5. A warning appears, indicating that to create a striped volume, the basic disk will be converted to a dynamic disk. If you convert the disk to dynamic, you will not be able to start installed operating systems from any volume on the disk. Click Yes to continue or No to cancel.

Striped volumes do not offer fault tolerance. Just as with spanned volumes, if one disk in the striped volume fails, all data from the entire striped volume is lost. You'll have to retrieve the data from a previous backup.

Mirrored Volumes

Mirrored volumes require only two disks. You cannot mirror to a third or fourth disk. Mirrored volumes store an exact copy of data from the first member of the mirrored volume to the second member. Because the data is written across both drives, you do get fault tolerance with mirrored volumes. Figure 4.31 shows an example of a mirrored volume.

FIGURE 4.31   A mirrored volume

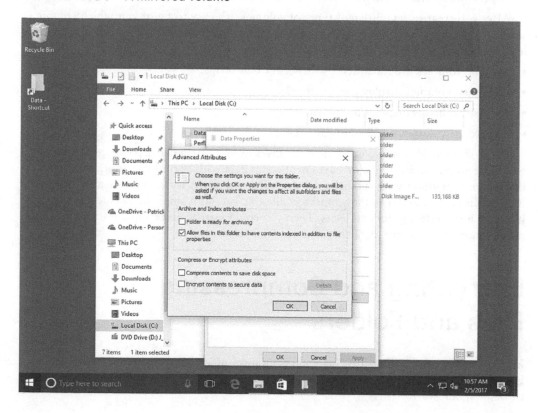

Create a Mirrored Volume

To create a mirrored volume, perform the following steps:

1. In Disk Management, right-click an empty disk and choose New Mirrored Volume. On the Welcome to the New Mirrored Volume Wizard screen, click Next.

2. Click the second disk in the Available box. Mirrored volumes require the same amount of disk space from each disk. When you add a disk to the Selected box, the "Total volume size in megabytes (MB)" box displays the most available free space from the disk with the smallest amount.

    You can reduce the amount of space, but it will be reduced on both disks. This makes sense because you're creating an exact copy of data stored on the source disk, so you don't need the destination disk to have additional free space that will never be used. After you have selected the disks, click Next.

3. On the Assign Drive Letter or Path screen, select a drive letter and click Next. The Format Volume screen is the same as the previous Format Volume screens. Set your format volume options and click Next. Click Finish.

4. A warning message appears, informing you that the basic disk will be converted to a dynamic disk. If you convert the disk to dynamic, you will not be able to start installed operating systems from any volume on the disk. Click Yes.

After you create a few different types of volumes, it's easy to figure out which volume is which—they're identified by a strip of color at the top of the volume. Here are the default legend colors for the different types of volumes:

-   Simple volumes are identified by their dark blue strips.
-   Spanned volumes display purple strips.
-   Striped volumes display aquamarine strips.
-   Mirrored volumes display burgundy strips.

In the real world, you wouldn't carve up disks as you do on client computers—there would be no point. But you may have client computers with two, three, four, or even six disks. On a computer with six disks, for example, you might want to create a spanned volume on disks 2, 3, and 4 so they appear in File Explorer as a single drive (such as drive E). It can be less confusing for end users. Then you could mirror disks 5 and 6 to create a mirrored volume for sensitive data that requires fault tolerance.

Encrypting and Compressing Files and Folders

Encrypting files and folders protects them from unwanted access. Microsoft uses the Encrypting File System (EFS) to encrypt individual files and folders in Windows Vista through Windows 10.

Encryption protects the contents of files and folders from unauthorized access. Windows uses EFS to allow users to encrypt information on hard disks, external flash disks, CDs, DVDs, backup tapes, and other types of physical media. Files and folders are not encrypted in Windows 10 by default; however, users can enforce encryption on data files, folders, and entire drives.

 Windows 10 Home does not fully support EFS.

Understanding Encrypting File System (EFS)

The data in an encrypted file is "scrambled" but still readable and usable by the user who encrypted the file. That user—and any other authorized users—can open and change the file as necessary. However, an unauthorized user who tries to open or copy the file receives an "Access Denied" message. Only the original owner and the computer's designated recovery agent can access encrypted files. The designated recovery agent is the Administrator account, by default, on a local computer or in a domain.

Certification Ready

How are files and folders encrypted using Encrypting File System (EFS)? Objective 4.3

A file created in or moved to an encrypted folder is automatically encrypted. The folder itself isn't encrypted; a user with appropriate file access permissions can see the names of the files in the folder.

 It's more efficient to encrypt at the folder level rather than the file level. New files added to the folder will also be encrypted.

When you mark a file for encryption, Windows generates a large, random number—a unique *encryption key*. The key is used to scramble the contents of the file. This encryption key is also encrypted with a personal file encryption certificate, which is stored in the Windows Certificate database. The file's encryption key is stored along with the file.

 Encrypted files can be significantly larger than unencrypted files, and the encryption/decryption process can add significant processing overhead.

When you're logged on to Windows and attempt to open an encrypted file, Windows retrieves your personal EFS certificate, decodes the file's unique encryption key, and uses that key to decode the contents of the file.

If you lose an encryption key or your EFS certificate, or one of them becomes damaged, you could lose your data. It's important to back up your encryption key(s) and certificate and keep them in a safe place. You should also consider creating a file recovery certificate.

Encrypt a File or Folder

To encrypt and decrypt a file or folder, perform the following steps:

1. In File Explorer, right-click the file or folder you want to encrypt and choose Properties. The Properties dialog box opens.

2. On the General tab, click Advanced. The Advanced Attributes dialog box opens (see Figure 4.32).

FIGURE 4.32 The Advanced Attributes dialog box

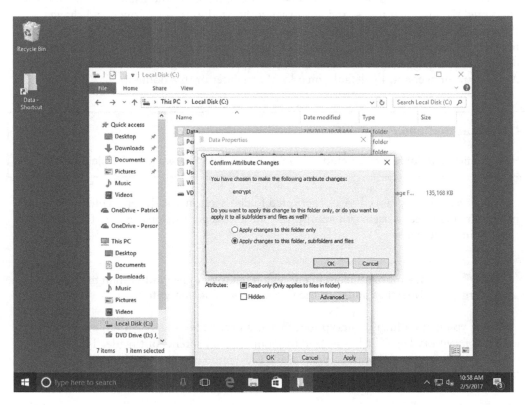

3. Select the "Encrypt contents to secure data" check box and click OK.

4. Click OK to accept your settings and close the Properties dialog box.

5. The Confirm Attribute Changes dialog box opens (see Figure 4.33). Click either "Apply changes to this folder only" or "Apply changes to this folder, subfolders and files."

6. Click OK.

FIGURE 4.33   The Confirm Attribute Changes dialog box

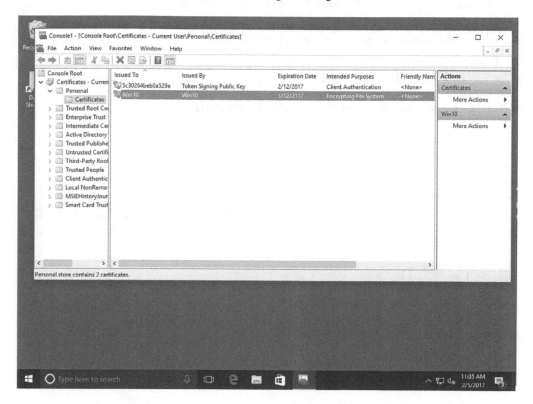

As Windows encrypts the folder, you are reminded to back up your encryption key. Microsoft recommends that you back up the encryption key immediately. Click the balloon reminder and follow the prompts. The encrypted folder and files will be displayed with a small golden lock, so you can see at a glance that it's encrypted.

Decrypt a File or Folder

GET READY. To decrypt a file or folder, perform the following steps:

1. Right-click the file or folder you want to decrypt and choose Properties.

2. Click the General tab and click Advanced.

3. Deselect the "Encrypt contents to secure data" check box and click OK.

Back Up Your EFS Certificate

To back up your EFS certificate, perform the following steps:

1. Click Start, type **mmc.exe,** and then press Enter. If you are asked to allow this app to make changes to your device, click Yes.

2. Click File ➢ Add/Remove Snap-in.

3. In the Add or Remove Snap-ins dialog box, click Certificates and click Add.

4. In the Certificates snap-in dialog box, My user account is already selected. Click Finish.

5. In the Add or Remove Snap-ins dialog box, click OK.

6. Expand the Personal folder by clicking its arrow.

7. Click Certificates. The user's personal certificates are listed (see Figure 4.34).

FIGURE 4.34   Personal certificates in Certificate Manager

8. Click the certificate that lists Encrypting File System in the Intended Purposes column. If there is more than one EFS certificate, select all of them.

9. Click Action ➢ All Tasks ➢ Export. The Export wizard starts.

10. Click Next.

11. On the Export Private Key page (see Figure 4.35), select the Yes, export the private key option, and click Next.

FIGURE 4.35   Using the Certificate Export Wizard

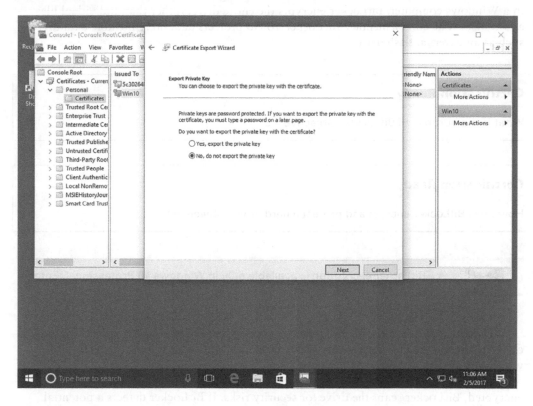

12. Click Personal Information Exchange and click Next.

13. Type the password you want to use, confirm it, and then click Next.

14. The wizard creates a file to store the certificate. Click Browse, navigate to the location where you want to save the file, and then type a name for the file. Click Save.

15. In the next screen, click Next.

16. Click Finish and click OK.

Be sure to back up the certificate file to a location that is different than where it's saved. For example, if you saved the file on your computer's hard disk, copy the file to removable media or a network location.

Understanding BitLocker

BitLocker Drive Encryption encrypts an entire fixed disk to prevent access by unauthorized users. BitLocker To Go protects removable drives, such as external flash drives. You can encrypt drives with BitLocker in Windows Professional, Enterprise, and Education editions only.

BitLocker Drive Encryption is another method of protecting data stored on a fixed drive in a Windows computer. BitLocker encrypts the entire drive, rather than individual files and folders. The complementary BitLocker To Go protects data on removable data drives, such as an external flash drive.

Certification Ready

What is the purpose of BitLocker? Objective 4.3

Certification Ready

How does BitLocker encrypt and protect a hard drive? Objective 5.2

 BitLocker encryption is available only in Windows 10 Professional, Enterprise, and Education editions.

When you add new files to a BitLocker-encrypted disk, the files are encrypted automatically. If you copy the files to another drive, BitLocker automatically decrypts the files, which means they're no longer protected.

Anytime you start a computer on which the operating system disk is BitLocker-encrypted, BitLocker scans the drive for security risks. If BitLocker detects a potential security risk such as a change to the startup files, it locks Windows (prevents it from running) and requires the user to provide the BitLocker recovery key to unlock Windows. This ensures that unauthorized users cannot access the system to steal files or somehow damage the system or data.

Some computers have a Trusted Platform Module (TPM) chip on the motherboard. If the chip is present, BitLocker uses the TPM chip to protect the BitLocker keys. When a user starts a computer with a TPM chip and with BitLocker enabled, BitLocker requests the keys from the TPM and unlocks the system.

BitLocker requires a hard disk with at least two partitions formatted with NTFS. One partition will be encrypted and contain the system partition. The other partition will be unencrypted and will be the active partition used to start the computer.

BitLocker features:

- **BitLocker Provisioning:** An administrator has the ability to enable BitLocker, prior to deploying the operating system from the Windows Preinstallation Environment (WinPE). BitLocker is applied to the formatted volume and encrypts the volume prior to running the Windows setup process.

- **Used Disk Space Only Encryption:** BitLocker requires that all data and free space on the drive be encrypted. With BitLocker, administrators have the ability to encrypt either the entire volume or just the space being used.

- **Standard User PIN and Password Change:** BitLocker requires that you need to be an administrator in order to configure BitLocker on operating system drives. However, users now have the ability to change the BitLocker PIN for the operating system or change the password on the data volumes.

- **Network Unlock:** Network Unlock allows administrators to manage desktop and servers that are configured to use BitLocker. This allows an administrator to configure BitLocker to unlock automatically any encrypted hard drive during a system reboot when that hard drive is connected to their trusted environment.

- **Support for Encrypted Hard Drives for Windows:** The advantage of this type of encryption is that encrypted hard drives that use Full Disk Encryption (FDE) get each block of the physical disk space encrypted. Because each physical block gets encrypted, it offers better encryption.

BitLocker Drive Encryption encrypts an entire drive. EFS protects individual files and folders on any drive on a per-user basis.

You can turn off BitLocker at any time by suspending it temporarily or decrypting the drive.

Turn On BitLocker Drive Encryption

To turn on BitLocker Drive Encryption, perform the following steps:

1. Right-click Start and choose Control Panel.

2. Click System and Security ➤ BitLocker Drive Encryption.

3. In the BitLocker Drive Encryption window (see Figure 4.36), click Turn On BitLocker for the operating system drive. When prompted, provide an administrative password or confirm to continue.

   BitLocker scans your computer to ensure that it meets the BitLocker system requirements.

4. In the BitLocker Setup Wizard, follow the prompts to choose how to store the recovery key.

5. When prompted, confirm that the Run BitLocker system check check box is selected and click Continue to encrypt the drive.

6. Restart the computer by clicking Restart now.

FIGURE 4.36   Turning on BitLocker

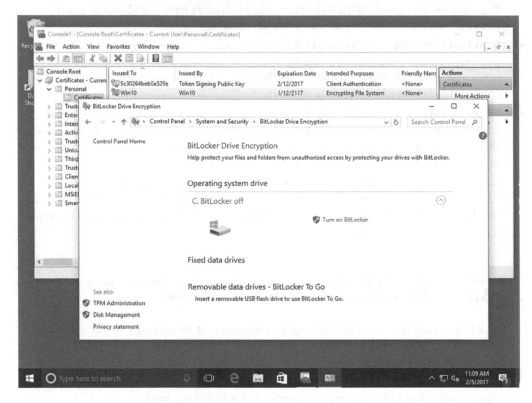

The encryption process might take several minutes to more than an hour. A completion message appears when the encryption process is finished.

Skill Summary

In this lesson, you learned:

- A software program (also known as an app) is a sequence of instructions written to perform a specified task for a computer. Today, most of these programs are installed as desktop apps or Windows Store apps. Desktop apps are traditional apps, such as Microsoft Office or Adobe Acrobat.

- The Program Compatibility Troubleshooter is a wizard-based solution that users or administrators can use to automatically configure an executable file to use an appropriate Windows 10 compatibility mechanism. Thus, the troubleshooter is not a compatibility mechanism in itself; it is simply a method for applying other mechanisms.

- The Windows Store provides a central location for you to purchase and download Windows apps that run on Windows 8 and later operating systems. Windows Store apps do not run on Windows 7 or earlier versions of Windows. Windows Store apps tend to be smaller and faster than desktop apps.

- Services run in the background on a Windows system to help the operating system run other programs. The Services console is the central management point of services in Windows 10.

- When it comes to Windows storage, there's more to it than just saving data on a disk. There are different types of disks (basic and dynamic) you need to know about, along with choices of partition styles such as the master boot record (MBR) and GUID partition table (GPT), which determine the number of partitions you are allowed to create along with the size limitations of those partitions.

- Encryption protects the contents of files and folders from unauthorized access. Windows uses Encrypting File System (EFS) to allow users to encrypt information on hard disks, external flash drives, CDs, DVDs, backup tapes, and other types of physical media. BitLocker Drive Encryption is another method of protecting data stored on a fixed drive in a Windows computer.

- BitLocker Drive Encryption is another method of protecting data stored on a fixed drive in a Windows computer. BitLocker encrypts the entire drive, rather than individual files and folders.

Knowledge Assessment

You can find the answers to the following sections in the Appendix.

Multiple Choice

1. Which of the following actions can be performed in the Programs and Features applet in Control Panel?

    A. Install an application

    B. Uninstall an application

    C. Encrypt an application's files

    D. Compress an application's files

2. Which of the following actions can be performed using Group Policy? (Choose all that apply.)

    A. Restrict user access to an application

    B. Encrypt a user's files

    C. Update an application

    D. Install applications from a network location

3. Which of the following locations is accessed to enter Safe Mode the next time the computer starts?

    A. The General tab

    B. The Boot tab

    C. The Startup tab

    D. Services console

4. In the System Configuration utility, which of the following tabs is accessed to start Performance Monitor?

    A. General

    B. Startup

    C. Services

    D. Tools

5. Which of the following represents the maximum disk size that NTFS can handle?

    A. 32 GB

    B. 256 GB

    C. 32 TB

    D. 256 TB

6. Which built-in account type used to run services has full access to a system?

    A. Local Service account

    B. Network Service account

    C. Local System account

    D. Root System account

7. Which of the following partitions or volumes can be created on a dynamic drive? (Choose all that apply.)

    A. Striped partition

    B. Striped volume

    C. Simple volume

    D. Spanned volume

    E. Mirrored partition

8. In which of the following locations are EFS certificates stored?

    A. EFS Certificate database

    B. Windows Certificate database

    C. Certificate library

    D. Documents library

9. Which of the following is used to indicate that a folder is compressed?

    A. Two small arrows pointing toward each other

    B. A golden lock

    C. 0s and 1s

    D. A series of question marks

10. Which of the following is the name of the chip that BitLocker can use on some computers to protect BitLocker encryption keys?

    A. Trusted Platform Module

    B. Trusted Protection Module

    C. Encryption Platform Module

    D. Trusted Hard Drive Module

Fill in the Blank

1. A(n) _____ is a program that runs within the operating system and helps a user perform a specific task, such as word processing, appointment scheduling, or accounting.

2. _____ is a collection of settings (policies) stored in Active Directory on a Windows network.

3. Windows uses _____ to handle requests for print spooling, file indexing, task scheduling, the Windows Firewall, and much more.

4.   _____ is used to enable or disable startup services, set boot options such as booting into Safe Mode, access tools like Action Center and Event Viewer, and more.

5.   Most Windows Vista through Windows 10 users use the _____ file system because it supports larger disks than FAT32 or FAT.

6.   Group Policy can be used to _____ (or publish) an application to all users or computers in a designated group.

7.   A _____ is a unique account that is the combination of an email address and a password that is used to sign in to services like Outlook.com, MSN.com, Hotmail.com, OneDrive, Windows Phone, or Xbox Live.

8.   Windows uses _____ to allow users to encrypt information on hard disks, external flash drives, CDs, DVDs, backup tapes, and other types of physical media.

9.   _____ is the process of decreasing the size of files or folders without affecting the files' contents.

10. _____ encrypts an entire drive, rather than individual files and folders on a disk.

True/False

1.   Use Programs and Features to install applications in Windows 10.

2.   Objects in Active Directory are linked to Group Policy Objects (GPOs).

3.   A Windows 10 system can have more than 100 services running at any one time.

4.   In System Configuration, the Tools tab enables you to enable or disable services.

5.   EFS and BitLocker Drive Encryption refer to the same thing.

Case Scenarios

You can find the answers to the following sections in the Appendix.

Scenario 4-1: Providing Redundancy on a Client Computer

You provide support for a commercial bioengineering lab. Mizuki is a chemist at the lab, and she recently inherited a computer from the IT department that has two large hard disks and runs Windows 10 Enterprise. One hard disk provides ample disk space for her programs and data files, but she would like to use the other disk for redundancy to better protect her system and files. Describe your recommended solution.

Scenario 4-2: Protecting Laptop Computers

Henry, a traveling salesperson at your company, left his laptop at the airport on his last trip and the laptop was never recovered. His new laptop arrived yesterday; you installed Windows 10 Enterprise and productivity applications and you also restored data from a backup. What should you do to the laptop to protect all programs and data on the computer in the event of loss or theft?

Scenario 4-3: Uninstalling Local Software

Henry, a traveling salesperson at your company, left on an extended business trip to Asia. He has called to request that the voice transcription software be deleted from his computer. He doesn't use the application and doesn't want it taking up space. Describe how to help him remove the software on his own.

Scenario 4-4: Running a Windows 7 Application on Windows 10

You use an inventory application that ran on your Windows 7 computer but it doesn't run on your new Windows 10 computer. Describe the various solutions available to you for getting this application to run on your Windows 10 computer.

Lesson

5

Managing Devices

Objective Domain Matrix

Technology Skill	Objective Domain Description	Objective Domain Number
Understanding Cloud Storage	Understand storage	5.2
Understanding Printing Devices	Understand printing devices	5.3
	Connect devices	5.1
Understanding System Devices and Device Drivers	Understand system devices	5.4
	Connect devices	5.1

Key Terms

audio device	OneDrive
cloud storage	OneDrive for Business
Device Manager	OneDrive Recycle Bin
Devices and Printers folder	plug-and-play (PnP) technology
driver	print device
fetching	print job
input devices	print queue
local printer	print spooler
network printer	video device

 Real World Scenario

Lesson 5 Case

Some of the computers you support at Interstate Snacks have two or more disks. To make the most of the storage space, you plan to span, stripe, or mirror the volumes, depending on the needs of each user. However, you are tired of always adding more disks or upgrading computers because the system runs out of disk space. Therefore, you also plan to run a pilot project using cloud storage and services such as Microsoft OneDrive.

Understanding Cloud Storage

Cloud services are becoming highly popular, and they provide convenient storage and application hosting for consumers and businesses alike.

If you've been in the IT industry for any length of time, you've probably seen outsourcing of data storage. Generally, when a company outsources the storage of its data, another company assumes the burden of maintaining all the storage devices and data backups. *Cloud storage* is remote data storage with backups but can also include application hosting. You can use applications like Microsoft Word and Outlook, along with many other applications, over the Internet. Client machines can run applications from the cloud and access data; in fact, they can maintain complete control of their data and security.

Certification Ready

What is the purpose of cloud storage, such as Microsoft OneDrive? Objective 5.2

Using OneDrive to Manage Files and Folders

OneDrive is a file hosting service that allows you to store and create files and folders and share them with other users and groups.

OneDrive is a free (up to 1 GB), secure file-hosting service that enables your users to store, sync, and share files across devices using the cloud. Office 365 comes with 1 GB of OneDrive storage for each user. Additional storage can be purchased. You can also use OneDrive to synchronize files and folders that you select across multiple devices. If you forget to include a file within your sync folder, you can use OneDrive to connect to your remote computer, locate the file, and then upload it to your OneDrive space. This process is called *fetching*.

The public offering of OneDrive is intended for personal use and is easily comparable to Dropbox. You store files in your OneDrive and access them from anywhere. *OneDrive for Business* is different from the public version of OneDrive because OneDrive for Business is based on SharePoint. By using SharePoint, OneDrive for Business can be used by team members to store and work on documents with others and it helps ensure that business files for your users are stored in a central location.

Accessing OneDrive from a Browser

You can access OneDrive from a browser using your Microsoft user account from anywhere you have an Internet connection. While OneDrive can be accessed from a browser at http://onedrive.live.com (as shown in Figure 5.1), OneDrive for Business is accessed from the Office 365 Portal (http://portal.office.com). After you are logged on to Office 365, you can click the OneDrive button to open the OneDrive Admin Console, on which you can upload, download, create, and share folders and files. If your computer is configured to support fetching, you can also connect to it remotely from the OneDrive for Business Console.

FIGURE 5.1   The OneDrive Console

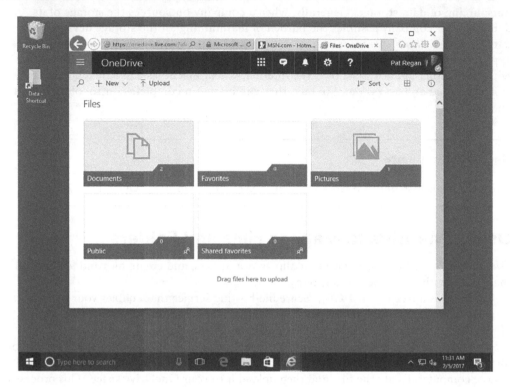

Uploading Files to OneDrive

If you have existing files on your computer that you want to upload to OneDrive, you can use either of the following options:

- From the OneDrive Dashboard, navigate to the folder in which you want to store the file. On the menu, click Upload, browse to the file you want from your computer, and then click Open.

- From the OneDrive app installed on your local computer, you can drag and drop the files you want to upload into the OneDrive folder. This automatically syncs with OneDrive. You can also configure OneDrive for the desktop to allow you to fetch files on your PC from other devices.

Recovering Files from OneDrive

Certification Ready

What is the primary tool to recover deleted files in OneDrive? Objective 5.2

Similar to deleting local files in Windows 10, if you accidentally delete a file, you have 30 days to recover it from the *OneDrive Recycle Bin*, a temporary storage place for deleted items.

By default, OneDrive stores your deleted files for at least 3 days and a maximum of 30 days. Unless you allocate more than 10 percent of your storage to deleted files, the deleted files will be held for 30 days. However, if you exceed 10 percent of your total OneDrive storage, the duration of the file will be reduced. Once the file is deleted from OneDrive, it will be deleted from all drives that are synced with OneDrive.

 Deleted files do not count toward your OneDrive storage limit.

To restore a deleted file, go to the OneDrive website (https://onedrive.live.com) and click Recycle Bin in the left pane. To restore all items, click Restore all items (as shown in Figure 5.2). To restore or permanently delete individual items, select them by clicking their check boxes and click Restore all items. To permanently delete all items, click Empty recycle bin.

FIGURE 5.2 Accessing the OneDrive Recycle Bin

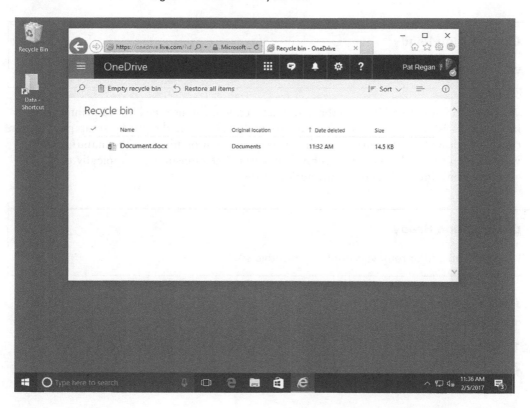

Understanding Printing Devices

Printing devices can be local or networked; they can even be available over the Internet. You can perform most printer support from the Devices and Printers applet.

Microsoft has historically used the term *"print device"* to refer to the actual hardware, but is now using the term "printer" in most consumer-level documentation. You will see both "printer" and "print device" in Microsoft documentation and in this lesson.

Understanding Local Printers

A *local printer* is connected directly to your computer via a cable, using a serial, parallel, USB, infrared, or other port type. Most printers come with a manufacturer's CD containing the printer software that must be installed for your operating system to talk to the printer. A good rule of thumb is if your printer ships with a manufacturer's CD, use the setup program on the CD to install the driver. A *driver* is a small program that enables hardware to interact with the operating system. If the correct print driver is not loaded, you may not be able to print documents, or the documents may contain strange characters or strange text or look distorted.

Certification Ready

What is a local printer? Objective 5.3

If you do not have a CD from the manufacturer, you can use the built-in printer drivers in Windows 10. However, it is almost always preferable to use the printer setup program on the CD or download the latest print driver setup installation file from the manufacturer's website than to use the built-in Windows 10 driver. The built-in driver typically provides access to a minimal subset of the printer's features.

Certification Ready

How can you add or remove a printer? Objective 5.1

Add a Local Printer

To add a local printer, perform the following steps:

1. Physically connect the printer to a computer with the appropriate cable.

2. Right-click Start and choose Control Panel.

3. In the Control Panel under Hardware And Sound, click View Devices And Printers. The Devices And Printers window displays (see Figure 5.3).

FIGURE 5.3   The Devices And Printers window

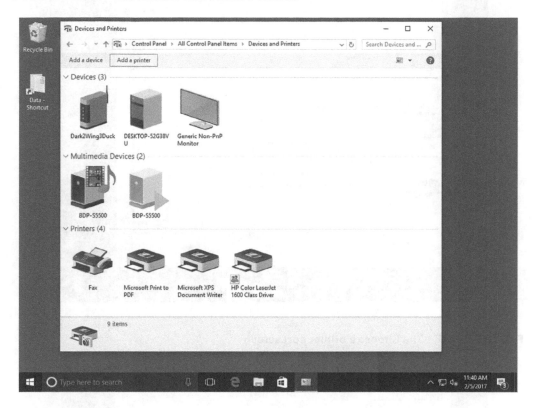

4. Select Add A Printer from the menu bar. The Add Printer Wizard starts.

5. On the "Choose a device or printer to add to this PC" page, click the "The Printer that I want isn't listed" option.

6. On the "Find a printer by other options" page (see Figure 5.4), click "Add a local printer or network printer with manual settings" and click Next.

7. On the Choose A Printer Port page, click the port that your printer is currently connected to: Use An Existing Port or Create A New Port. Figure 5.5 shows the default existing port. Your choices for creating a new port are Local Port or TCP/IP Port (whereby you enter the IP address or name of a printer). After you select a port, click Next.

FIGURE 5.4   The Find a printer by other options screen

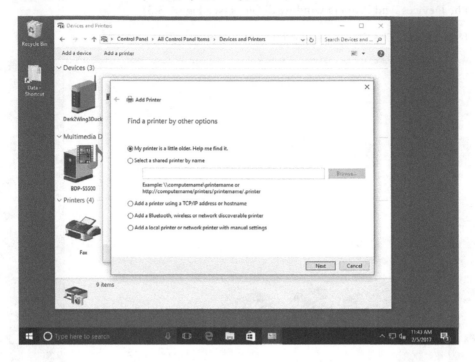

FIGURE 5.5   The Choose a printer port screen

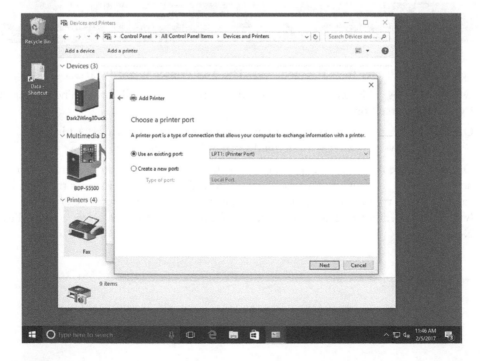

8. The Install The Printer Driver page asks for a printer driver and displays a list of manufacturers and printers. Click the manufacturer of the printer and click the printer (see Figure 5.6). If you do not see your printer, click the Windows Update button to get a more extensive list of printers to choose from.

FIGURE 5.6   Selecting your printer

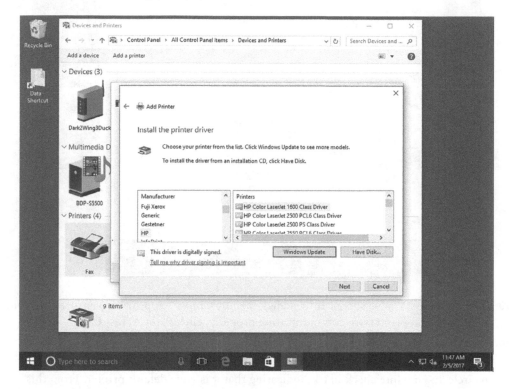

9. When you've found your printer, click the Have Disk button to open the Install From Disk dialog box. Ensure the CD is in the CD/DVD drive, browse to the appropriate printer model, and then click OK.

10. Type a name for your printer and click Next.

11. The Printer Sharing page (see Figure 5.7) allows you to share the printer so other people can connect to and use the printer across the network. The printer is local for you, but for all others connecting across the network, it's a networked printer. If you would like to share the printer, type the respective information for the Share Name, Location, and Comment text boxes. If you do not want to share the printer, click the "Do not share this printer" option.

12. Click Next.

FIGURE 5.7   Sharing your printer (or not sharing your printer)

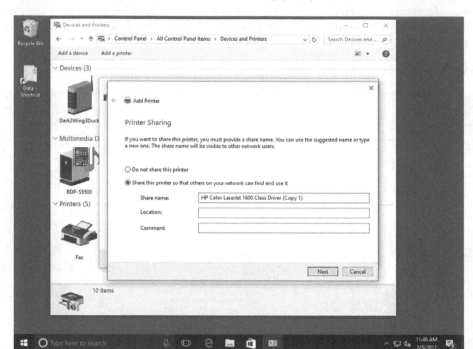

13. The message "You've successfully added *<printername>*" appears. To ensure that your computer and printer are communicating properly, click Print A Test Page.

14. If the test page prints properly, click Finish.

Your newly added printer should display in the Devices and Printers window with a green circle and a white check mark, indicating that it is your default printer. From this point forward, whenever you tell the computer to print, it automatically prints to your default printer. You can always choose to print to a different printer by selecting a different printer from the list of printers when you print a document.

Remove a Local Printer

To remove a local printer, perform the following steps:

1. Open Devices And Printers.

2. Right-click the printer that you want to remove and choose Remove Device.

3. Close the Devices And Printers window.

You can't remove a printer that has print jobs in the queue.

Understanding Network Printers

A *network printer* generally has a network adapter and is connected to a network. The printer receives an IP address and is a node on the network much like a networked computer. You can share a local (directly connected) printer with others on a network; in this case, the printer is considered to be both local (to the computer to which it is connected) and networked.

Certification Ready

What is a network printer? Objective 5.3

A true network printer is most commonly connected to and shared from a network server. While you can use the "Add a local printer or network printer with manual settings" option in the Add Printer Wizard, you can also use the "Select a shared printer by name" option and specify a UNC to the printer. Alternatively, you can open a UNC to a server, such as \\LON-SVR1, right-click the shared printer, and choose Connect.

Some network printers on the market today use proprietary connectivity methods and can only be accessed by installing a driver that is supplied by the manufacturer.

Printing a Document

Figure 5.8 shows a document that is ready to be printed in Word 2016. You can access this page by clicking the File menu within the Word document, and then clicking Print. Alternatively, press Ctrl+P.

FIGURE 5.8   Printing a Word 2016 document

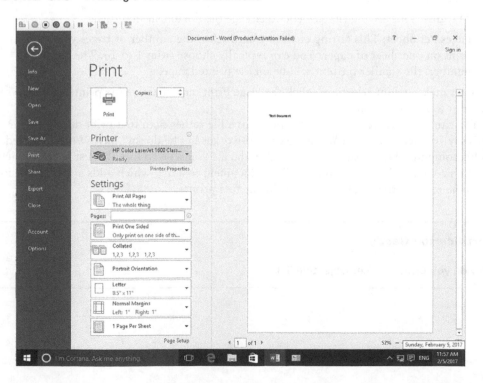

The first option at the top of the page is the number of copies; the default is to print one copy but you can change this by typing a number or clicking the up and down arrows to increase or decrease the number.

The print device displays directly under the Printer heading. A status message indicates whether or not the printer is ready to print. If the printer is not ready to print, because it's out of paper or offline, the status message indicates the problem so you can fix the issue before attempting to print. You can click the arrow to the right of the printer name and select a different printer if others are available.

The Settings section of the Print page includes many print options:

- **Print All Pages:** The default setting prints the entire document; however, you can click this button and specify to print the current page or a custom page range. You can also use the Pages text box to print a range of pages. For example, if you have a 100-page document but want to print only pages 5 through 10, type **5-10** in the Pages text box.

- **Print One Sided:** The default is to print on one side of the paper. You can change the setting to manually print on both sides of the paper. Printers with built-in duplexers can print on both sides of the paper automatically.

- **Collated:** This setting applies to multiple copies of a document. It affects whether multiple copies are printed in order (one complete set, and then another, and so on) or all copies of page 1 first, and then all copies of page 2, and so on.

- **Orientation:** Select to print the document in portrait (upright) or landscape (lengthwise) format.

- **Size:** This option enables you to select the paper size. Letter size (8.5" x 11") is the default paper size for most printers.

- **Margins:** This setting enables you to change the document margins.

- **Pages Per Sheet:** This setting enables you to select the number of pages you want to print on one sheet of paper. You can typically choose from 1 to 16. The larger the number, the smaller the text will be on the printed page.

After making your selections, click the large Print button above the printer name to send the print job to the printer.

You can also choose to print a document to a file rather than to a print device. Why? Let's say you need to send a Word file to a co-worker but he doesn't have Word installed on his computer. He doesn't need to modify the file you send to him, he just needs to view the file's contents. You can print the Word document to a file, which adds a .prn extension. When he receives the file, he can print the file to a printer.

Certification Ready

How do you print to a file? Objective 5.3

Print to a File

To print to a file from Word, perform the following steps:

1. Launch Word.

2. Open the document you want to print to a .prn file.

3. Select File ➤ Print.

4. On the Print page, click the arrow to the right of the printer name and select Print to File at the bottom of the list.

5. Click Print at the top of the page. In the Print to file dialog box, navigate to the location on your computer where you want to save the file, type a file name in the File name text box, and then click OK.

Print a .prn File

To print a .prn file to a local printer, perform the following steps:

1. Open a command prompt window by clicking Start, typing **cmd** in the Ask Me Anything search box, and then clicking cmd.exe in the resulting list.

2. Use the cd command to navigate to the location of the file. For example, if the file is named doc.prn and you saved it to the root of drive C, type **cd c:** and press Enter to execute the command.

3. Execute the following command to send the file to the directly connected printer:

   `copy /B doc.prn \\`*`computername`*`\`*`printer_sharename`*

   This command sends a binary (/B) copy of doc.prn to the device PRN, which is the system name for the default printer. A binary copy prevents anything in the file from changing during the process.

Understanding Print Queues

The *print spooler* is an executable file that manages the printing process, which includes retrieving the location of the correct print driver, loading the driver, creating the individual print jobs, and scheduling the print jobs for printing.

A *print job* is a file or set of files that have been sent to a printer. The printer processes the file or files in the print job and produces the document. The print job specifies which printer it is supposed to print to, the media size, the number of copies, and the priority.

Some printers can accept multiple pages of data at one time, but larger documents can take a while to print. You can think of a *print queue* as a holding area until the printer is finished printing the entire document. If you have a large document that cannot be entirely stored in a printer, the print job is sent to a print queue, which stores it until the printer can accept it. The printer then prints page by page until the entire document has been printed.

On occasion, a print job might have been sent that was not intended, or you might decide it is not necessary to print a job. In that situation, you need to delete the print job from the print queue.

By default, all users can pause, resume, restart, and cancel their own documents. To manage documents that are printed by other users, however, you must have the Allow manage documents permissions.

When the print device is available, the spooler retrieves the next print job and sends it to the print device. By default, the spool folder is located at C:\Windows\System32\Spool\Printers. If you have a server that handles a large number of print jobs or several large print jobs, make sure the drive where the spool folder is located has sufficient disk space.

Certification Ready

What is the purpose of a print queue? Objective 5.3

Explore a Print Queue

To explore a print queue, perform the following steps:

1. Right-click Start and choose Control Panel.

2. In the Control Panel, under Hardware and Sound, click View devices and printers. The Devices and Printers window displays.

3. Double-click your printer. A window similar to Figure 5.9 displays. The printer information displayed in this window includes:

   - The printer name

   - The printer's status (in this example the Error - printing)

   - The number of documents in the queue

   - The owner of each document

FIGURE 5.9 Viewing printer information

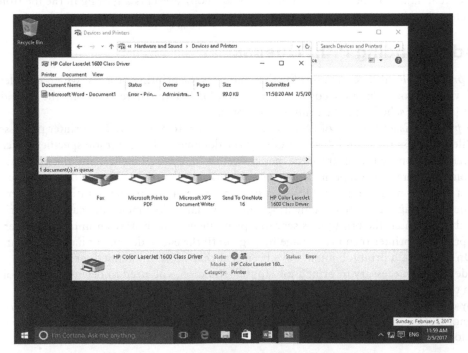

In this example, the first document in the print queue is in an error status and nothing else can print until either the error is resolved so the job can print or the job is cancelled and the next job will be allowed to print. If you have checked that your printer is turned on, has paper, and the ready lamp is lit, chances are you can get that job to print and then the subsequent jobs will print in turn.

The print queue window has three menus at the top: Printer, Document, and View:

Printer   From this menu, you can choose a default printer, set printing preferences (default orientation), print on both sides of the paper, select the page order, add a watermark to pages, and set up color profiles so you can ensure that the colors you see on your screen are the colors that will be printed. Most printers today come with color profiles you can download from the manufacturer of the printer. You can also pause printing, cancel all documents (deletes all documents from the queue), share a printer (or stop sharing if it was previously shared), use the printer offline, and open the properties of the printer to make changes.

Document   This menu is grayed out and thus cannot be accessed unless a document is selected. In the previous example, where the first print job has an error status, you could select that document and from the Document menu choose to restart the printing of the document or cancel the printing of the document. If you cancel the printing of the document, the next document in the queue (if any) begins printing. Other options from the Document menu allow you to pause, resume, or view document properties.

View   This menu has two selections. Status Bar shows the number of documents in the queue on the status bar and Refresh refreshes the screen to show the most current view of the print queue.

On occasion, the print spooler might freeze or become unresponsive. You can restart the print spooler by following these steps:

1.   Open the Services console located in Administrative Tools.

2.   Right-click Print Spooler and choose Restart.

You can also stop and start the service.

Understanding Internet Printing

If you run Windows Server 2016, you can create a website hosted by Internet Information Services (IIS) using the Internet Printing role service. Clients can then use a web browser to connect and print to shared printers on the server using the Internet Printing Protocol (IPP). By default, Windows 10 has the Print and Document Services ➤ Internet Printing Client Windows feature installed; it is located under the Turn Windows features on or off option in the Control Panel.

Certification Ready

How do you set up Internet printing? Objective 5.3

You should restart the print queue at this point to ensure that print jobs reach the printer. Restart the Print Spooler service in the Services console to clear the print queue. (You learned about services in Lesson 4.)

Understanding System Devices and Device Drivers

A computer is a collection of hardware devices, each of which requires a piece of software called a device driver in order to function. Windows 10 includes a large library of device drivers, but it is still sometimes necessary to obtain them yourself.

The main *video device* on a computer is the video adapter or card. This is an internal circuit board that's either in the form of a physical card inserted into a slot on the motherboard or is manufactured as part of the motherboard. Other types of video devices include webcams, video capture cards, and TV tuners, to name a few.

Certification Ready

Which types of video devices are supported by Windows 10? Objective 5.4

The main *audio device* in a computer is a sound card. Like a video card or adapter, it is either in the form of a circuit board that's inserted into a motherboard slot or hard-wired into the motherboard. Additional audio devices include microphones, headsets, and speakers. Headsets are always external devices, but microphones and speakers can be either internal or external.

Certification Ready

Which types of audio devices are supported by Windows 10? Objective 5.4

Input devices are items such as keyboards, mice, trackballs, touchpads, digital pens, and joysticks (for gaming). On desktop computers, input devices are almost always external devices that plug into different ports on the computer. On a laptop computer, keyboards and touchpads are built in, although you can connect external input devices as well.

Certification Ready

Which types of infrared input devices are supported by Windows 10? Objective 5.4

Many external devices, such as headsets and input devices, connect to a computer using wireless technology. A wireless keyboard or mouse, for example, comes with a small Bluetooth receiver that you plug into a USB port on the computer. The mouse contains a Bluetooth transmitter that communicates with the receiver. As you move the mouse around, it transmits signals using Bluetooth radio signals rather than a wire. If your computer already has Bluetooth technology built in, you may be able to set up Bluetooth to communicate directly with the external Bluetooth device without the need for the USB receiver.

Many wireless mice use infrared technology and are referred to as optical mice. These mice have an infrared light-emitting diode (LED) inside the mouse that detects the surface over which it is moved. This technology lets you use the mouse on a wider variety of surfaces compared to legacy trackball mice that required a mouse pad to operate.

Nearly all modern devices that you attach to a computer port are automatically detected by the operating system. This is part of *plug-and-play (PnP) technology*. As long as a PnP device is plugged into your computer and powered on (if the device requires power, like a printer), Windows detects the device and automatically installs the drivers.

Certification Ready

Do you need to install drivers for PnP devices? Objective 5.1

The first time you connect a device, you should see a bubble message on the status bar that states "Installing device driver software." When it installs the device driver successfully, you'll see "Your device is ready to use." The device has now been added to Device Manager. You can unplug the device and plug it in again, but the device driver installs only one time.

Managing Devices

In most cases, the information the device driver provides is integrated into the Windows interface. For example, the Properties dialog box for a printer includes generic system information, such as which port the printer is connected to and who is permitted to use it. Other tabs, and particularly the Device Settings tab, as shown in Figures 5.10 and 5.11, are based on hardware-specific information provided by the device driver.

FIGURE 5.10   The General tab of a printer's Properties dialog box

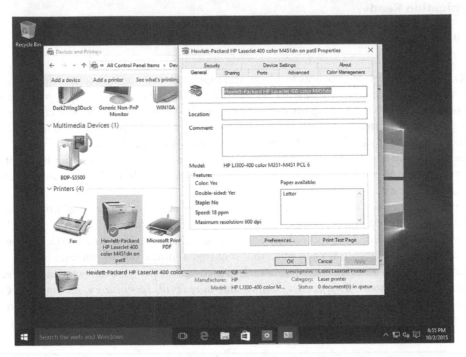

FIGURE 5.11   The Device Settings tab of a printer's Properties dialog box

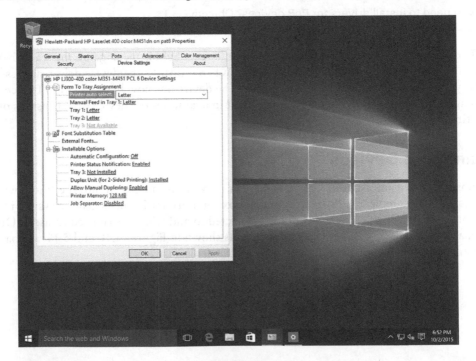

In addition to providing information about a device, drivers also permit the operating system to modify the hardware configuration settings of the device. For example, when you configure a printer to print a document in landscape mode instead of portrait mode, the printer device driver generates the appropriate command and sends it to the hardware.

The process of installing a hardware device consists primarily of identifying the device and installing a device driver for it. This process can occur during the operating system installation or at a later time, but the steps are fundamentally the same.

A major part of the Windows 10 installation process consists of identifying the devices in the computer and installing the appropriate drivers for them. The Windows 10 installation package includes hundreds of drivers for many different devices, which is why many installations finish without any user involvement. Sometimes, however, you might have to supply device drivers yourself.

Installing and Updating Device Drivers

A device driver is a computer program that controls or operates a device that is attached to a computer. A driver provides the interface to hardware devices, enabling operating systems and other computer programs to utilize hardware functions.

Drivers need to be updated. Sometimes a vendor may need to fix an issue with a driver; when this happens there is an update to the driver to improve functionality.

There are different ways to download and install drivers. Microsoft drivers can be downloaded using the Windows Update utility. Drivers from different vendors may be downloaded from the vendor's website.

Once the new drivers are downloaded, they can be installed by using Device Manager. We will discuss using Device Manager later in this chapter.

Using the Devices and Printers Folder

Windows 10 includes the *Devices and Printers folder* to quickly allow users to see all the devices connected to the computer and to configure and troubleshoot these devices. It will also allow you to view information about the make, model, and manufacturer and give you detailed information about the sync capabilities of a mobile phone or other mobile devices.

The Devices and Printers folder gives you a quick view of devices connected to your computer that you can connect or disconnect from your computer through a port or network connection. This includes mobile devices such as music players and digital cameras, USB devices, and network devices. (See Figure 5.12.) It does not include items installed inside your computer such as internal disk drives, expansion cards, or RAM, and it will not display legacy devices such as keyboards and mice connected through a PS/2 or serial port.

FIGURE 5.12   Devices and Printers

To open the Devices and Printers folder, open the Control Panel and, under Hardware and Sound, click View devices and printers while in Category view or double-click Devices and Printers in Large Icons or Small Icons view.

When you right-click a device icon in the Devices and Printers folder, you can choose from a list of tasks that vary depending on the capabilities of the device. For example, you might be able to see what's printing on a network printer, view files stored on a USB flash drive, or open a program from the device manufacturer. For mobile devices that support the new Device Stage feature in Windows, you can also open advanced, device-specific features in Windows from the shortcut (right-click) menu, such as the ability to sync with a mobile phone or change ringtones.

Most PCs use USB connections for peripheral devices and PnP is an integral part of the USB standard. When you connect a printer, camera, scanner, or another type of device to a computer running Windows 10 using a USB port, the system usually detects it, adds it to the Devices and Printers folder, and installs the appropriate device driver for it.

You can also manually install a device by selecting Add a device, which displays the "Choose a device or a printer to add to this PC" page.

Using Device Manager

The Windows 10 tool for managing devices and their drivers is called *Device Manager*. You can use Device Manager to get information about the devices installed in the computer, as well as install, update, and troubleshoot device drivers.

Although it is not immediately apparent, Device Manager is a snap-in for the Microsoft Management Console (MMC). This means that there are many ways that you can access Device Manager, including the following:

- Open Hardware and Sound in the Control Panel and click the Device Manager link.

- Open the Computer Management console from the Administrative Tools program group in the System and Security section of Control Panel and click Device Manager in the left pane.

- Run the MMC shell application (Mmc.exe), click File ➤ Add/Remove Snap-in, and click Device Manager from the list of snap-ins provided.

- Click Start, type Device Manager or the file name of the Device Manager snap-in (Devmgmt.msc), and then execute the resulting file.

- Search for Device Manager using Cortana and execute the resulting file.

Each of these procedures launches the Device Manager and displays a window with an interface like that shown in Figure 5.13.

FIGURE 5.13   The Windows 10 Device Manager

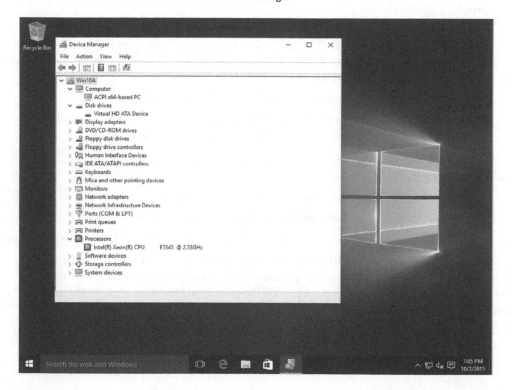

Device Manager is capable of displaying information in the following four modes, which can be selected from the View menu:

- **Devices by Type:** Displays a list of device categories, which you can expand to show the devices in each category. This is the default Device Manager view.

- **Devices by Connection:** Displays a list of the interfaces that hardware devices use to communicate with the computer. Expanding a connection shows the devices using that connection.

- **Resources by Type:** Displays a list of resource types, including Direct Memory Access (DMA), Input/Output (I/O), Interrupt Request (IRQ), and Memory, which you can expand to show the resources of each type and the devices that are using them.

- **Resources by Connection:** Displays a list of resource types, including Direct Memory Access (DMA), Input/Output (I/O), Interrupt Request (IRQ), and Memory, which you can expand to show the connection associated with each individual resource and the device using each connection.

To examine the properties of a device, simply locate it in the tree display and double-click it to open its Properties dialog box.

The tabs on the Properties dialog box vary depending on the nature of the device you select, but virtually all devices have the following four tabs:

- **General:** Displays the name of the device, its type, manufacturer, and location in the system. The Device Status box indicates whether the device is functioning and, if not, provides troubleshooting help.

- **Driver:** Displays the device driver's provider, date, version, and digital signer. The tab also provides buttons you can use to display driver details, update, roll back (used when an upgrade of a device driver fails or causes problems with a system), or uninstall the driver, and enable or disable the device.

- **Detail:** Displays extensive information about the driver and its properties.

- **Resources:** Displays the hardware resources being used by the device and indicates whether there are any conflicts with other devices in the computer.

With Device Manager, you can disable any device in the computer, using any of the following procedures:

- Select the device and choose Disable from the Action menu.

- Right-click the device and choose Disable from the shortcut menu.

- Open the device's Properties dialog box and on the Driver tab, click the Disable button.

Disabling a device does not affect the hardware in any way or uninstall the device driver; it simply renders the device inoperative until you enable it again. Obviously, you cannot disable devices that are necessary for the system to function, such as the processor, and some devices that are in use require you to restart the system before they can be disabled.

NOTE Disabling a device releases the hardware resources it was using back to the operating system. If you restart the computer with the device disabled, Windows might reassign those hardware resources to other devices. If you re-enable the device, the computer might allocate different hardware resources to it than it had originally.

When you update a driver using Device Manager, you can point to a location on your computer where you have already saved the new driver, or you can run a search of your computer and the Internet. To update a device driver, use the following procedure.

Update a Device Driver

Log on to Windows 10 using an account with Administrator privileges, and perform the following steps:

1. Open Device Manager and locate the device that you want to update.

2. Double-click the device you want to update, so that its Properties dialog box appears.

3. Click the Driver tab, as shown in Figure 5.14.

FIGURE 5.14   Viewing driver information

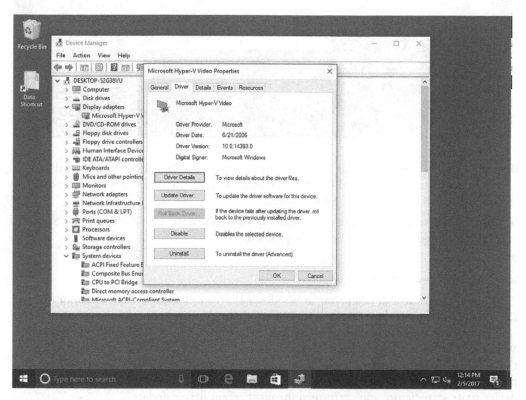

4. Click the Update Driver button. The "How do you want to search for driver software?" page appears, as shown in Figure 5.15.

FIGURE 5.15   The "How do you want to search for driver software?" page

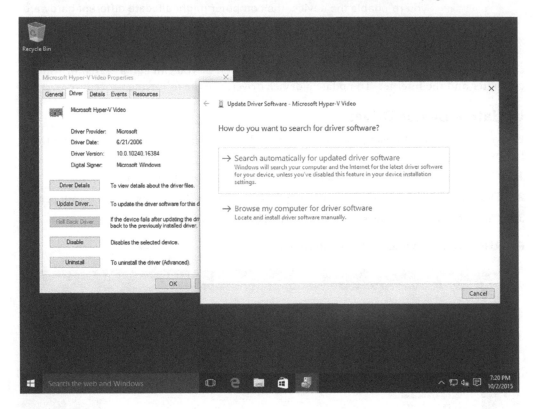

5. Click "Browse my computer for driver software" to specify a location for the driver or to select from a list of installed drivers. Click "Search automatically for updated driver software" to initiate a search for a driver.

6. Click Next when you locate the driver you want to install. The Windows Has Successfully Updated Your Driver Software page appears.

7. Click Close.

8. Close the Device Manager window.

When you update a device driver in Windows 10, the operating system does not discard the old driver completely. It is not uncommon for new drivers to cause more problems than they solve, and many users find that they would prefer to go back to the old version. Windows 10 makes this possible with the Roll Back feature, which you initiate by clicking the Roll Back Driver button on the Driver tab of the device's Properties dialog box. This procedure uninstalls the current driver and reinstalls the previous version, returning the device to its state before you performed the most recent driver update.

Installing a new hardware device or a new device driver is a risky undertaking. There is always the possibility of a problem that, depending on the devices involved, could be trivial or catastrophic. For a peripheral device, such as a printer, a hardware misconfiguration or faulty driver would probably just cause the new device to malfunction. However, if the device involved is a graphics adapter, a bad driver could prevent the system from functioning.

Before installing new drivers, you should make sure you have a good backup. Backups are discussed in Lesson 8.

Disabling and Enabling a Device in Device Manager

Log on to Windows 10 using an account with Administrator privileges, and perform the following steps:

1. Right-click Start ➤ Device Manager (or use the integrated search window and type **device manager**).
2. Click the triangle next to the appropriate category to expand the item list; you can also double-click the category name.
3. Right-click the hardware item and select Properties.

You can select Disable directly from the context menu if desired.

4. Choose the Driver tab.
5. Click the Disable button. (This is a toggle button; it will be labeled Disable if the device is enabled and Enable if the device is disabled.)
6. The device driver and the device will be disabled and will no longer function. There will be a down arrow on the item in Device Manager, and the General tab will show that the device is disabled. Close the Properties dialog box for that device.

Uninstalling and Reinstalling a Device Driver

Log on to Windows 10 using an account with Administrator privileges, and perform the following steps:

1. Right-click Start ➤ Device Manager (or use the integrated search window and type **device manager**).
2. Click the triangle next to the category for the device to uninstall to expand the item list; you can also double-click the category name.
3. Right-click the hardware item and select Properties. Note: you can select Uninstall directly from the context menu.

4. Choose the Driver tab.

5. Click the Uninstall button.

6. Click OK in the Confirm Device Uninstall dialog box.

   A progress box appears during uninstall. Once the driver is uninstalled, Device Manager will no longer show the device.

7. From Device Manager, choose the Action menu item and select Scan For Hardware Changes; you can right-click the machine name in Device Manager and select Scan For Hardware Changes from the context menu.

Windows 10 will initiate the process of discovering the PnP device and will reinstall the device driver configuration into the operating system. The hardware will be available again within Device Manager.

Troubleshooting Problem Devices

The Action Center (see Figure 5.16) shows important notifications related to the security and maintenance of your computer. When problems occur, you will be alerted to investigate them further.

FIGURE 5.16   Viewing the Action Center

To configure how messages are displayed in the Action Center, open Windows 10 Settings and then click Settings ➢ Notifications & Actions. Then under the Notifications section, you can enable or disable the following options:

- Get notifications from apps and other senders
- Show notifications on the lock screen
- Show alarms, reminders, and incoming VoIP calls on the lock screen
- Hide notifications when I'm duplicating my screen
- Get tips, tricks, and suggestions as you use Windows

To troubleshoot hardware or driver problems, consider some of the following techniques:

- Open the Properties dialog box for the device and check the Device Status box on the General tab. If the device is malfunctioning, this tab informs you of its status and enables you to launch a troubleshooter.
- Open the Device Manager and delete the device entirely. Then restart the system and allow Windows 10 to detect and install the device again. This process will cause Windows to re-allocate hardware resources to the device, which could resolve the problem if it was caused by a hardware resource conflict.
- If the device or driver malfunction prevents the system from running properly, as in the case of a bad graphics driver that prevents an image from appearing on the screen, you can start the computer in Safe Mode by pressing the F8 key as the system starts. Safe Mode loads the operating system with a minimal set of generic device drivers, bypassing the troublesome ones, so you can uninstall or troubleshoot them.

Device Manager also displays all of the devices installed on your computer. When a device is experiencing problems, Device Manager uses symbols to provide information about the particular error condition.

When there is an issue with a device, you will see one of the following symbols (each symbol represents a specific type of problem):

- **Blue Question Mark inside White Circle:** The driver is installed, but may not provide full functionality.
- **Red X:** The device is installed in the computer and is consuming resources, the protected mode driver is not loaded, or the device was installed improperly.
- **Yellow Warning Symbol with Black Exclamation Point:** The device is in a problem state; the device might be functioning. A problem code will be displayed with the device.
- **Blue *I* on White Field:** Use automatic settings was not selected for the device or the resource was manually selected; does not indicate a problem or disabled state.
- **Problem Code:** This is the code that explains the problem with the device.
- **White Circle with Down Arrow:** The device was disabled by an administrator or user.

Windows 10 uses built-in hardware diagnostics to detect hardware problems on your computer. When problems are identified, a message appears that lets you know about the problem. If you select the message, you will be taken to the Action Center, which provides a central location to view any problems with your hardware or software.

When there is a problem, you will see two types of messages in the notification area (the bottom-right corner of your desktop):

- **Red Items (White Flag, Red Circle with White *x*):** These are important messages that indicate a significant problem that needs to be addressed. For example, your firewall is turned off, or spyware or antivirus applications need to be updated.

- **Yellow Items:** These are messages that suggest tasks that can make your computer run better. For example, updating an application or configuring Windows Update to automatically download and install updates rather than checking with you beforehand.

How you troubleshoot a device depends upon the type of problem you encounter. For example, when you notice a device with the black exclamation point in a yellow triangle, you can double-click the device to investigate the problem further. Figure 5.17 shows that the device cannot start and the specified request is not a valid operation for the target device.

FIGURE 5.17   Looking at problem devices in Device Manager

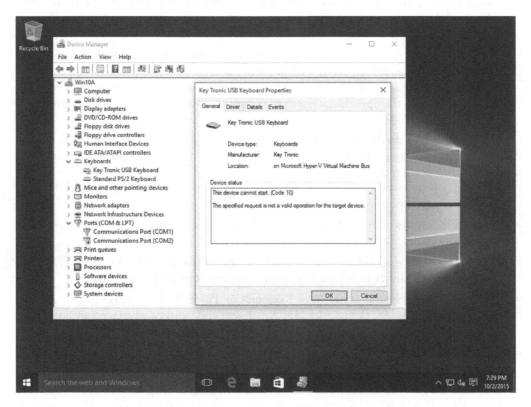

Another item of interest when troubleshooting device problems is to look for an Other Devices folder. This folder contains devices that are detected by Windows but lack a driver for the device.

Skill Summary

In this lesson, you learned:

- Cloud storage is remote data storage with backups, but can also include application hosting. You can use applications like Microsoft Word and Outlook, along with many other applications, over the Internet. Client machines can run applications from the cloud and access data; in fact, they can maintain complete control of their data and security.

- OneDrive is a file-hosting service that allows you to store and create files and folders and share them with other users and groups.

- OneDrive for Business is different from the public version of OneDrive because OneDrive for Business is based on SharePoint. By using SharePoint, OneDrive for Business can be used by team members to store and work on documents with others and it helps ensure that business files for your users are stored in a central location.

- Printing devices can be local or networked; they can even be available over the Internet. You can perform most printer support from the Devices and Printers applet.

- Some printers can accept multiple pages of data at one time but larger documents can take a while to print. You can think of a print queue as a holding area until the printer is finished printing the entire document.

- A computer is a collection of hardware devices, each of which requires a piece of software called a device driver in order to function. Windows 10 includes a large library of device drivers, but it is still sometimes necessary to obtain them directly from the vendor.

- Windows 10 includes the Devices and Printers folder to quickly allow users to see all the devices connected to the computer and to configure and troubleshoot these devices. It will also allow you to view information about the make, model, and manufacturer and give you detailed information about the sync capabilities of a mobile phone or other mobile devices.

- The Windows 10 tool for managing devices and their drivers is called Device Manager. You can use Device Manager to get information about the devices installed in the computer, as well as install, update, and troubleshoot device drivers.

Knowledge Assessment

You can find the answers to the following sections in the Appendix.

Multiple Choice

1. Which of the following actions can be used to recover a file that was accidentally deleted in Microsoft OneDrive?

    A. Using the Windows Recycle Bin

    B. Using the OneDrive Recycle Bin

    C. Using the Sync utility

    D. Using the OneDrive Recovery utility

2. In OneDrive, by default, how long will a deleted file be available in the OneDrive Recycle Bin?

    A. 3 days

    B. 5 days

    C. 30 days

    D. 90 days

3. Which of the following actions is the easiest way to let someone know that a new document is available on OneDrive?

    A. Call them on the phone; leave a message if they are not there.

    B. Send them a document with the link embedded.

    C. Send a notification after sharing the document or folder.

    D. Sync your computer with their computer.

4. Which of the following is a holding area for print jobs?

    A. Print trap

    B. Print cache

    C. Print drive

    D. Print queue

5. Which of the following services allows you to print to a printer via a website?

    A. Internet Printing

    B. Web Printing

    C. Cache Printing

    D. HTTP Printing

6. Which of the following tools can be used to quickly determine if a device has a bad device driver?

    A. Disk Manager

    B. Device Manager

    C. Driver Manager

    D. Control Panel

7. Which of the following tools is usually used to manage printers on a Windows 10 machine?

    A. Device Manager

    B. Devices and Printers folder

    C. USB Manager

    D. Print Queue Manager

8. Which of the following tasks can be completed with Device Manager? (Choose all that apply.)

    A. Update a driver's software.

    B. Disable a driver.

    C. Uninstall a driver.

    D. Change a device's hardware ID.

    E. Scan for hardware changes.

9. Which of the following refers to the set of files sent to the printer that specifies what the printer is supposed to print?

    A. Print queue

    B. Print job

    C. Print spooler

    D. Print driver

10. In Device Manager, a white circle with a down arrow indicates which of the following?

    A. The device is disabled.

    B. The device driver is not loaded.

    C. There is a problem with the device.

    D. The wrong driver is loaded.

Fill in the Blank

1. _____ can be used to view device IRQ and DMA settings.

2. A(n) _____ is a file or set of files that have been sent to a printer, which are used to produce the document.

3. A(n) _____ is a small program that enables hardware to interact with the operating system.

4. A Windows _____ can be used to pause printing, cancel all documents, and resume or restart a document.

5. _____ can be used to determine the version of files that a device driver installs and their complete paths.

6. _____ technology automatically detects a device and installs the drivers.

7. Microsoft cloud storage is called _____.

8. OneDrive for Business is stored in _____.

9. A(n) _____ is a printer that has a network adapter that is connected to a printer.

10. The _____ is an executable file that manages the printing process and creates the individual print jobs.

True/False

1. OneDrive and OneDrive for Business are the same.

2. Print jobs can be viewed in the print queue.

3. Device Manager can be used to update print drivers.

4. In Device Manager, a red X indicates that the driver has not been installed.

5. Device Manager is found in the Computer Management console.

Case Scenarios

You can find the answers to the following sections in the Appendix.

Scenario 5-1: Troubleshooting Print Jobs

John is trying to print a large document, but nothing is printing from the printer. You receive several complaints that when others try to print to the same printer, it is not working. What should you do to troubleshoot the printer problem?

Scenario 5-2: Troubleshooting a Printer Driver

Axel runs the warehouse for Mighty Bubbles Beer Distributor. He called you to report that the new wireless laser printer he recently purchased does not work. He connected it to the USB port on his computer running Windows 10 Professional and turned on the printer, but the printer does not appear in the Devices and Printers window. How should you advise Axel to help troubleshoot the problem?

Scenario 5-3: Changing Print Drivers

You have a new Canon printer. Unfortunately, it did not come with any drivers. So, you visit the Canon website and download the driver. You then print the document, but the printed page contains what looks like programming code. When other users try to print, their documents do not print. Describe your recommended solution.

Scenario 5-4: Using Cloud Services

The sales and marketing department at your company consists of two salespeople, a graphic designer, a copywriter, and a layout person.

Tonya and Aaron are the salespeople. Tonya is responsible for the western United States and Aaron covers the eastern United States. They tend to use the same files for all sales presentations, client follow-ups, and so on. When one modifies a template, it's important that the other gets the updated file as soon as possible.

The marketing employees share several Word documents and PowerPoint presentations, in addition to a large folder of graphical images. It's important for them to have shared access to a Marketing folder that contains the shared files.

What should you do to help the sales and marketing employees work more efficiently?

Lesson

6

Understanding File and Print Sharing

Objective Domain Matrix

Technology Skill	Objective Domain Description	Objective Domain Number
Understanding File and Printer Sharing Basics	Understand file and printer sharing	4.2
Configuring HomeGroup Connections	Understand file and printer sharing	4.2
Configure File System and Share Permissions	Understand file and printer sharing	4.2
Configuring Printer Sharing	Understand file and printer sharing	4.2

Key Terms

advanced sharing	network discovery
basic sharing	network location
effective permissions	NTFS permissions
explicit permissions	print driver
file system permissions	printer permissions
HomeGroup	Public folder
inherited permissions	shared folder
mapping a drive	

 Real World Scenario

Lesson 6 Case

As the IT technician at Interstate Snacks, Inc., you've been asked to set up file and printer sharing for all of the computers at a remote warehouse. The employees there do not need constant access to the network at the main Interstate facility. All of the computers at the remote location are running Windows 10 Professional. There are two printers in the warehouse. One printer is attached to the supervisor's computer and the other printer is attached to a computer in the middle of the warehouse that all employees use to print pallet labels for outgoing shipments. Some folders on the supervisor's computer contain confidential files that need to be protected from access by other employees.

Understanding File and Printer Sharing Basics

Windows 10 provides many ways to share files or printers on a network. The first step is to ensure that file and printer sharing is turned on in the advanced sharing settings in Network and Sharing Center. Some networking methods, such as HomeGroup, also require that your network location be set to Home network.

Microsoft offers several ways for Windows 10 users to share resources such as files and printers, either on the same computer (between accounts) or on a network, without the need for a server. For example, you can share files from any folder on your computer by setting up basic or advanced sharing, or by moving files to the Public folder. Another method is by using a HomeGroup, the networking feature that's built in to Windows 10.

> This lesson assumes you are working on a peer-to-peer network in a small office or home office setting. The network does not have a server and does not use a domain.

To share files and printers with users on other computers, you need to have a wired or wireless network set up. In a typical wired environment, each computer has a network adapter that is connected to other computers and a hub, switch, or router with Ethernet cables. Wireless networks are easier to set up and maintain. Each computer's wireless network adapter connects "over the air" to a router or wireless access point within range.

A *network location* is a collection of security settings that's appropriate for the type of network to which you want to connect. Windows 10 offers three broad categories of network locations:

- **Public Network:** This network location type is assigned to any new networks when they are first connected and is considered to be shared with the world, with no protection between the local computer and any other computer. Therefore, the Windows Firewall rules are configured to be the most restrictive including blocking file sharing, network discovery, and automatic setup of network printers, TVs, and other devices.

- **Private Network:** This network location type is for home or small office networks, or where you know and trust the people and devices on the network. This setting allows your PC to connect to a homegroup and devices on the network, such as printers.

- **Domain Network:** This network location type is detected when the local computer is a member of an Active Directory domain, and the local computer can authenticate to a domain controller for that domain through one of its network connections.

> *Network discovery* is a Windows feature that enables your computer to find other computers and devices (such as printers) on a connected network. It also lets you control whether other computers can see your computer on the same network.

Whether wired or wireless, you must turn on file and printer sharing on each computer that will share files and/or printers. To do so, right-click the network icon in the notification area of the taskbar and choose Open Network and Sharing Center. In the task pane on the left, click the Change advanced sharing settings link. Click the down arrow to the right of Private, Guest or Public, or All Networks. The advanced sharing settings are shown in Figure 6.1.

FIGURE 6.1 Advanced sharing settings in Windows 10

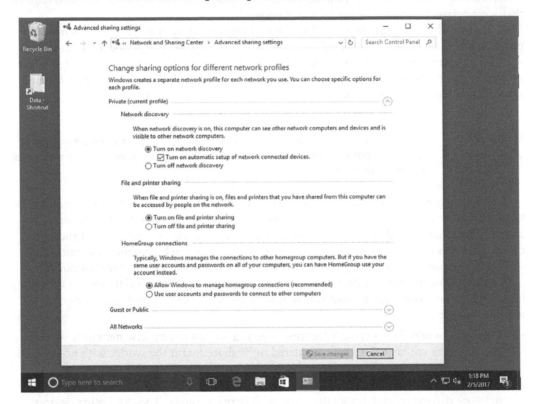

Notice that Network discovery and File and printer sharing are turned on. These settings allow you maximum flexibility for sharing files in a small office or home office environment.

Finally, if your network includes a mix of computers running Windows XP and higher, and you want to share files between the computers, you should use a workgroup. A workgroup is a logical grouping of networked computers that can "see" each other on a network. You're prompted to set up a workgroup when installing Windows, and many computers are set up to be a part of a workgroup named WORKGROUP by default. To see if your computer is part of a workgroup, right-click the Start button and choose System.

Administrators can install two types of printers, either a local or a network printer. Network printers can be shared local printers or printers that connect directly to a network.

When an administrator installs a physical printer, Microsoft refers to it as a print device. Then, the administrator needs to create a logical printer; this is referred to as the printer. This printer provides the software interface between the print device and the applications.

When you create the printer, you are also loading the print driver.

When you print a document, the printer uses the logical printer and printer driver to configure the document into a form that is understood by the printer.

The print job is sent to the local spooler, which allows you to print and queue additional documents while the first document is being printed.

If a print job is sent to the local print device, it will save it, temporarily, to the local hard drive's spool file. When the printer becomes available, it will send the print job to the local print device. If is determined that the print job is for a network print device, Windows will send the job to the print server's spooler. The print server's spooler will save it to the print server's hard drive spool file. Then, when the network print device becomes available, the job will print.

Installing Printers

Use the Add Printer Wizard to install the printer, if you have permissions to add a local printer or a remote shared printer. After the printer is installed, it will appear in the Devices and Printers folder as well as in the Device Manager.

Add a Local Printer

To add a local printer perform these actions:

1. Right-Click the Start button, and then click and open Control Panel.
2. Under Hardware and Sound, click View Devices and Printers.
3. Start the Add Printer Wizard by clicking Add a printer.
4. Click the "The printer that I want isn't listed" option.
5. Then, select "Add a local printer or network printer with manual settings" and click Next.
6. When the Add Printer dialog box appears, specify the port to which the printer is connected.
7. If Plug and Play does not detect and install the correct printer automatically, you will be asked to specify the printer driver (the vendor and printer model). If the printer is not listed, you may have to use the Have Disk option.
8. When the Type a Printer Name dialog box appears, specify the name of the printer. If you want this to be the default printer for the system, select the Set as the default printer option. Click the Next button.
9. In the Printer Sharing dialog box, specify the share name. You can also specify the Location or Comments.
10. When the printer is added, you can now print a Windows test page by clicking the Print a test page button. Click the Finish button.

Add a Network Printer

To add a network printer perform these steps:

1. Click the Start button and open the Control Panel.

2. Under Hardware and Sound, click View Devices and Printers.

3. To start the Add Printer Wizard, click Add a printer.

4. Select Add a Network, Wireless, or Bluetooth printer.

5. If the printer is not automatically found, click The Printer that I want isn't listed option.

6. If you have a printer published in Active Directory (assuming you are part of a domain), choose "Find a printer in the directory, based on location or feature".
    If you know the UNC, choose Select a shared printer by name. If you know the TCP/IP address, choose the last option. Click the Next button.

7. In the Type a printer name dialog box, specify the printer name. If you want this to be the default printer for the system, select the Set as the default printer option. Click the Next button.

8. When the printer is successfully added, you can print a Windows test page by selecting the Print a test page button. Click the Finish button.

Add Additional Print Drivers

To add additional print drivers perform these steps:

1. Open Devices and Printers.

2. Click the Print Server Properties button.

3. Select the Drivers tab.

4. Click the Change Driver Settings button.

5. Click the Add button.

6. When the Welcome to the Add Printer Driver Wizard screen appears, click the Next button.

7. Select the appropriate processor and operating system drivers and click the Next button.

8. If necessary, provide a path for the printer driver and click the OK button.

9. When the wizard is complete, click the Finish button.

Configuring HomeGroup Connections

When you run Windows 10 within a domain, Windows servers and clients have several tools and mechanisms available to share files and printers. Today, many households have multiple computers. A *homegroup* is a group of computers on a home network that can share files and printers. To protect your homegroup, you use a password. As with share permissions, other people cannot change the files that you share unless you give them permission to do so. Homegroups are relatively limited when compared to folder sharing, because you can only share the contents of the libraries in the user's profile.

HomeGroup is available with Windows 7, Windows 8/8.1 (including Windows RT 8.0/8.1), and Windows 10. Windows RT, Starter, and Home Basic editions can join a homegroup, but you cannot create a homegroup from them. For the system to use homegroups, the system cannot use a public network. If a system is part of a domain, you cannot create your own homegroup, but you can join one that is created by someone on your network.

If the system does not detect a homegroup, the Network and Sharing Center in the Control Panel contains a link that provides access to the Create a Homegroup Wizard.

Create a Homegroup

Log on to Windows 10 using an account with Administrator privileges. Make sure that the system is configured to use the Private network location. Perform the following steps:

1. Right-click Start and choose Control Panel.

2. In the search box, type **homegroup**. In the search results, click HomeGroup. The HomeGroup page appears as shown in Figure 6.2.

FIGURE 6.2   Opening the Control Panel HomeGroup

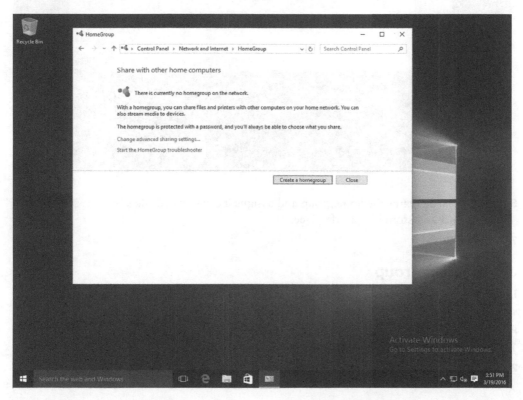

3. Click Create A Homegroup.

4. In the Create A Homegroup Wizard, click Next.

5. On the Share With Other Homegroup Members page (as shown in Figure 6.3), select the libraries that you want to share and click Next.

FIGURE 6.3   Sharing libraries and folders with homegroup members

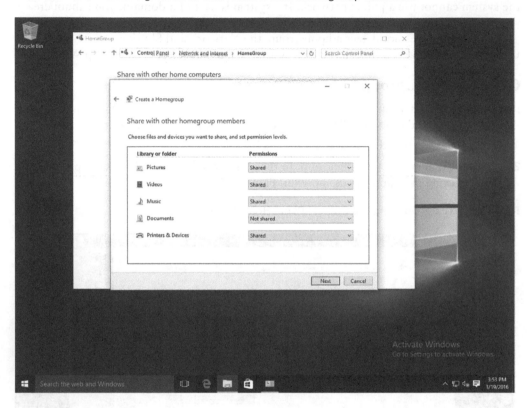

6. The wizard creates the homegroup and assigns it a password. Be sure to record this password and store it in a safe place.

7. Click Finish.

Join a Homegroup

Log on to Windows 10 using an account with Administrator privileges. Make sure that the system is configured to use the Private network location. To join an existing homegroup, perform the following steps:

1. Right-click Start and choose Control Panel.

2. In the search box, type **homegroup**. In the search results, click HomeGroup.

3. On the HomeGroup page, click Join Now.

4. In the Join A Homegroup Wizard, click Next.

5. On the Share With Other Homegroup Members page, select the libraries that you want to share and click Next.

6. On the Type The Homegroup Password page, in the Type The Password text box, type the password supplied by the Create A Homegroup Wizard and click Next.

7. On the You Have Joined The Homegroup page, click Finish.

After you have created and joined a homegroup, you can manage the homegroup settings using the HomeGroup page, as shown in Figure 6.4. The HomeGroup options include:

- **Change What You're Sharing With The Homegroup:** Select the libraries and printers you want to share in their entirety with your homegroup.

- **Allow All Devices On The Network Such As TVs And Game Consoles To Play My Shared Content:** Share media with all devices on your network. For example, you can share pictures with an electronic picture frame or share music with a network media player. Unfortunately, shared media is not secure. Anyone connected to your network can receive your shared media.

FIGURE 6.4   Managing a homegroup

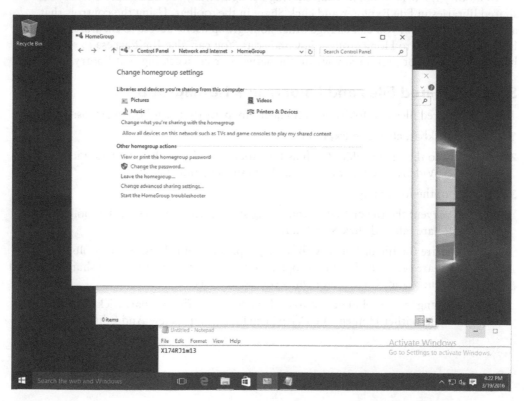

- **View Or Print The Homegroup Password:** View or print the password for your home-group.
- **Change The Password:** Change the password for your homegroup.
- **Leave The Homegroup:** Leave your homegroup.
- **Change Advanced Sharing Settings:** Change the settings for network discovery, file sharing, Public folder sharing, password-protected sharing, homegroup connections, and file sharing connections.
- **Start The HomeGroup Troubleshooter:** Troubleshoot homegroup problems.

Remove a Computer from a HomeGroup

To remove a computer from a homegroup, follow these steps on the computer you want to remove.

1. Right-click Start and choose Control Panel.
2. In the search box, type **homegroup**. In the search results, click HomeGroup.
3. Click Leave The Homegroup.
4. Click Finish.

   To modify the default homegroup sharing configuration, you can select one of your shared libraries in File Explorer and click Share in the toolbar. Using the controls that appear in the ribbon, you can change other homegroup users' access to the library from Homegroup (view) to Homegroup (view and edit). You can also limit access to specific homegroup users, or prevent anyone on the network from accessing that library.

Specify Shared Files and Folders in a Homegroup

To specify shared files and folders in a homegroup, perform the following steps:

1. On the taskbar, click File Explorer.
2. Navigate to the file or folder (such as Desktop, Downloads, Documents, Pictures, Music, or Videos) you want to exclude from sharing and click it.
3. Do one of the following:
   - To prevent the file or folder from being shared with anyone, in the toolbar, click the Share tab and click Stop Sharing.
   - To share the file or folder with some people but not others, in the toolbar, click the Share tab, click Specific People, select each person you want to share with, and then click Add. Click Share when you are finished.
   - To change the level of access to a file or folder, in the toolbar, click the Share tab and click either Homegroup (View) or Homegroup (View And Edit).

Creating Shares

Windows 10 provides Public folders and traditional file sharing capabilities to meet your networking needs. Public folders are a quick and easy way to share files with network users and with other users on your computer. Basic and advanced sharing allows you to control who may access specific files and folders located in your libraries. Advanced sharing offers the most options and is therefore the best choice for protecting confidential information.

Certification Ready

What are the primary differences between Public, basic, and advanced shares?
Objective 4.2

HomeGroup isn't the only way to share files and folders in Windows 10. You can also use traditional Windows file sharing to share individual files or folders or move files or folders to a Public folder.

Traditional Windows file sharing offers greater control over sharing with Public folders. In traditional file sharing, depending on whom you choose to share files or folders with, you can generally apply permissions to restrict users to simply viewing (reading) files as well as allow them to modify and/or delete files.

Let's look at Public folders first, because this method is the more convenient of the two methods.

Configuring Public Folders

The *Public folder* is an easy and convenient way to share files on your computer. You can share files in your Public folders with other people using the same computer and with people using other computers on your network. Any file or folder you put in a Public folder is automatically shared with the people who have access to your Public folders.

Certification Ready

For what purpose would you use Public folders? Objective 4.2

The folders that make up the Public library are stored in the C:\Users\Public folder. The Public folder contains subfolders (Public Documents, Public Music, Public Pictures, Public Videos, and more) that help you get organized; however, those folders do not have any files in them until you or other people use your computer to add files to them.

By default, Public folder sharing is turned off, except when the system is part of a homegroup. To enable or disable Public folders, open the Network and Sharing Center and click Change advanced sharing settings. When Public folder sharing is turned on, anyone on your computer or network can access these folders. When Public folder sharing is turned off, only people with a user account and password on your computer can access the public folders.

Configure Public Folders

To configure Public folders, perform the following steps:

1. Log on to LON-CL1 as **adatum\administrator** with the password of **Pa$$w0rd**.

2. On the taskbar, right-click the network status icon and choose Open Network And Sharing Center.

3. In the Network And Sharing Center window, click Change Advanced Sharing Settings.

4. Under All Networks, select the "Turn on sharing so anyone with network access can read and write files in the Public folders" option.

5. Click Save Changes and close the Network And Sharing Center.

After you turn on Public folder sharing, local users can navigate to C:\Users\Public to open the public folders. If you want the Public folders to be available over the network, you can share the Public folder so that it can be easily accessed using a UNC.

Configuring File Sharing

Most users are not going to log on to a server directly to access their data files. Instead, a drive or folder will be shared (known as a *shared folder*), and they will access the data files over the network. To help protect against unauthorized drive or folder access, you should use share permissions along with NTFS permissions (if the shared folder is on an NTFS volume). When a user needs to access a network share, she will use the universal naming convention (UNC), which is *servername**sharename*.

Certification Ready

What are the two methods for sharing a folder? Objective 4.2

Certification Ready

What permissions are available for Windows 10 file sharing? Objective 4.2

Traditional Windows file sharing allows you to restrict access to specific shared files and folders, and choose which users have access. *Basic sharing* allows you to share a file or folder with a specific user and restrict the user to Read or Read/Write actions.

Advanced sharing offers the greatest amount of control; for example, you can:

- Share files, folders, or an entire drive.
- Choose users or groups with which to share files and folders.

- Limit the number of users who can use a file or folder at the same time, mainly for security purposes.

- Set permissions on shared files and folders, such as allowing users Read, Change, or Full Control permissions.

- Choose which files are available to users offline.

You'll learn about permissions later in this lesson.

To set up basic or advanced shares, you must make sure that file sharing and network discovery are turned on. You should also turn on password-protected sharing for security purposes. File sharing, network discovery, and password-protected sharing options are enabled by default in the Network and Sharing Center (Advanced sharing settings page).

Set Up a Basic Share

To set up a basic share for a specific user, perform the following steps:

1. In File Explorer, navigate to the file or folder you want to share.

2. Right-click the file or folder and choose Properties. Click the Sharing tab in the Properties dialog box and click Share. The File Sharing dialog box opens (see Figure 6.5). You can also right-click the file or folder and choose Share With ➤ Specific People.

FIGURE 6.5 Windows 10 basic sharing

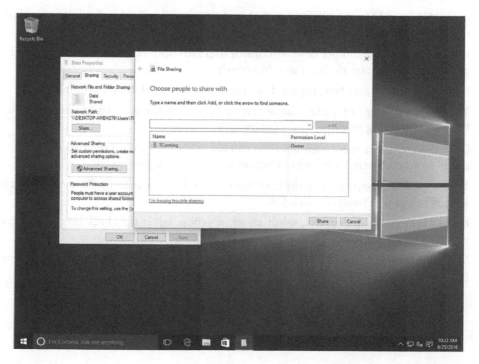

3. Click the arrow next to the text box, click a name from the list, and then click Add. Alternatively, if you know the user name of the person you want to add, type it in the text box and click Add.

4. In the Permission Level column, click the down arrow for the new user and select Read or Read/Write. Read allows the user to open and view items but not make changes or delete them. Read/Write allows users to open, modify, and delete items. You can also click Remove to remove the user.

5. When you're finished, click Share. If you're prompted for an administrator password or confirmation, type the password or provide confirmation.

6. After you set up a basic share for a user, Windows lets you send a confirmation to that user via email, or you can copy and paste a link to the shared item and send it to the user via email or instant message, for example.

7. When you're finished, click Done.

Set Up an Advanced Share

To set up an advanced share, perform the following steps:

1. In File Explorer, navigate to the folder or drive you want to share. This exercise assumes you are not working with Public folders.

2. Right-click the item to be shared and choose Properties. Click the Sharing tab in the Properties dialog box and click the Advanced Sharing button. If you're prompted for an administrator password or confirmation, type the password or provide confirmation.

3. In the Advanced Sharing dialog box, select the Share This Folder check box (as shown in Figure 6.6).

4. Use the "Limit the number of simultaneous users to" spin box to select the number of users who may access the item simultaneously.

5. In the Comments text box, type a description of the shared item (optional).

6. To specify users or groups or change permissions, click the Permissions button. The Permissions dialog box opens (see Figure 6.7).

7. Click Add to add a user or group. (You can also click Remove to remove a user or group from the share.) The Select Users or Groups dialog box opens.

8. Type a user or group name in the text box or click Locations to find a user or group to add. When you're finished, click OK.

9. In the Permissions dialog box, select a user or group, select the check boxes for the permissions you want to assign, and then click OK.

10. When you're finished, click OK to close the Advanced Sharing dialog box. Close the Properties dialog box.

FIGURE 6.6 The Advanced Sharing dialog box

FIGURE 6.7 The Permissions dialog box

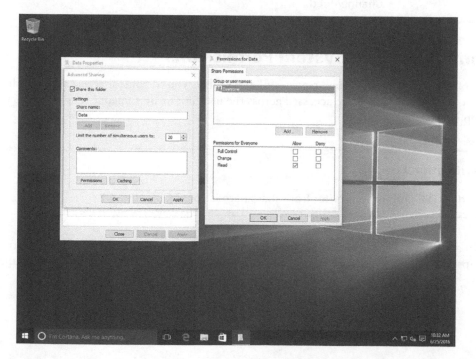

Share permissions are set for folders when they are shared in workgroups and domain-based networks and are only associated with the folders. These permissions determine the type of access that others will have to the folders when they connect to them over the network.

Share permissions only apply when you are accessing a shared folder via the UNC. If you log on locally and access the files directly without using the UNC, these permissions will not apply. Share permissions are not granular; therefore, the permission you assign to the share will automatically apply to the files and subfolders within the share itself.

In Windows 10, you will create and manage shares and share permissions from the folder properties Sharing tab. To see the permissions, click Advanced Sharing, select the Share this folder check box, and click the Permissions button. Table 6.1 shows the available permissions.

TABLE 6.1 Understanding Share Permissions

Permission	Description
Read	Enables user/group to view file and subfolder names, view data in files, and run programs.
Change	Enables user/group to add files and subfolders to the shared folder, change data in files, delete subfolders and files, and change any permission associated with Read.
Full Control	Enables user/group to change file permissions (NTFS only), take ownership of files (NTFS only), and perform tasks associated with Change/Read.

Configuring File System Permissions

The NTFS file permission tool is powerful and enables you to control access to your files and folders whether they are accessed across the network or by someone logging on to the computer locally.

Certification Ready

How do NTFS permissions differ from share permissions? Objective 4.2

In addition to the permissions you set when sharing a folder, Windows offers a more comprehensive set of permissions called *NTFS permissions*. These permissions are available on volumes formatted with the NTFS file system.

NTFS permissions differ from share permissions in two ways:

- They apply to files and folders on NTFS volumes.
- They apply whether the user attempts to access them over the network or locally.

Figure 6.8 shows the Security tab in the Properties dialog box. This tab is present because the folder is located on an NTFS volume. As you can see, there are a number of different permissions available for selected users and groups (see Table 6.2).

FIGURE 6.8   Managing NTFS permissions

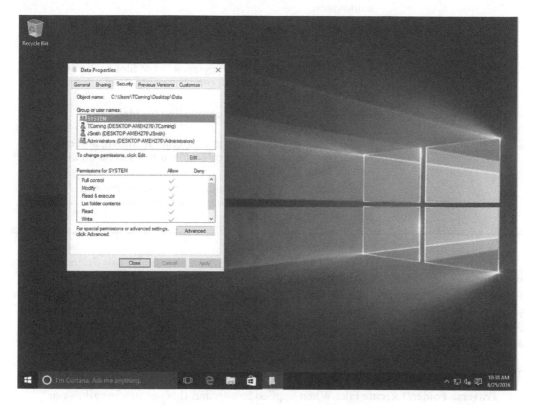

TABLE 6.2   NTFS Permissions

Permission	Description
Read	**Folder**: Enables user/group to read the contents of the folder.
	File: Enables user/group to read the contents of the file.
Read & Execute	**Folder**: Enables user/group to read the contents of the folder and execute programs in the folder.
	File: Enables user/group to read the contents of the file and execute the program.

TABLE 6.2   NTFS Permissions *(continued)*

Permission	Description
Write	**Folder**: Enables user/group to create files and folders. **File**: Enables user/group to create a file.
Modify	**Folder**: Enables user/group to read and write permissions. User can delete files within the folder and view the contents of subfolders. **File**: Enables user/group to read and write permissions. User can modify the contents of the file.
List Folder Contents	**Folder**: Enables user/group to view a list of files in the selected folder; user is not allowed to read the contents of a file or execute a file. **File**: There is no equivalent permission for files.
Full Control	**Folder**: Enables user/group to add, change, move, and delete items. User can also add and remove permissions on the folder and its subfolders. **File**: Enables user/group to change, move, delete, and manage permissions. User can also add, change, and remove permissions on the file.

Groups or users that are granted Full Control permission on a folder can delete any files in that folder regardless of the permissions protecting the file. In addition, the permissions for List folder contents are inherited by folders but not files, and it should only appear when you view folder permissions. In Windows 10, the Everyone group does not include the Anonymous Logon group by default, so permissions applied to the Everyone group do not affect the Anonymous Logon group.

Each of the standard permissions consists of a logical group of advanced permissions. The available advanced permissions are as follows:

- **Traverse Folder/Execute File:** When applied to a folder, this permission allows or prevents a user or group to move through folders to reach other files or folders, even if the user has no permission for the parent folder. When applied to a file, this permission allows the user or group to run program files. By default, the Everyone group is granted the Bypass traverse checking user right, which is applied to folders only. Setting the Traverse folder permission on a folder does not automatically set the Execute file permission on all files within that folder.

- **List Folder/Read Data:** When applied to a folder, this permission allows or prevents the user or group to see a list of files and subfolders in the folder. When this permission is applied to a file, you can open and read the file.

- **Read Attributes:** When applied to files and folders, this permission allows or prevents the viewing of file or folder attributes, such as read-only and hidden.

- **Read Extended Attributes:** When applied to files and folders, this permission allows or prevents the viewing of extended attributes of a file or folder. Extended attributes are defined by programs and may vary by program.

- **Create Files/Write Data:** When applied to a folder, this permission allows or prevents a user or group to create new files within the folders. When applied to a file, this permission allows the user or group to add to or modify the file, including overwriting existing content.

- **Create Folders/Append Data:** When applied to a folder, this permission allows you to create subfolders within the folder. When applied to a file, this permission allows the user or group to add data to the end of a file, but not to change, delete, or overwrite existing data.

- **Write Attributes:** When applied to files or folders, this permission allows or prevents changing the attributes of files or folders, such as read-only or hidden.

- **Write Extended Attributes:** When applied to files or folders, this permission allows or prevents changing the extended attributes of a file or folder.

- **Delete Subfolders and Files:** When applied to files or folders, this permission allows the user or group to delete subfolders and files.

- **Delete:** When applied to files and folders, this permission allows or prevents deleting the file or folder.

- **Read Permissions:** When applied to a file or folder, this permission allows or prevents viewing the permissions of the file or folder.

- **Change Permissions:** When applied to a file or folder, this permission allows or prevents the user or group changing the permissions of a file or folder.

- **Take Ownership:** When applied to a file or folder, this permission allows or prevents taking ownership of the file or folder. As an owner, you can change permissions regardless of permissions that you are explicitly granted to the file or folder.

To simplify administration, you can use groups to grant permissions. By assigning NTFS permissions to a group, you are granting permissions to one or more people simultaneously, reducing the number of entries in each access list as well as the amount of effort required to grant multiple people access to certain files or folders.

Understanding Effective NTFS Permissions

The folder and file structure on an NTFS drive can be complicated, with many folders and nested folders. In addition, because you can assign permissions to groups and at different levels on an NTFS volume, figuring out the effective permissions of a particular folder or file for a particular user can be tricky.

There are two types of permissions used in NTFS:

- *Explicit permissions*: Permissions granted directly to a file or folder
- *Inherited permissions*: Permissions that are granted to a folder (parent object or container) that flow into child objects (subfolders or files inside the parent folder)

In a file system, a folder with subfolders is considered the parent folder. The subfolders are considered child folders. After you set permissions on a parent folder, new files and subfolders that are created in the folder inherit these permissions.

To stop permissions from being inherited, select the "Replace all existing inheritable permissions on all descendants with inheritable permissions from this object" check box in the Advanced Security Settings dialog box. You are then prompted to confirm if you are sure you want to proceed. You can also clear the "Allow inheritable permissions from parent to propagate to this object" check box. When you clear this check box, Windows responds with a Security dialog box. In the Security dialog box, when you click the Copy button, the explicit permission is copied from the parent folder to the subfolder or file. You can then change the subfolder's or file's explicit permissions. If you click the Remove button, you remove the inherited permission altogether.

By default, any objects within a folder inherit the permissions from that folder when they are created, as shown in Table 6.3. However, explicit permissions take precedence over inherited permissions, as shown in Table 6.4. So, if you grant different permissions at a lower level, the lower-level permissions take precedence.

For example, say you have a folder called Data. Within the Data folder, you have Folder1, and within Folder1, you have Folder2. Folder2 has File1. If you grant Allow full control to a user account, the Allow full control permission will flow down to the subfolders and files within the Data folder.

TABLE 6.3 Inherited Permissions

Object	NTFS Permissions
Data	Grant Allow full control (explicit)
Folder1	Allow full control (inherited)
Folder2	Allow full control (inherited)
File1	Allow full control (inherited)

In comparison, if you grant Allow full control on the Data folder to a user account and you grant Allow read permission to Folder1, the Allow read permission will overwrite the inherited permissions and will then flow down to Folder2 and File1.

TABLE 6.4   Explicit Permissions Overwrite Inherited Permissions

Object	NTFS Permissions
Data	Grant Allow full control (explicit)
Folder1	Allow read (explicit)
Folder2	Allow read (inherited)
File1	Allow read (inherited)

If a user has access to a file, he can still gain access to the file even if he does not have access to the folder containing the file. Of course, because the user doesn't have access to the folder, the user cannot navigate or browse through the folder to get to the file. Therefore, the user will have to use the UNC or local path to open the file.

When you view permissions of a file or folder, they will appear in one of the following ways:

- **Checked:** Permissions are explicitly assigned.
- **Cleared (Unchecked):** No permissions are assigned.
- **Shaded:** Permissions are granted through inheritance from a parent folder.

Besides granting the Allow permission, you can also grant the Deny permission. The Deny permission always overrides other permissions that have been granted, including when a user or group has been given Full control. For example, if a group is granted Read and Write permission and one person within the group is denied the Write permission, the user's effective right is the Read permission.

When you combine applying Deny versus Allowed with explicit versus inherited permissions, the hierarchy of precedence of permission is as follows:

1. Explicit Deny
2. Explicit Allow
3. Inherited Deny
4. Inherited Allow

Because users can be members of several groups, it is possible for them to have several sets of explicit permissions for a particular folder or file. When this occurs, the permissions are combined to form the *effective permissions*, which are the actual permissions when logging in and accessing a file or folder. These consist of explicit permissions plus any inherited permissions.

When you calculate effective permissions, you must first calculate the explicit and inherited permissions for an individual or group and then combine them. When combining user and group permissions for NTFS security, the effective permission is the cumulative permission. The only exception is that Deny permissions always apply.

For example, you have a folder called Data. Within the Data folder, you have Folder1, and within Folder1, you have Folder2. If User 1 is a member of Group 1 and Group 2 and you assign the following:

- The Allow write permission to the Data folder to User 1
- The Allow read permission to Folder1 to Group 1
- The Allow modify permission to Folder2 to Group 2

User 1's effective permissions would be as shown in Table 6.5.

TABLE 6.5 Calculating Effective Permissions

Object	User 1 NTFS Permissions	Group 1 Permissions	Group 2 Permissions	Effective Permissions
Data	Allow write (explicit)			Allow write
Folder1	Allow write (inherited)	Allow read (explicit)		Allow read and write
Folder2	Allow write (inherited)	Allow read (inherited)	Allow modify* (explicit)	Allow modify*
File1	Allow write (inherited)	Allow read (inherited)	Allow modify* (inherited)	Allow modify*

* The Modify permission includes the Read and Write permissions.

As another example, say you have a folder called Data. Within the Data folder, you have Folder1, and within Folder1, you have Folder2. If User 1 is a member of Group 1 and Group 2 and you assign the following permissions:

- The Allow write permission to the Data folder to User 1
- The Allow read permission to Folder1 to Group 1
- The Deny modify permission to Folder2 to Group 2

User 1's effective permissions would be as shown in Table 6.6.

TABLE 6.6 Effective Permissions Affected by Deny Permissions

Object	User 1 NTFS Permissions	Group 1 Permissions	Group 2 Permissions	Effective Permissions
Data	Allow write (explicit)			Allow write
Folder1	Allow write (inherited)	Allow read (explicit)		Allow read and write

Object	User 1 NTFS Permissions	Group 1 Permissions	Group 2 Permissions	Effective Permissions
Folder2	Allow write (inherited)	Allow read (inherited)	Deny modify (explicit)	Deny modify
File1	Allow write (inherited)	Allow read (inherited)	Deny modify (inherited)	Deny modify

The concept of inheritance is important to keep in mind when setting NTFS permissions. Remember the following:

- When users copy files and folders, the files and folders inherit the permissions of the destination folder.

- When users move files and folders within the same volume, they retain their permissions.

- When users move files and folders to a different volume, they inherit the permissions of the destination folder.

Effective permissions for an object, such as a folder, are permissions granted to a user or group based on the permissions granted through group membership and any permissions inherited from the parent object. Windows does not include share permissions as part of the effective permissions.

NTFS permissions are cumulative. For example, if you give a user in the sales group Read permissions to a folder and its contents, and the user is also a member of the marketing group, which has been given the Write permission to the same folder, the user will have Read/Write permissions. In this type of situation, if you do not want the user to be able to write to the folder, you can use the Deny permission and select the specific user account. The Deny permission always overrides the Allow permission.

Viewing Effective Permissions on a Resource

In Windows 10, the Effective Access tab enables you to view the effective NTFS permissions for a user, group, or device account on a resource. To access this tab, right-click the file or folder, choose Properties, click the Security tab, and then click Advanced.

For example, let's say you create a folder called Data and then share the folder, allowing the Sales group full control. You also configure the NTFS permissions for JSmith, a member of the group, with the following settings: Read & Execute, List Folder Contents, and Read. What would JSmith's effective permissions be?

To determine JSmith's effective permissions, right-click the Data folder and choose Properties. Click the Security tab and click Advanced. Once you are in the Advanced Security Settings for Data dialog box, click Select a user and then search for JSmith's account. Once you find his account, select it and then click View effective access to see the permissions he has for the folder.

As shown in Figure 6.9, even though JSmith has Full Control to the share due to his membership in the Sales group, NTFS permissions restrict him to only reading, listing folder contents, and executing files within the folder. He cannot create files, folders, or make any changes to the documents.

FIGURE 6.9   Viewing a user's effective permissions

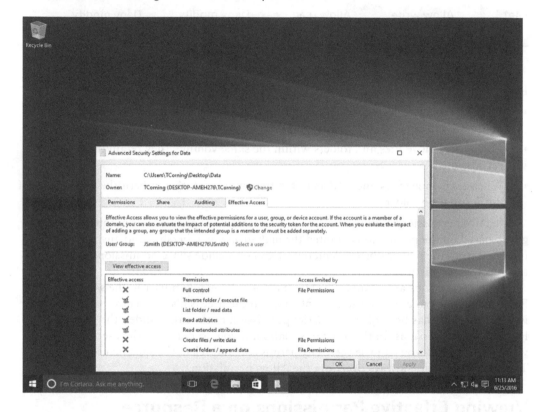

Review Permissions Using the Effective Access Tab

To view the effective permissions for the local Administrator account, log on to your computer with administrative credentials and perform the following steps:

1. Click the File Explorer icon on the taskbar.
2. Click Local Disk (C:).
3. Right-click the Windows folder and choose Properties.
4. Click the Security tab and click Advanced.
5. Click the Effective Access tab.

6. Click Select a user.

7. In the Enter the object name to select field, type Administrator and then click OK.

8. Click View effective access.

9. Review the current permissions for the local Administrator account on C:\Windows and click OK.

10. Click OK and then close the Windows Properties dialog box.

When planning your NTFS/Share permissions on storage spaces or any volumes in which files and folders are shared, the best approach is to set the Share permissions to provide Full Control to the appropriate user group and then use NTFS permissions to further lock down access to the resource. This process ensures that resources are secured regardless of how they are accessed (remotely or locally).

Combining NTFS and Share Permissions

It is very common to combine share and NTFS permissions when providing access to resources on NTFS volumes. When this happens, you must have a good understanding of the cumulative effects to ensure that your resources remain protected. Now that you have a better understanding of NTFS permissions and share permissions, you need to understand what happens when you combine the two permissions on the same resource.

For example, let's say you create and share a folder with the following settings:

- Share permission (Share tab): Sales group, Read

- NTFS permission (Security tab): Sales group, Full Control

When users connect to the share over the network, both the share and NTFS permissions combine, and the most restrictive set is applied. In the preceding example, the share permission of Read is more restrictive than the NTFS permission, so users can read the folder and its contents. If the same users were to log on locally to the computer in which this share is located, they would bypass the share permissions and their level of access would be based on the NTFS permission. In this example, they would have Full Control.

Mapping Drives

Drive mapping allows you to create a shortcut to a shared folder across a network. Instead of finding and connecting to the shared drive each time you log on, you can create a mapped drive that is available at all times. Just double-click the mapped drive to access the shared folder.

Certification Ready

What is a mapped drive? Objective 4.2

Once you share a folder or drive on your computer with other users, an easy way for them to get to the shared item is by *mapping a drive*. A mapped drive is a shortcut to a shared folder or drive on another computer across a network. File Explorer makes this process easy and straightforward.

By default in Windows 10, network drive letters start from the end of the alphabet (Z: is the first default drive letter that displays) and work down, so as not to interfere with local drives (which start with A: and work up). When mapping a drive, you can select any drive letter that's not already in use.

A mapped network drive is displayed in File Explorer under This PC in the navigation pane.

Map a Drive

To assign a drive letter to a shared folder on the network, perform the following steps:

1. Open File Explorer.

2. On the Home tab, click Easy Access (as shown in Figure 6.10) and click Map As Drive.

FIGURE 6.10   Selecting the Map network drive command

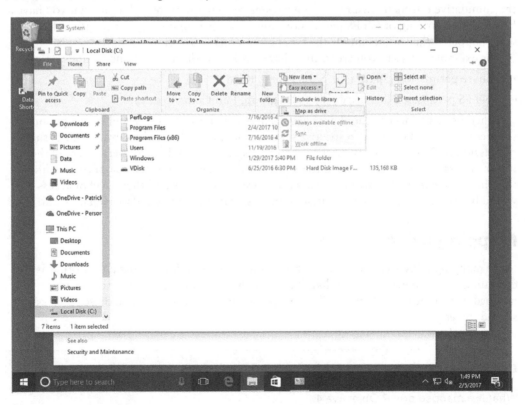

3. In the Map Network Drive window, in the drop-down menu, click a drive letter of your choice (see Figure 6.11).

FIGURE 6.11   Selecting a drive letter from the drop-down list

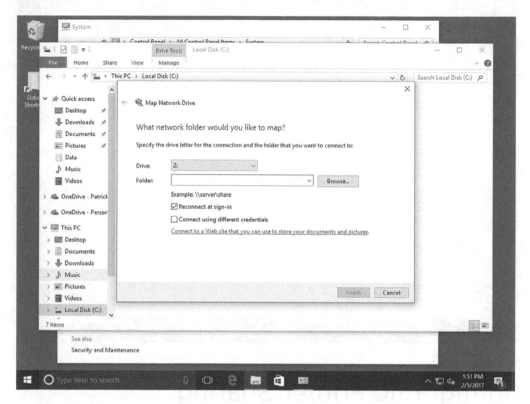

4. Click Browse and navigate to the shared folder you want to map to. Alternatively, type the UNC path of the folder. A UNC is a naming format that specifies the location of a resource on a local area network. The UNC format is *computername* *sharename**filepath*. The *computername* and *sharename* variables refer to the computer or server on which the folder resides. The *filepath* variable is the name of the folder you're mapping.

5. Select the shared folder and click OK.

6. By default, the Reconnect At Sign-in check box is selected. This means the drive mapping will persist until you manually disconnect it (using the Disconnect network drive entry in the Tools menu in File Explorer). When you're done, click Finish.

The mapped drive displays in the File Explorer navigation pane (see Figure 6.12). Click it to access the shared folder.

FIGURE 6.12   A shared folder with a drive mapping

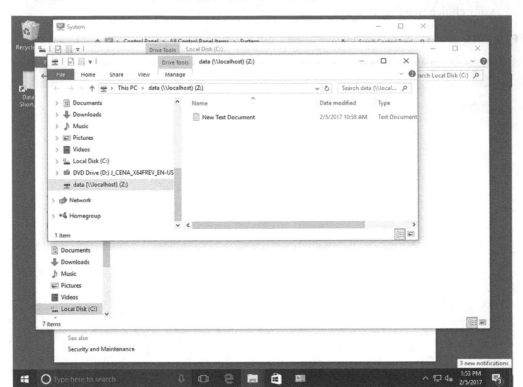

Configuring Printer Sharing

Printers are considered objects. Therefore, as with NTFS files and folders, you can assign permissions to a printer so that you can specify who can use the printer, who can manage the printer, and who can manage the print jobs.

When you open the printer's Properties dialog box, you can configure sharing using the Sharing tab. You can change the share name and specify whether you want to render the print jobs on the client computer or not.

To configure the print sharing permissions, click the Security tab, as shown in Figure 6.13. Windows 10 provides three levels of *printer permissions*:

- **Print:** Allows users to send documents to the printer.

- **Manage this Printer:** Allows users to modify printer settings and configurations, including the access control list (ACL) itself.

- **Manage Documents:** Provides the ability to cancel, pause, resume, or restart a print job.

FIGURE 6.13   Printer permissions

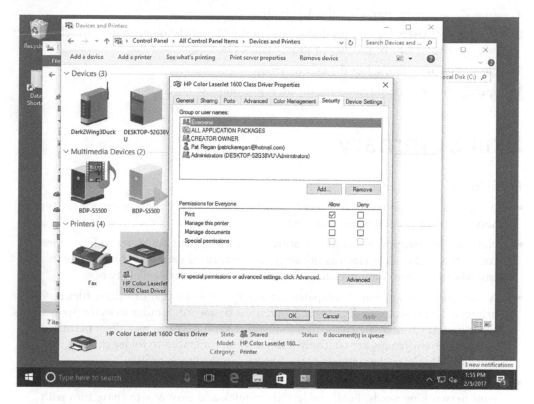

By default, the Print permission is assigned to the Everyone group. If you need to restrict who can print to the printer, you remove the Everyone group and add another group or user and assign the Allow print permission to the group or user. Of course, it is still recommended that you use groups instead of users. As with file permissions, you can also deny print permissions.

Share a Printer

To share a printer in Windows 10, perform the following steps:

1. Right-click Start and choose Control Panel.
2. Under Hardware And Sound, click View Devices and Printers.
3. Right-click the printer and choose Printer Properties.
4. To share a printer, click the Sharing tab.
5. If you need to share the printer, select the Share This Printer check box, and in the Share Name text box, specify the share name of the printer.

6. Click the Security tab.

7. To add a group or user, click the Add button.

8. In the Select Users Or Groups dialog box, in the "Enter the object names to select" text box, type the name of the user or group. Click OK.

9. On the Security tab, select the user or group.

10. Specify the print permissions for the user or group and click OK.

Skill Summary

In this lesson, you learned:

- A network location is a collection of security settings that's appropriate for the type of network to which you want to connect.

- Network discovery is a Windows feature that enables your computer to find other computers and devices (such as printers) on a connected network. It also lets you control whether other computers can see your computer on the same network.

- A homegroup is a group of computers on a home network that can share files and printers. To protect your homegroup, you use a password. Similar to share permissions, other people cannot change the files that you share unless you give them permission to do so. Homegroups are relatively limited when compared to folder sharing, because you can only share the contents of the libraries in the user's profile.

- Windows 10 provides Public folders and traditional file sharing capabilities to meet your networking needs. Public folders are a quick and easy way to share files with network users and with other users on your computer. Basic and advanced sharing allow you to control who may access specific files and folders located in your libraries. Advanced sharing offers the most options and is therefore the best choice for protecting confidential information.

- To provide access to a drive or folder, you can share the drive or folder, and users will access the data files over the network. To help protect against unauthorized drive or folder access, you should use share permissions along with NTFS permissions (if the shared folder is on an NTFS volume). When a user needs to access a network share, she will use the universal naming convention (UNC), which is \\servername\sharename.

- Printers are considered objects. Therefore, as with NTFS files and folders, you can assign permissions to a printer so that you can specify who can use the printer, who can manage the printer, and who can manage the print jobs.

Knowledge Assessment

You can find the answers to the following sections in the Appendix.

Multiple Choice

1. Which of the following is *not* a network location in Windows 10?

    A. Private

    B. Office

    C. Domain

    D. Public

2. Which of the following should be used for file sharing when a peer-to-peer network has a mix of Windows 10, Windows 8/8.1, and Windows 7 computers?

    A. Public folders

    B. HomeGroup

    C. A workgroup

    D. A domain

3. Which of the following actions can be performed with a homegroup? (Choose all that apply.)

    A. Share libraries

    B. Share attached printers

    C. Allow users to view but not modify or copy shared files

    D. Choose which folders users may access

4. After sharing a folder on a Windows 10 computer with other users, which of the following can be done to make it easy for those users to access the shared folder?

    A. Create a workgroup.

    B. Create effective permissions.

    C. Create NTFS permissions.

    D. Map a drive.

5. Which of the following statements is not true regarding NTFS permissions?

    A. Copied files and folders inherit permissions of the destination folder.

    B. Copied files and folders retain permissions of the source folder.

    C. Files and folders moved within the same partition retain their permissions.

    D. Files and folders moved to a different partition inherit the permissions of the destination folder.

6. Which of the following Windows 10 permissions allows users to view and change files and folders, create new files and folders, and run programs in a folder?

    A. Write

    B. Modify

    C. Read and Execute

    D. Full control

7. Which of the following Public folders is not created by default?

    A. Public Documents

    B. Public Music

    C. Public Pictures

    D. Public Projects

8. Which Windows 10 feature is used to turn Public folders on or off?

    A. Advanced sharing settings

    B. The This PC window

    C. Network and Sharing Center window

    D. Devices and Printers window

9. Which Windows 10 feature is used to add a printer?

    A. Devices and Printers

    B. Device Manager

    C. Printer Troubleshooter

    D. Programs and Features

10. When sharing a folder, which share permission should be configured?

    A. Deny Full Control

    B. Allow Full Control

    C. Allow Read

    D. Allow Modify

Fill in the Blank

1. A _____ is a collection of security settings that's appropriate for the type of network to which a user wants to connect.

2. Each default library in Windows 10 has _____, created to easily share documents, music, and so on with network users.

3. _____ allows a user to share a file or folder with another user and restrict that user to Read or Read/Write actions.

4. After setting permissions on a parent folder, new files and subfolders that are created in the folder _____ these permissions.

5. _____ permissions apply to users who log on locally or remotely.

6. The _____ is a network location that has the most restrictive firewall rules, including blocking file sharing and network discovery.

7. _____ allows users to share files, folders, or an entire drive, and set permissions on shared files and folders (Read, Change, or Full Control).

8. _____ is the built-in file and printer sharing feature in Windows 10 that's designed for small office or home office networks.

9. When users connect to the share over the network, both the share and NTFS permissions combine, and the most _____ set is applied.

10. _____ permissions for an object, such as a folder, are permissions granted to a user or group based on the permissions granted through group membership and any permissions inherited from the parent object.

True/False

1. Network users can join two or more homegroups at a time.

2. When creating a homegroup, a user can share libraries but not printers.

3. Public folder sharing in Windows 10 is turned off by default, except on a homegroup.

4. Share permissions apply to users who connect to a shared folder over a network.

5. A user has full permissions over his own print jobs.

Case Scenarios

You can find the answers to the following sections in the Appendix.

Scenario 6-1: Picking an Appropriate File Sharing Method

Arnie, a supervisor in a small content translation company, wants to share a status spreadsheet with seven co-workers on a regular basis. His computer runs Windows 10. The peer computers all run Windows 10 and are connected through a wireless network. Which method of file sharing should be set up for the supervisor?

Scenario 6-2: Creating and Configuring a Homegroup

Meredith's Pet Shop has three computers in the back office, all running Windows 10. For all three computers, Meredith wants to share all files in their Documents and Pictures libraries and share a printer attached to one of the computers. Describe your recommended solution.

Scenario 6-3: Restricting Permissions

You are setting permissions on a network share named Marketing. Currently, the accounts for Bob and Aileen have Full Control over the Marketing folder. However, you want to restrict both users so that they can revise files within the Marketing folder and create new ones, but they cannot execute programs. Which permissions should be applied?

Scenario 6-4: Mapping a Network Drive

Samuel needs to be able to access the \Projects\Documents\98-349\ folder on the network often and quickly. He doesn't want to click through several folders to get to the one he needs. Describe your recommended solution.

Lesson 7

Maintaining, Updating, and Protecting Windows 10

Objective Domain Matrix

Technology Skill	Objective Domain Description	Objective Domain Number
Exploring Built-In Maintenance Tools	Understand maintenance tools	6.2
	Understand storage	5.2
	Configure desktop settings	1.2
Configuring and Managing Updates	Configure updates	6.3
Defending Your System from Malicious Software	Configure antivirus settings	3.3

Key Terms

action	security update
Action Center	service pack
critical update	signature
cumulative patch	spyware
Current Branch (CB) servicing	Task Scheduler
Disk Cleanup	trigger
Disk Defragmenter	Trojan horse
firewall	virus
fragmented	Windows 10 Anniversary Update
hotfix	Windows Defender
Long-Term Servicing Branch (LTSB) servicing	Windows Firewall
	Windows Insider program
malicious software	Windows registry
Microsoft Windows Malicious Software Removal Tool	Windows Update
	worm
out-of-band patches	
Patch Tuesday	

 Real World Scenario

Lesson 7 Case

A primary part of your IT technician position at Interstate Snacks involves maintaining company computers. To keep support costs down, you use free tools that are built in to Windows or downloadable from the Microsoft website. The tools include Disk Defragmenter, Disk Cleanup, Windows Update, and Windows Defender. With the exception of Disk Cleanup, these tools have built-in scheduling features. You plan to use Task Scheduler to automate Disk Cleanup to run once a week and to start the accounting software every day at 8:30 a.m. for all accounting employees.

Exploring Built-in Maintenance Tools

Windows 10 comes with many built-in maintenance tools that help to keep computers running at top performance. These tools include Disk Defragmenter, Disk Cleanup, Task Scheduler, and the Action Center Maintenance feature.

Microsoft began bundling computer maintenance utilities in its early versions of Windows and has improved and expanded on them ever since. The latest utilities provide nearly any type of maintenance you might need, such as defragmenting disks, removing unnecessary files, scheduling tasks, troubleshooting problems, backing up files, and more.

In the following sections, you learn about some of the most popular Windows built-in utilities: Disk Defragmenter, Disk Cleanup, Task Scheduler, and the Maintenance section of Action Center.

Using Disk Defragmenter

Disk Defragmenter can speed up your computer's performance by defragmenting data on your hard disk. In Windows 10, the utility is set to automatically run once a week.

Certification Ready

What is Disk Defragmenter? Objective 6.2

Certification Ready

What is the smallest addressable unit on a hard disk that is used to store files?
Objective 5.2

A hard disk is divided into many sectors, each of which can hold a small amount of data for a file. The hard disk's arm moves across a disk to "read" each sector in order to display a file or run a program. As more and more files are added to the disk, the information becomes *fragmented*, which means it is spread across sectors on different parts of the disk.

Disk Defragmenter is a utility that helps improve your computer's performance by moving sectors of data on the hard disk, so that files are stored sequentially. This minimizes the movement a hard disk's arm must make to read all of the sectors that make up a file or program.

 Solid state drives (SSDs) differ from hard disks. An SSD uses solid state memory to store data rather than writing data to sectors. Therefore, an SSD does not need to be defragmented.

Disk Defragmenter first analyzes your hard disk to determine the level of fragmentation, and then it defragments the disk if necessary.

In Windows 10, Disk Defragmenter is scheduled to run once a week by default. Although you may continue to use your computer while your hard disk is being defragmented, you might notice a performance hit if you're working on large files or running several programs at once. If you're often working on your computer when the hard disk is being analyzed and defragmented, you can change the schedule for when Disk Defragmenter runs automatically.

Run Disk Defragmenter

To run Disk Defragmenter, perform the following steps:

1. Click Start and type **Disk Defragmenter**. From the results, click Defragment and Optimize Drives.

2. In the Optimize Drives window (as shown in Figure 7.1), click to select a drive and click Optimize.

3. After the disk is optimized, click the Close button.

FIGURE 7.1   The Disk Defragmenter window

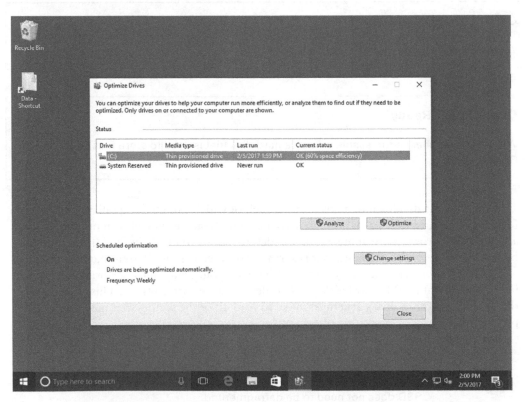

The defragmentation process can take several minutes to well over an hour to complete, depending on the size and level of fragmentation of the hard disk.

IT technicians and other advanced users may want to use the command-line version of Disk Defragmenter, in order to run reports and use advanced commands. To use the command-line version of the utility, click Start, type **cmd** in the Ask Me Anything search box, select cmd.exe from the resulting list, and then in the command window, type **defrag/?** and press Enter. Reissue the command using any of the command-line parameters that display.

Change the Disk Defragmenter Schedule

To change the Disk Defragmenter schedule, perform the following steps:

1. In the Optimize Drives window (refer to Figure 7.1 if necessary), click Change settings. The Optimize Drives: Optimization schedule dialog box opens (see Figure 7.2).

FIGURE 7.2   Optimize Drives: Optimization Schedule dialog box

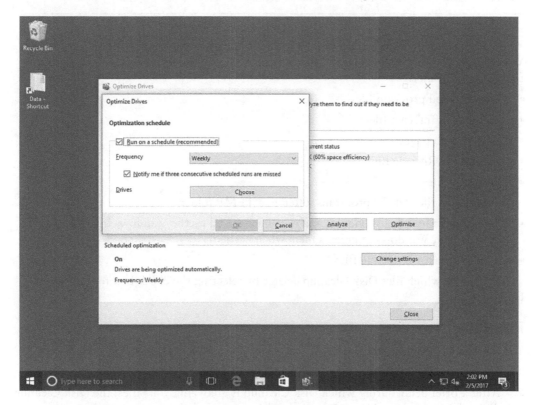

2. To change how often Disk Defragmenter runs, click the Frequency drop-down arrow and click Daily, Weekly, or Monthly.
3. To change the time of day when Disk Defragmenter runs, click the Time drop-down arrow and click a time.

4. To change the volumes that are scheduled to be defragmented, click the Choose button. Deselect any volumes you don't want scanned and click OK.

5. Click OK and click Close.

Using Disk Cleanup

Disk Cleanup helps you remove unnecessary files from your computer, such as down-loaded program files, temporary Internet files, files that are left after running software, and much more.

Certification Ready

How does Disk Cleanup help you maintain a Windows 10 computer? Objective 6.2

Another handy maintenance tool in Windows 10, and many previous versions of Windows, is *Disk Cleanup*. This utility removes many different kinds of unnecessary files from your computer:

- Downloaded program files
- Temporary Internet files
- Offline web pages
- Files in the Recycle Bin
- Setup log files
- Temporary files left by programs, often in a TEMP folder
- Thumbnails for photos, videos, and documents used by the Windows interface (if you delete them, Windows re-creates them when needed)
- Windows error reporting files

You choose which files Disk Cleanup deletes by selecting the check box for each type of file.

Run Disk Cleanup

To run Disk Cleanup, perform the following steps:

1. Click Start. Type **Disk Cleanup** and press Enter.

2. After a brief delay during which Disk Cleanup is analyzing your files, the Disk Cleanup dialog box opens (see Figure 7.3), showing how much disk space you will gain by running the program. You can select the types of files you want the utility to delete; those that are deselected will not be deleted. For many of the file types, you can click View Files to see a list of files that will be deleted.

3. When you're ready, click Clean Up System Files.

FIGURE 7.3   The Disk Cleanup dialog box

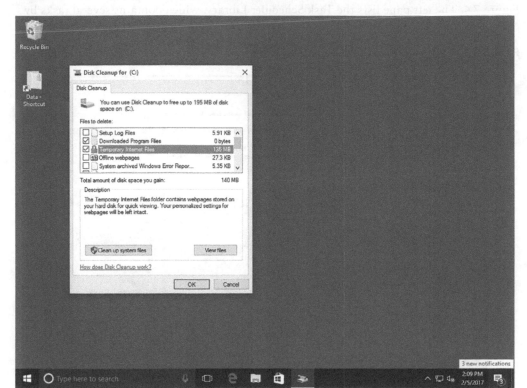

Using Task Scheduler

Many, but not all Windows utilities have their own scheduling feature. For those utilities that you want to automate, you can use Task Scheduler. You can also use Task Scheduler to open programs on specific days and times, or at Windows startup.

Certification Ready

When you schedule a task using Task Scheduler, what is used to specify when the schedule is executed? Objective 6.2

Task Scheduler enables you to schedule and automate a variety of actions, such as starting programs, displaying messages, and even sending emails. You create a scheduled task by specifying a *trigger*, which is an event that causes a task to run, and an *action*, which is the action taken when the task runs.

The main Task Scheduler window with the Task Scheduler Library selected is shown in Figure 7.4. The left pane lists the Task Scheduler Library, which contains several tasks by Microsoft and other vendors.

FIGURE 7.4   The main Task Scheduler window with the built-in libraries expanded

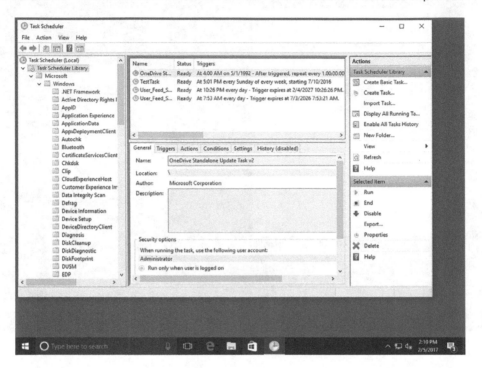

When you select Task Scheduler (Local), as shown in Figure 7.5, the middle pane shows three panes. The Overview pane provides you with an overview of Task Scheduler, the Task Status pane displays a summary of tasks that started in a certain time period (for example, within the last 24 hours), and the Active Tasks pane displays scheduled tasks. The information displayed in the middle pane can vary greatly from computer to computer.

On the right of the screen, the Actions pane provides commands for connecting to another computer and scheduling tasks for that computer, creating basic and more advanced tasks, and viewing tasks and their histories.

Notice in Figure 7.5 that there are two commands in the Actions pane for creating tasks: Create Basic Task and Create Task. When you use the Create Basic Task command, the Create Basic Task Wizard walks you through the essentials of creating a task. The Create Task command displays the Create Task dialog box (see Figure 7.6), which is the manual way of creating tasks that gives you more control and options.

FIGURE 7.5   The Task Scheduler (Local)

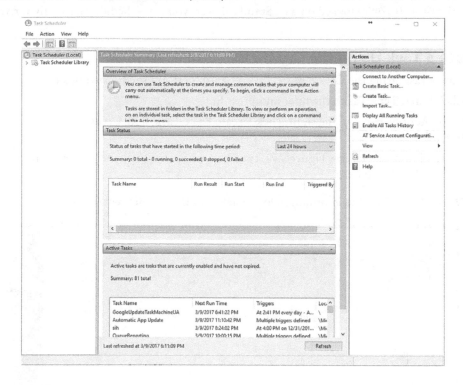

FIGURE 7.6   The Create Task dialog box

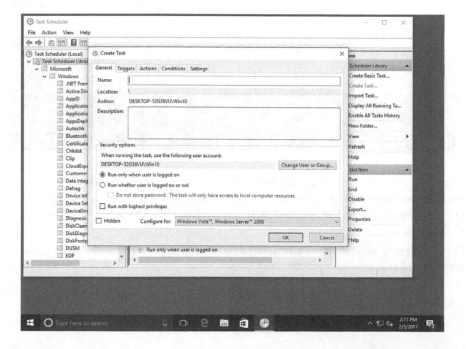

To schedule tasks for all users on your computer, you must be logged on as the Administrator. If you're logged on as a Standard user, you can schedule tasks only for your user account.

Create a Task Using the Create Basic Task Wizard

To create a task using the Create Basic Task Wizard, perform the following steps:

1. Click Start. Type **Task Scheduler** and press Enter.

2. In the Actions pane on the right, click Create Basic Task. The Create Basic Task Wizard opens.

3. On the initial screen (see Figure 7.7), type a name for the task and its description (optional). Click Next.

FIGURE 7.7   Entering information for a basic task in the initial wizard screen

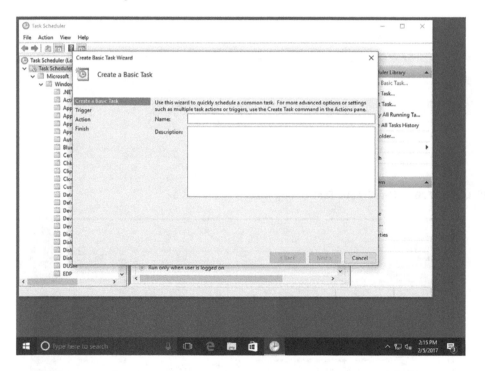

4. The Task Trigger screen enables you to select the frequency with which the task should occur or an event that triggers the task (see Figure 7.8). The default selection is Daily. For our example, because this task will run weekly, click the Weekly option and click Next.

5. On the Weekly screen, select a starting date as well as the time and day of the week the task should run (see Figure 7.9). Click Next.

FIGURE 7.8 You can create a task to run daily, weekly, monthly, one time, and more.

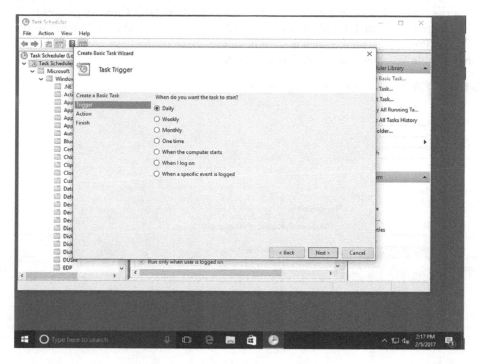

FIGURE 7.9 Selecting frequency and recurrence of the task

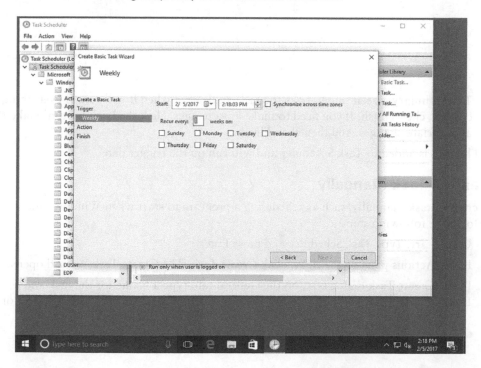

6.   On the Action screen, click Start a program and click Next.

7.   On the Start a Program screen, click Browse to find the Disk Cleanup program. Navigate to and click C:\Windows\system32\cleanmgr.exe and click Open. On the Start a Program screen, which now indicates the path to the Disk Cleanup program executable (as shown in Figure 7.10), click Next.

FIGURE 7.10   Selecting the program to run

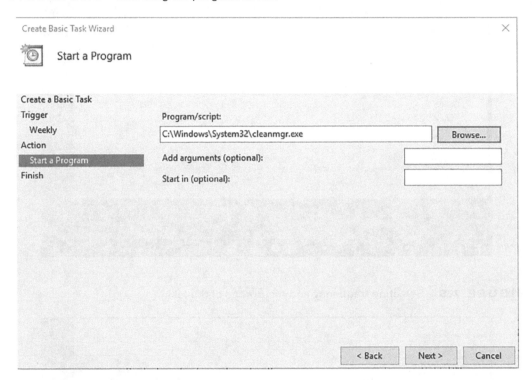

8.   The Summary screen summarizes the task, indicating when it will run. If everything is correct, click Finish. If you need to make any changes, click the Back button, make the appropriate changes, and then click Finish.

The task is added to Task Scheduler and will run on the trigger date.

Create a Task Manually

To create a task manually, such as scheduling a program to start when Windows starts, perform the following steps:

1.   Click Start. Type **Task Scheduler** and press Enter.

2.   In the Actions pane on the right, click Create Task. The Create Task Wizard opens.

3.   In the Create Task dialog box, on the General tab, type a Name for the task and a Description (optional). In the Security options section, you can click Change User or

Group to change the account or group the task runs under, and select whether the task should run when the user is logged on or not. Be sure to select the appropriate operating system in the Configure for drop-down list.

4. Click the Triggers tab and click New. In the New Trigger dialog box, click the Begin the task drop-down arrow (see Figure 7.11) and click one of the options, such as At startup.

FIGURE 7.11 The New Trigger dialog box

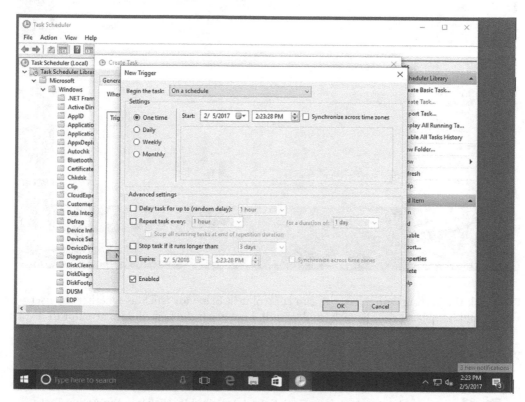

With this option selected, the New Trigger dialog box changes. Configure advanced settings, if needed, and click **OK**.

5. In the Create Task dialog box, click the Actions tab and click New. In the New Action dialog box, click Browse, navigate to the program's executable file (in this example, navigate to C:\Program Files\Internet Explorer\ and locate the Internet Explorer 11 executable named iexplore.exe), select it, and then click Open.

6. Click OK.

7. In the Create Task dialog box, click the Conditions tab. In addition to the trigger, you can specify conditions under which the task should run (see Figure 7.12). For example, the power conditions are selected in an effort to avoid running a laptop's battery down unnecessarily. Make selections as appropriate.

FIGURE 7.12   Selecting conditions for the new task

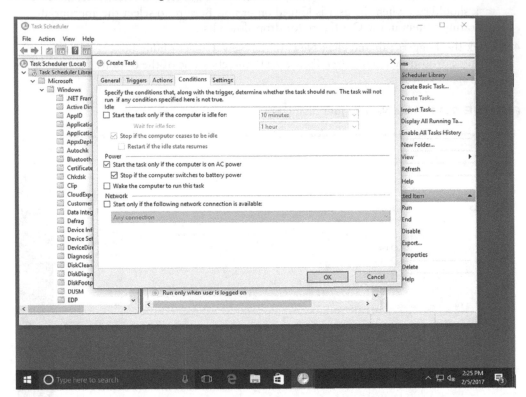

8. Click the Settings tab. Here you can control task behavior (such as whether the user should be able to run the task on demand), how often the task should attempt to restart if it fails, and so on. Make selections as appropriate.

9. When you're finished configuring settings, click OK.

 To delete a task from Task Scheduler, double-click it in the Active Tasks pane and click Delete in the Actions pane.

The task is added to Task Scheduler. You can see the task listed in the Active Tasks pane at the bottom of the main Task Scheduler window.

Using Security and Maintenance (formerly called Action Center)

Windows 10 Security and Maintenance is an improvement upon Security Center in previous versions of Windows. Within Security and Maintenance, you can view notifications for security features (firewall, antivirus software, and so on) and maintenance (backups, updates, and so on).

In Windows 10, the action center is where you'll find app notifications and quick actions.

FIGURE 7.13   Action Center Icon

The old Action Center is still here, but has been renamed Security and Maintenance. This is where you go to change your security settings.

In the search box on the taskbar, type **Security and Maintenance** and then select Security and Maintenance from the menu.

FIGURE 7.14   Security and Maintenance from the Menu

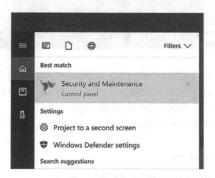

Action Center provides a single interface in which you can view the status of security and maintenance features (see Figure 7.15). Action Center alerts you to problems you need to correct and usually provides a way to fix them.

The quickest way to open Action Center is from the desktop. Click the Comment icon in the notification area of the taskbar. If no issues are pending, the Security and Maintenance section is collapsed. When an issue needs your attention, errors are indicated by a red circle with a white X and warnings are indicated by a yellow triangle with a black exclamation point.

FIGURE 7.15 Action Center

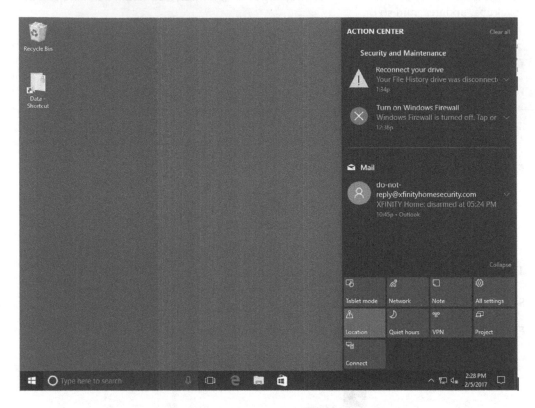

In Windows 10, Security and Maintenance is where you'll find app notifications as well as quick actions, which gives quick access to commonly used settings and apps. You can change the settings at any time from the Settings app.

Select the Start button, and then select Settings, then go to System ➤ Notifications & Actions.

You can do any of the following:

- Choose the quick actions you'll see in Action Center.

- Turn notifications, banners, and sounds on or off for some or all notification senders.

- Choose whether to see notifications on the lock screen.

- Choose whether to see notifications when you're duplicating your screen.

- Turn tips, tricks, and suggestions about Windows on or off.

Using System Information

System Information displays a wealth of information about your computer's hardware, drivers, and system software. If you're having any type of system-related issues, you should check System Information for possible clues as to the source of the problem.

System Information is a utility that displays details about your computer's hardware components, software, and drivers. You can use System Information to simply gather information about your computer or to diagnose issues. To open System Information, click Start, type **system info,** and press Enter. The main System Information window is shown in Figure 7.16.

FIGURE 7.16   The System Information window

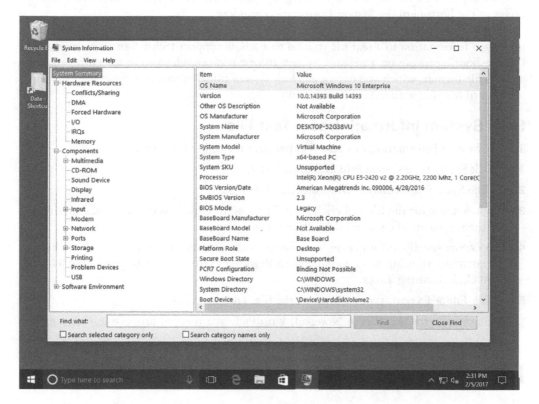

The left pane includes the following categories:

- **System Summary:** This category displays general information about your computer. You can view the name of the operating system, the name of the computer (system), the type of processor, and much more.

- **Hardware Resources:** This category displays details about your computer's hardware, such as whether any conflicts exist and the status of input/output (I/O) devices.
- **Components:** This category displays information about hardware devices and their drivers, such as disk drives, network adapters, and computer ports.
- **Software Environment:** This category displays details about system drivers, current print jobs and network connections, services, startup programs, and other system-related items.

System Information provides a search feature that enables you to quickly find specific information about your system. Just type the information you're looking for in the Find What box at the bottom of the window. For example, to see which programs launch at startup, type **startup** in the Find What box and click Find. You can narrow your search by selecting either the Search selected category only or Search category names only check boxes at the bottom of the System Information window.

When attempting to diagnose a system problem, it can be useful to export information in System Information to a text file to send to a fellow support technician or post on a troubleshooting forum on a website. System Information enables you to save information to an .nfo file format, which you can open from System Information, or export information to a standard text file with a .txt file extension.

Save System Information to a Text File

To save System Information to a text file, perform the following steps:

1. Click Start. Type **system info** and press Enter.

2. In the System Information window, click File ➤ Save.

3. Type a name for the file and click Save. The resulting file is very long and contains all of the information collected by System Information.

4. To export specific information from System Information to a text file, such as the list of currently running tasks, expand the Software Environment category in the left pane and click Running Tasks.

5. Click File ➤ Export, type a name for the file, and then click Save.

You can open the text files in Notepad, WordPad, or any word processing program.

Maintaining the Windows Registry

The Windows registry is a database of configuration settings for your computer. It's often referred to as the "brains" of a Windows operating system. The registry is self-sufficient and rarely requires maintenance, but you can use a reputable registry cleaner occasionally to remove settings that are no longer used.

The *Windows registry* is a database in Windows that stores user preferences, file locations, program configuration settings, startup information, hardware settings, and more. In addition, the registry stores the associations between file types and the applications that use them. For example, the registry holds the information that tells Windows to open the default media player program (usually Windows Media Player) when you double-click a music or movie file.

The registry is made up of keys, subkeys, and values, as shown in Figure 7.17. Registry keys are similar to folders in File Explorer in that the keys can have subkeys (like subfolders). Subkeys have values that make up the preferences, configuration settings, and so on of the operating system. Whenever you change a preference, install software or hardware, or essentially make any changes to the system, the changes are reflected in the Windows registry.

FIGURE 7.17 A portion of the Windows registry

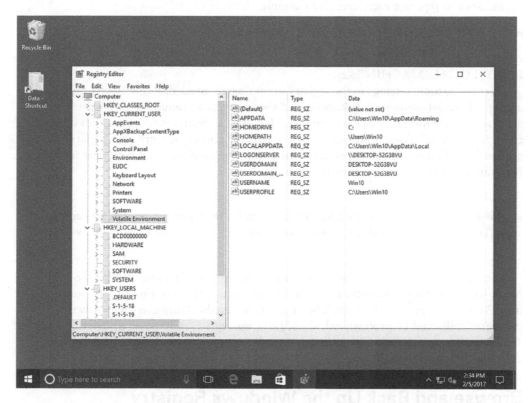

The registry is organized according to several logical sections, often referred to as hives, which are generally named by their Windows API definitions. The hives begin with HKEY and are often abbreviated to a three- or four-letter short name starting with "HK." For example, HKCU is HKEY_CURRENT_USER and HKLM is HKEY_LOCAL_ MACHINE. Windows Server 2016 has five Root Keys/HKEYs:

- **HKEY_CLASSES_ROOT:** Stores information about registered applications, such as the file association that tells which default program opens a file with a certain extension.

- **HKEY_CURRENT_USER:** Stores settings that are specific to the currently logged-on user. When a user logs off, the HKEY_CURRENT_USER is saved to HKEY_USERS.
- **HKEY_LOCAL_MACHINE:** Stores settings that are specific to the local computer.
- **HKEY_USERS:** Contains subkeys corresponding to the HKEY_CURRENT_USER keys for each user profile actively loaded on the machine.
- **HKEY_CURRENT_CONFIG:** Contains information gathered at run time. Information stored in this key is not permanently stored on disk, but rather regenerated at boot time.

Registry keys are similar to folders, which can contain values or subkeys. The keys within the registry follow a syntax similar to a Windows folder or file path, using backslashes to separate each level. For example:

`HKEY_LOCAL_MACHINE\Software\Microsoft\Windows`

refers to the subkey "Windows" of the subkey "Microsoft" of the subkey "Software" of the HKEY_LOCAL_MACHINE key.

Over time, some settings in the registry are no longer needed. Registry settings take up a relatively small amount of disk space, and the settings can remain in the registry without affecting the performance of the computer. However, a registry setting can also become corrupt. Microsoft doesn't provide tools to repair the registry directly, but registry cleaners are available that remove unnecessary settings (for programs that are no longer installed, for example) and can repair many problems.

 Some registry cleaners can actually harm your computer. Be sure to get a reputable program to avoid contaminating your PC with spyware and viruses.

You should back up your registry before running any maintenance program on it. Microsoft provides the Registry Editor utility to make changes to the registry and back it up. To open Registry Editor, click Start and type **regedit**. Only users with advanced computer skills and IT professionals should edit the registry. Changing or deleting a critical setting can prevent your computer from operating upon reboot. However, nearly anyone can safely back up the registry.

Browse and Back Up the Windows Registry

To back up the Windows registry, perform the following steps:

1. Open Registry Editor by clicking Start, typing **regedit,** and pressing Enter.
2. Expand keys in the left pane to view the associated subkeys. To view Microsoft-related subkeys, for example, click the gray arrow (>) to the left of the HKEY_CURRENT_USER key, click the SOFTWARE subkey, and then click the Microsoft subkey. Browse the list of Microsoft subkeys.

3. Similarly, expand the HKEY_LOCAL_MACHINE key, expand the SOFTWARE subkey, and then expand the Microsoft subkey. Another set of Microsoft-related subkeys appears.

4. Collapse (close up) all keys by clicking the down arrow to the left of each expanded entry in the left pane.

5. Click File ➤ Export, navigate to the location where you want to save the registry backup file, type a name for the backup in the File Name text box, and then click Save.

A best practice is to save registry backups to an external location, such as a USB flash drive, a CD/DVD, or a network drive.

Configuring and Managing Updates

Intruders and some viruses, worms, rootkits, spyware, and adware gain access to a system by exploiting security holes in Windows, Internet Explorer, Microsoft Office, or other software applications. Therefore, the first step you should take to protect yourself against malware is to keep your system up to date with the latest service packs, security patches, and other critical fixes.

Certification Ready

Why is it important to keep your system updated with the newest Windows updates?
Objective 6.3

Microsoft routinely releases security updates on the second Tuesday of each month, commonly known as *Patch Tuesday*. Although most updates are released on Patch Tuesday, there might be occasional patches (known as *out-of-band patches*) released at other times when the patches are deemed critical or time-sensitive.

Because computers are often used as production systems, you should test any updates to make sure they do not cause problems for you. Although Microsoft performs intensive testing, occasionally problems do occur, either as a bug or as a compatibility issue with third-party software. Therefore, always be sure you have a good backup of your system and data files before you install patches so that you have a back-out plan, if necessary.

Microsoft classifies updates as Important, Recommended, or Optional:

- **Important Updates:** These updates offer significant benefits, such as improved security, privacy, and reliability. They should be installed as they become available and can be installed automatically with Windows Update.

- **Recommended Updates:** These updates address noncritical problems or help enhance your computing experience. Although these updates do not address fundamental issues with your computer or Windows software, they can offer meaningful improvements.

- **Optional Updates:** These updates include updates, drivers, or new software from Microsoft to enhance your computing experience. You need to install these manually.

Depending on the type of update, Windows Update can deliver the following:

- **Security Updates:** A *security update* is a broadly released fix for a product-specific, security-related vulnerability. Security vulnerabilities are rated based on their severity, which is indicated in the Microsoft security bulletin as critical, important, moderate, or low.

- **Critical Updates:** A *critical update* is a broadly released fix for a specific problem addressing a critical, non-security-related bug.

- **Service Packs:** A *service pack* is a tested, cumulative set of hotfixes, security updates, critical updates, and updates, as well as additional fixes for problems found internally since the release of the product. Service packs might also contain a limited number of customer-requested design changes or features. After an operating system is released, many corporations consider the first service pack release as the time when the operating system has matured enough to be used throughout the organization.

Not all updates can be retrieved through Windows Update. Sometimes, Microsoft might offer the fix for a specific problem in the form of a hotfix or cumulative patch that you can install. A *hotfix* is a single cumulative package that includes one or more files that are used to address a problem in a software product, such as a software bug. Typically, hotfixes are made to address a specific customer situation, and they often have not gone through the same extensive testing as patches retrieved through Windows Update. A *cumulative patch* is multiple hotfixes combined into a single package.

Upgraded builds of Windows 10 will occasionally be made available, and will be identified by a version number based on year and month. The original version was 1507, because it was released in July of 2015. Microsoft's first major update was version 1511, which consisted of general bug fixes and improvements, streamlined activation, restored colored window title bars, integrated Skype, and improvements to the Edge browser. You can also use the Find My Device option under Settings ≻ Update & Security to use built-in tracking, so you can track your laptop or tablet—via GPS and location services—if you lose it.

In August of 2016, Microsoft released the *Windows 10 Anniversary Update*. It introduced a number of new features and enhancements over the previous November Update release, including new extension support for Microsoft Edge, biometric authentication support with Windows Hello, improvements to Cortana, and Windows Inking.

Configuring Windows Update Options

Windows Update provides your Windows 10 users with a way to keep their computers current by checking a designated server. The server provides software that patches security issues, installs updates that make Windows and your applications more stable, fixes issues with existing Windows programs, and provides new features. The server can be hosted by Microsoft or it can be set up and managed in your organization by running the Windows Server Update Services (WSUS) or System Center 2012 R2/2016 Configuration Manager.

When you first install Windows 10, you can choose how you want Windows Update to function. On a Windows 10 computer, you can open Settings and click Update & Security to open the Windows Update page (see Figure 7.18).

FIGURE 7.18   The Windows Update page

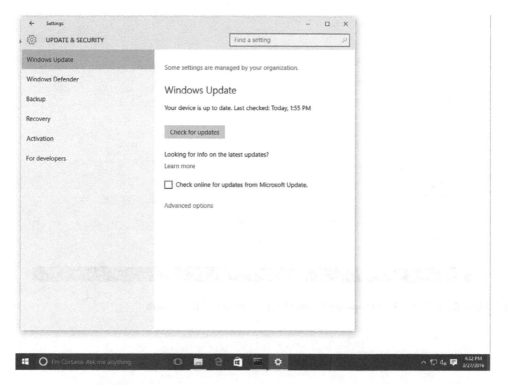

By clicking Advanced options, you can configure for Automatic Updates, get updates for other Microsoft products when Windows is updated, defer upgrades, and view update history (as shown in Figure 7.19).

For corporations, you can also use WSUS or System Center 2012 R2/2016 Configuration Manager to keep your systems updated. Smaller organizations might use WSUS or cloud-based services such as Microsoft Intune to keep systems up to date. The advantage of using one of these systems is that it allows you to test the patch, schedule the updates, and prioritize client updates. Once you determine a patch is safe, you can enable it for deployment.

When you click the Choose how updates are delivered option, the Updates from more than one place page appears (see Figure 7.20). Unless you are part of a corporation that is using WSUS or System Center 2012 R2/2016 Configuration Manager, you must use your Internet connection to retrieve updates from Microsoft. Starting with Windows 10, you can enable the Updates from more than one place option, which also allows you to get updates from other computers on the same network as your local computer and from computers on the Internet.

FIGURE 7.19   The Windows Update Advanced Options page

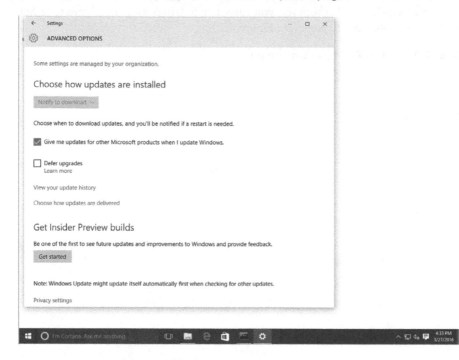

FIGURE 7.20   The Updates From More Than One Place page

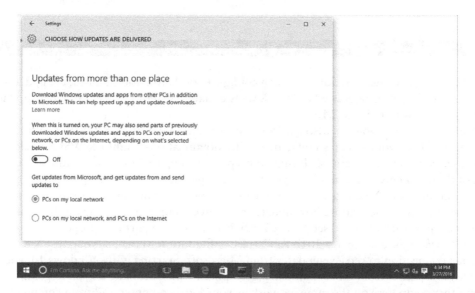

When you click Change active hours, you can configure when your system can be upgraded. The Restart options specifies when your machine can be rebooted, so that it can finish installing updates. In March 2017, Microsoft added a snooze option that prompts you when Windows 10 updates are available. Instead of automatically installing the update,

Windows 10 will wait up to three days before requiring the update to be installed. The snooze feature is designed to give you ample time to finish and save any crucial work.

Under Advanced options, you can select the "Give me updates for other Microsoft products when I update Windows" option. Some Windows 10 editions let you defer feature upgrades to your PC. By selecting the Defer upgrades option, new Windows features won't be downloaded or installed for several months. This option is usually used to help avoid problems with an update that might cause problems within your organization. You can also select the "Use my sign in info to automatically finish setting up my devices after an update" option.

> **WARNING**   Deferring upgrades does not affect security updates, but it does prevent you from getting the latest Windows features as soon as they are available.

Managing Update History and Rolling Back Updates

You can view your update history by clicking the Update History option. On the Update History page, each update includes the KB article number and the date installed. If you click Successfully installed on <date> for a specific update, it provides a short description of the update.

At the top of the Update History page, you can click Uninstall Updates to open the Control Panel Installed Updates page, as shown in Figure 7.21. To uninstall or roll back an update, right-click the desired update and choose Uninstall. You are then prompted to uninstall the update. When you click Yes, the update will be uninstalled.

FIGURE 7.21   The Control Panel Installed Updates page

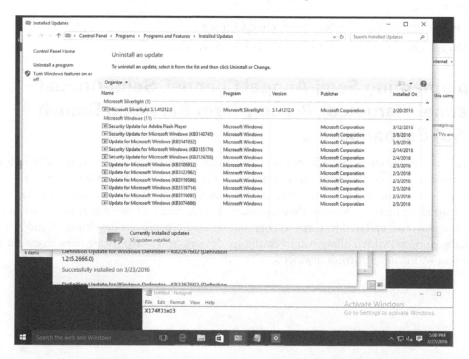

Implementing Insider Preview

In the past, the *Windows Insider program* (which was previously accessible to developers only) allowed users to sign up for early builds of the Windows operating system. Today, the Windows Insider program has been expanded to include enterprise testers and advanced users. This enables Microsoft to get feedback before a new feature or update is released to the general public and is a way to test upcoming Windows features before they are released to the general public.

If you decide to use the Insider Preview, you need to keep in mind that you will often be receiving updates to Windows that might not be fully tested. There are risks that these updates might take your system down and possibly corrupt data. So, you want to make sure that you only implement Insider Preview on test machines and make sure you have backups of all important data and programs.

Enable the Insider Preview Build

To enable the Insider Preview Build Updates, perform the following steps:

1. Log on to a computer running a genuine, activated copy of Windows 10 with an active Internet connection.
2. Click Start ➤ Settings.
3. In the Settings window, click Update & Security ➤ Windows Insider Program.
4. In the Get Insider Preview builds section, click Get Started.
5. Sign in with a Microsoft account.
6. When you are warned that the prerelease software and services may not be fully tested, click Next.
7. On the Before You Confirm page, click Confirm.
8. On the One More Step to Go page, click Restart Now.

Implementing Semi-Annual Channel, Semi-Annual Channel (Targeted), & Long-Term Servicing Branch (LTSB) Scenarios

Enterprise companies are usually not willing to upgrade to the newest version of Windows, and most responsible corporations would deploy the monthly updates that Microsoft publishes every month. However, these corporations are not usually willing to deploy new or updated features because they can cause a wide range of problems. So rather than force the new and updated features to corporations, Microsoft has developed Windows 10 servicing options, which allow you to configure devices into one of three tiers based on how often you want these features deployed.

As part of the association between Windows 10 and Office 365 ProPlus, Microsoft has adopted a common terminology to make it easier to understand the servicing process. There have been some name changes; Microsoft will be utilizing:

- **Semi-Annual Channel:** We will be referring to Current Branch (CB) as "Semi-Annual Channel (Targeted)," while Current Branch for Business (CBB) will simply be referred to as "Semi-Annual Channel."

- **Long-Term Servicing Channel:** The Long-Term Servicing Branch (LTSB) will be referred to as the Long-Term Servicing Channel (LTSC).

The new servicing terms can be found here:

https://docs.microsoft.com/en-us/windows/deployment/update/waas-overview

The Windows 10 servicing options or scenarios are shown in Table 7.1.

TABLE 7.1   The Windows 10 Servicing Options

Servicing Option	Availability of New or Upgraded Features	Minimum Length of Servicing Lifetime	Supported Editions
Semi-Annual Channel (Targeted) - (formerly called Current Branch (CB) servicing)	Receives upgrades immediately after Microsoft makes them publicly available.	18 months	Home, Pro, Education, Enterprise, IoT Core, Windows 10 IoT Core Pro (IoT Core Pro)
Semi-Annual Channel - (formerly called Current Branch for Business (CBB) servicing)	Defers receiving feature upgrades for four months after Microsoft makes them publicly available.	18 months	Pro, Education, Enterprise, IoT Core Pro
Long-Term Servicing Channel (LTSC) - (formerly called Long-Term Servicing Branch (LTSB))	Are available immediately after being published by Microsoft, but allows for long-term deployment of selected Windows 10 releases in low-change configuration (up to 10 years).	10 years	Enterprise LTSB

For systems that are configured for the *Semi-Annual Channel (Targeted)*, you will deploy the new features within four months after they are publicly released. This gives a corporation four months to deploy the new or updated features.

The Semi-Annual Channel servicing is a slower track, which gives you four months to test and evaluate the new or updated features, and then four months to test and deploy the new or updated features. Unless you are controlling your updates with Windows Server Update Services (WSUS), System Center Configuration Manager (SCCM), or some similar technology, you can use the Defer Upgrades option to move a computer into CBB servicing.

Long-Term Servicing Channel (LTSC) is similar to Windows 10 Enterprise, but will be a stripped-down version. It does include Internet Explorer 11, and is compatible with the Windows 32-bit version of Microsoft Office. It does not include Microsoft Edge, Windows Store Client, Cortana, Outlook Mail, Outlook Calendar, OneNote, Weather, News, Sports, Money, Photos, Camera, Music, or Clock. LTSC is intended for scenarios during which changes to software running on devices is limited to essential updates (vulnerabilities and other important issues).

Defending Your System from Malicious Software

One of the most challenging problems for computer users and administrators is to prevent viruses, worms, and other types of malware from infecting your computer. To protect against malicious software, make sure your system is updated, you are using a firewall to limit exposure to malware, and you are using an up-to-date antimalware software package.

Malicious software, sometimes called malware, is software designed to infiltrate or infect a computer system without the owner's informed consent. It is usually associated with viruses, worms, Trojan horses, spyware, rootkits, and dishonest adware. As a network administrator or computer technician, you will need to know how to identify malware, how to remove malware, and how to protect a computer from malware.

Because it is quite common for a computer to be connected to the Internet, there are more opportunities than ever for your computer to be infected by malware. In addition, over the last couple of years, the amount of malware that has been produced is staggering. You also have to make sure that if a computer gets infected on a network, it does not spread to other computers.

Many early forms of malware were written as experiments or practical jokes (known as pranks). Most of the time, these were intended to be harmless or merely annoying. However, as time went by, malware turned into a type of vandalism or a tool to compromise private information. In addition, malware can be used as a denial-of-service (DoS) tool, to attack other systems, networks, or websites, causing those systems to have performance problems or to become inaccessible.

Malware can be grouped into these categories:

- Viruses
- Worms
- Trojan horses
- Spyware and dishonest adware

A computer *virus* is a program that can copy itself and infect a computer without the user's consent or knowledge. Early viruses were usually some form of executable code that was hidden in the boot sector of a disk or as an executable file (a file name with an .exe or .com extension).

Later, as macro languages were used in software applications such as word processors and spreadsheets to enhance the power and flexibility of these programs, macros could be embedded within the documents. Unfortunately, these documents can infect other documents and can cause a wide range of problems on a computer system as the macro code is executed when you open the document.

Today's websites can be written in various programming and scripting languages and can include executable programs. Therefore, as you access the Internet, your system is under constant threat.

A *worm* is a self-replicating program that replicates itself to other computers over the network without any user intervention. Different from a virus, a worm does not corrupt or modify files on a target computer. Instead, it consumes bandwidth as well as processor and memory resources, slowing your system down or causing your system to be unusable. Worms usually spread by using security holes found within the operating system or TCP/IP software implementations.

A *Trojan horse* is a program named after the Trojan horse story in Greek mythology. A Trojan horse is an executable program that appears as a desirable or useful program. Since it appears to be a desirable or useful program, users are tricked into loading and executing the program on their systems. After the program is loaded, it can cause your computer to become unusable or it can bypass your system's security, allowing your private information (including passwords, credit card numbers, and social security numbers) to be read. Also, a Trojan horse may execute adware.

Spyware is a type of malware that is installed on computers and collects personal information or browsing habits, often without the user's knowledge. Spyware can also install additional software and redirect your web browser to other sites or change your home page.

One type of spyware is the keylogger, which records every key a user presses. When you type in credit card numbers, social security numbers, and passwords, that information gets recorded and is eventually sent to or read by someone without the user's knowledge. It should be noted that not all keyloggers are bad, since some corporations used them to monitor their corporate users.

Adware is any software package that automatically plays, displays, or downloads advertisements to a computer after the software is installed on it or while the application is being used. While adware may not necessarily be bad, it is often used with ill intent.

Many protection companies sell stand-alone antivirus, antispyware, and firewall programs that are bundled into Internet security products that usually provide additional features (such as antispam and anti-phishing filters, parental controls, and password vaults). At a minimum, every computer should have antivirus and antispyware software installed, along with a firewall. Every computer should also use the security settings found in the latest web browsers.

Understanding Windows Firewall

Windows Firewall comes with Windows 10 and other Windows versions to protect your computer from traffic entering through communications ports.

A *firewall* is a software program or device that monitors traffic entering and leaving a computer. This term comes from the building trades, where it refers to a special barrier designed to delay the advance of fire from one area to another. In the computer world, threats and attacks from malicious insiders are the "fire" advancing on computers connected to the Internet.

> Networks have firewalls, too—they are similar to computer firewalls, but are usually much more robust.

Microsoft provides Windows Firewall with Windows 10. The firewall is turned on automatically in new installations. To access Windows Firewall, click Start, type **firewall,** and press Enter. The Windows Firewall page indicates whether or not the program is enabled (see Figure 7.22) and what it's protecting.

FIGURE 7.22   The Windows Firewall page

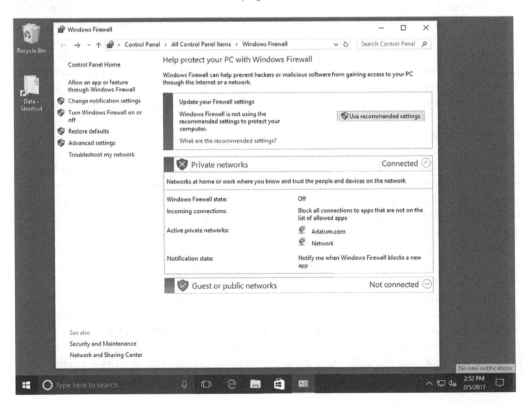

Sometimes a firewall works too well, blocking communications that you want to allow! For example, a newly installed program that needs to communicate with the Internet might not work because it's blocked by the firewall. In this case, click the Allow an app or feature through Windows Firewall command in the task pane of the Windows Firewall page. The Allowed Apps page appears (see Figure 7.23). To change settings, click the Change settings button. Click the Allow another program button. Scroll through the list to locate the program, select it, click Add, and then click OK.

FIGURE 7.23   The Windows Firewall Allowed Apps page

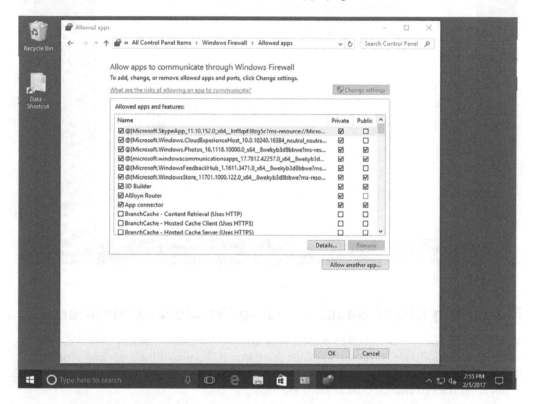

It's best to have only one firewall running on a computer. If you install an Internet security product, the new software should automatically turn off Windows Firewall. If you check Action Center and see that two firewalls are running, open the Windows Firewall page, click Turn Windows Firewall on or off in the task pane, click the Turn off Windows Firewall option (as shown in Figure 7.24), and then click OK. Reboot your computer and immediately check Action Center again to verify that only one firewall is enabled.

FIGURE 7.24   The Windows Firewall Customize Settings page

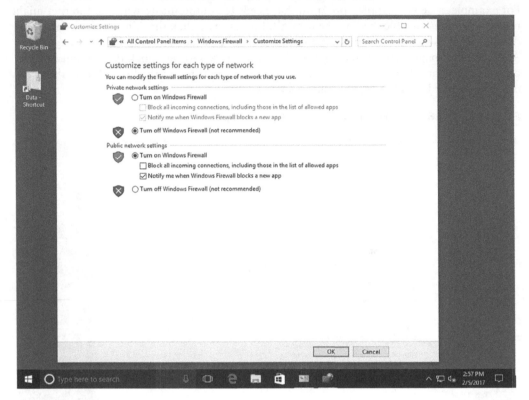

Managing Client Security Using Windows Defender

Windows Defender is designed to protect your computer against viruses, spyware, and other types of malware. It protects against these threats by providing real-time protection in which it notifies you if malware attempts to install itself on your computer or when an application tries to change critical settings.

Certification Ready

How does Windows Defender help protect your system? Objective 3.3

Windows Defender automatically disables itself if you install another antivirus product.

At the heart of Windows Defender are its definition files, which are downloaded from Windows Update. The definition files, which contain information about potential threats, are used by Windows Defender to notify you of potential threats to your system.

To access Windows Defender from the Windows 10 menu, click Start, type Windows Defender, and click Windows Defender in the results. Figure 7.25 shows the Windows Defender Home tab.

FIGURE 7.25   Viewing the Windows Defender Home tab

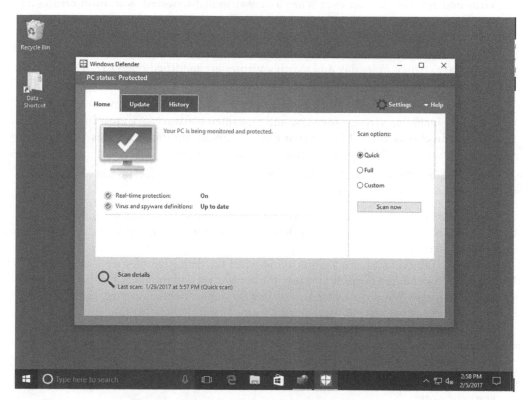

The Home tab allows you to check the status of Windows Defender, including whether Windows Defender is up to date and whether Windows Defender is protecting your system. It also gives you the option to initiate a scan.

On the Home tab, you should always watch for a green message indicating "Your PC is being monitored and protected" and you should also make sure your system is up to date. Other components include:

- **Real-Time Protection:** Real-time protection uses signature detection methodology and heuristics to monitor and catch malware behavior. Signature detection uses a vendor's definition files to detect malicious programs, which look for known patterns in files and processes. If the program contains code that matches the signature, the program most likely contains the virus. This works well when the threat has already been identified, but what happens in between the time the virus is released and the definition file is made available? That's where heuristics can help. It is used to monitor for suspicious activity by a program. Suspicious activity includes a program trying to copy itself into another program, a program trying to write to the disk directly, or a program trying to manipulate critical system files required by the operating system. These are indicators of possible malware activity that heuristics can detect.

- **Virus and Spyware Definitions:** When a new virus is discovered, Microsoft creates a new virus signature/definition update. Each definition file contains a piece of the actual virus code that is used to detect a specific virus or malware. During scans, the content on the computer is compared with information in the definition files. Because new viruses are created every day and existing viruses are modified regularly, it's important to keep your definitions updated.

- **Scan Options (Quick, Full, and Custom):** A Quick scan checks the areas that malicious software, including viruses, spyware, and unwanted software, are most likely to infect. A Full scan checks all the files on your disk, including running programs. A Custom scan is designed to check only locations and files you specify.

- **Scan Details**   This area of the Home tab provides information on when the last scan was performed on the computer.

The Update tab provides you with information about your virus and spyware definitions. It is important to keep these definitions current to ensure that your computer is protected at all times.

The Update tab provides information about when the definition files were created and the last time you updated them. It also lists the current version numbers for the virus and spyware definitions. Windows Defender updates the definition files automatically, but you can manually check for updates by clicking Update definitions on this tab.

The History tab provides information about items that have been detected in the past and the actions that were taken with them.

The categories of items are as follows:

- **Quarantined Items:** These items were not allowed to run but were not removed from your computer.

- **Allowed Items:** These items were allowed to run on your computer.

- **All Detected Items:** These items include all items detected on your computer.

Remove a Quarantined Item

To remove an item that has been quarantined, perform the following steps:

1. Open Windows Defender.
2. Click the History tab.
3. Click Quarantined Items.
4. Click View Details.

5. Select the detected item and read the description.

6. Click Remove.

If you click Windows Defender Settings, you will open the Windows 10 Settings, Update & Security ➤ Windows Defender page, as shown in Figure 7.26. The Settings page is where you can fine-tune how Windows Defender works.

FIGURE 7.26   The Windows Defender Settings page

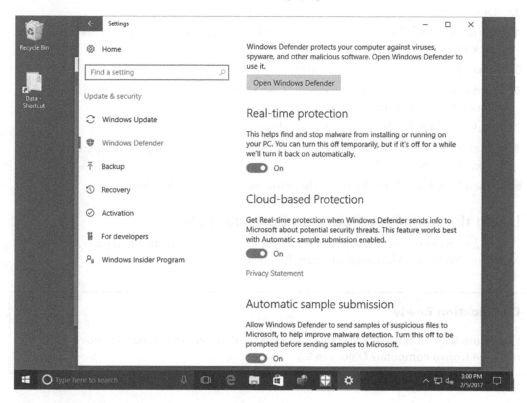

On the Settings page, you can:

- Enable or disable real-time protection.
- Select if you want to use cloud-based protection.
- Select the files and locations you want to exclude from the scanning process.
- Select the file types you want to exclude from the scan.
- Select the processes you want to exclude.
- Display the Windows 10 version information.
- Open Windows Defender.

To keep your system more secure, you should schedule a Windows Defender scan.

Schedule a Windows Defender Scan

To schedule a Windows Defender scan, log on with administrative privileges and then perform the following steps:

1. Click Start and type **taskschd.msc**. From the results, click Task Scheduler.

2. In the left pane, expand Task Scheduler Library ➤ Microsoft ➤ Windows ➤ Windows Defender.

3. Double-click Windows Defender Scheduled Scan.

4. In the Windows Defender Scheduled Scan Properties (Local Computer) dialog box, click the Triggers tab and click New.

5. In the Begin the task field, choose On a schedule.

6. Under Settings, select One time and in the Start field, change the time to 5 minutes from your current time.

7. Make sure the Enabled check box is selected and click OK.

8. To close the Windows Defender Scheduled Scan Properties (Local Computer) dialog box, click OK.

9. Open Windows Defender to see the status of the scan on the Home tab.

Using the Malicious Software Removal Tool

If your antimalware software cannot remove a virus or worm from a computer, try the Microsoft Windows Malicious Software Removal Tool (MSRT).

Certification Ready

How is the Microsoft Windows Malicious Software Removal Tool used to remove malware from a computer? Objective 3.3

Computers can become infected even with the best protection software running in the background. If you know your computer is infected with malware, such as Blaster, Mydoom, EyeStyle, or Poison, download and run the MSRT. This utility scans your computer for dangerous malware and attempts to remove it immediately.

Microsoft releases an updated version of the MSRT on Patch Tuesday each month, or more often if security threats are detected before the next Patch Tuesday updates. Microsoft recommends that you run the tool regularly, such as every week or two, as a supplement to your real-time antivirus software.

Windows MSRT helps keep Windows computers free from malware. MSRT finds and removes threats and reverses the changes made by these threats and or as a stand-alone tool.

MSRT can be downloaded from `https://www.microsoft.com/en-us/download/ malicious-software-removal-tool-details.aspx`.

Windows Update automatically downloads and runs MSRT in the background. This tool does not replace antimalware such as Windows Defender Antivirus.

After MSRT scans the computer and removes threats, it will display a report that lists the threats. It also generates a log file, `%windir%\debug folder\mrt.log`.

Skill Summary

In this lesson, you learned:

- Windows 10 comes with many built-in maintenance tools that can help to keep computers running at top performance. These tools include Disk Defragmenter, Disk Cleanup, Task Scheduler, and the Action Center Maintenance feature.

- Disk Defragmenter is a utility that helps improve your computer's performance by moving sectors of data on the hard disk, so that files are stored sequentially. This minimizes the movement a hard disk's arm must make to read all the sectors that make up a file or program.

- Task Scheduler enables you to schedule and automate a variety of actions, such as starting programs, displaying messages, and even sending emails. You create a scheduled task by specifying a trigger, which is an event that causes a task to run, and an action to be taken when the task runs.

- Intruders and some viruses, worms, rootkits, spyware, and adware gain access to a system by exploiting security holes in Windows, Internet Explorer, Microsoft Office, or other software applications. Therefore, the first step you should take to protect yourself against malware is to keep your system up to date with the latest service packs, security patches, and other critical fixes.

- One of the most challenging problems for computer users and administrators is to prevent viruses, worms, and other types of malware from infecting your computer. To protect against malicious software, make sure your system is updated, you are using a firewall to limit exposure to malware, and you are using an up-to-date antimalware software package.

Knowledge Assessment

You can find the answers to the following sections in the Appendix.

Multiple Choice

1. Which of the following Windows built-in utilities helps delete unnecessary files from a computer?
   A. Disk Defragmenter
   B. Disk Cleanup
   C. Task Scheduler
   D. Registry Editor

2. Which of the following Windows built-in utilities helps improve a computer's performance by moving sectors of data on the hard disk?
   A. Disk Defragmenter
   B. Disk Cleanup
   C. Task Scheduler
   D. Registry Editor

3. In Task Scheduler, which of the following commands creates a task using a wizard?
   A. Create Task
   B. Create Scheduled Task
   C. Create Task Automatically
   D. Create Basic Task

4. In Windows Defender, which of the following scans is *not* an available option?
   A. Quick
   B. Full
   C. Partial
   D. Custom

5. Which of the following is *not* part of the Maintenance section in Action Center?
   A. Check for solutions to problem reports
   B. Virus protection
   C. Backup
   D. Check for updates

6. If Action Center detects a maintenance or security issue that needs attention, which of the following indicates errors that require immediate attention?
   A. A red circle with a white X.
   B. A yellow triangle with a black exclamation point.

    C. An orange flashing triangle.

    D. A green box.

7. By default, the Windows 10 Disk Defragmenter utility is set to run how often?

    A. Every day

    B. Once a week

    C. Biweekly

    D. Once a month

8. Which of the following programs are always updated on Patch Tuesday?

    A. Windows Defender

    B. The Microsoft website

    C. The Malicious Software Removal Tool

    D. The Windows Firewall

9. Which of the following tools should be used to remove malware such as Mydoom from an infected computer?

    A. Malicious Software Removal Tool

    B. Windows Firewall

    C. Windows Defender

    D. Task Scheduler

10. Which of the following Windows 10 Servicing options receives updates immediately after Microsoft makes them publicly available?

    A. CB

    B. CBB

    C. LTSB

    D. CTSB

Fill in the Blank

1. A hard disk that is _____ has file data spread across many different sectors.

2. _____ is a utility that removes many kinds of unnecessary files from a computer.

3. In Task Scheduler, a _____ is an event that causes a task to run.

4. The _____ is a database in Windows that stores user preferences, file locations, program configuration settings, startup information, hardware settings, and more.

5. Microsoft provides regularly scheduled updates to the Windows operating system via the _____ feature.

6. _____ delivers updates for Microsoft software in addition to the Windows operating system.

7. _____ describes a wide variety of malicious software, such as viruses and worms that attack computers.

8. A _____ is a collection of updates issued from Microsoft after the last version of Windows or another Microsoft product was released.

9. _____ is Microsoft's free antimalware program.

10. _____ is used to view the computer's hardware, drivers, and system software.

True/False

1. Microsoft includes Windows built-in maintenance tools in the Maintenance Tools folder in Accessories.

2. Disk Cleanup can be run on demand, but the utility does not have its own scheduling feature.

3. Windows Update provides hotfixes and service packs for Windows computers.

4. Windows Defender protects only against spyware.

5. Windows Firewall is enabled automatically in new installations of Windows 10.

Case Scenarios

You can find the answers to the following sections in the Appendix.

Scenario 7-1: Automating Computer Maintenance and Program Launching

Maria is a busy freelance writer who uses her computer several hours a day to research and write articles for several national magazines and newspapers. Her computer, which runs Windows 10 Professional, must be running at peak performance with little downtime. Maria has little time to devote to computer maintenance tasks. She also uses Internet Explorer 11 and Microsoft Word 2016 every day and would like them to start automatically when Windows starts. Maria asks you for insight on how to maintain her computer with relatively little effort, and how to configure her computer to start programs automatically. Describe your recommended solution.

Scenario 7-2: Removing Viruses Safely

You are a support person for a computer consulting company. Rajeem is an independent tax consultant who calls you to report that he believes he infected his computer with a virus after downloading and installing a tax-related utility from the web. Describe your recommended solution.

Scenario 7-3: Gathering System Information

In an effort to troubleshoot an issue on a client computer, you posted a message on an online PC support forum. The forum moderator posts a message asking you to list all of the programs that launch at startup on the affected computer. Describe the easiest way to provide this information.

Scenario 7-4: Distributing Windows Updates Across a Network

You support Richman Investments, a brokerage firm that employs 20 brokers. Each broker has his own client computer, and the firm has a server running Windows Server. All the client computers are configured identically.

Over the past six months, some Windows updates have caused the computers to hang, leaving the brokers without computers to conduct business. Describe how to ensure that the Windows updates that install on client computers will not cause usability issues.

Lesson 8

Understanding Backup and Recovery Methods

Objective Domain Matrix

Technology Skill	Objective Domain Description	Objective Domain Number
Understanding Local, Network, and Automated Backup Methods	Understand backup and recovery methods	6.1
Restoring Previous Versions of Files and Folders	Understand backup and recovery methods	6.1
Configuring System Recovery	Understand backup and recovery methods	6.1

Key Terms

backup
File History
restore
restore point
safe mode

Windows 10 File Recovery drive
Windows 10 System Restore
Backup and Restore (Windows 7)
Windows Recovery Environment
(Windows RE or WinRE)

Understanding Local, Network, and Automated Backup Methods

With Windows 10, backups are better than ever. In this section, you'll learn about local, manual, and network backups and how to automate them.

Certification Ready

How are local, network, and automated backups created? Objective 6.1

A *backup* is a properly secured copy of files and folders—and sometimes settings— usually saved in a compressed format. A backup is created so you can *restore* the files and settings in the event of data loss from a hard disk failure, accidental erasure or disk formatting, or natural events. Most users hope they never need backups. When they do need backups, however, they need them *now*! And if they don't have backups, it's often too late—their files might be gone forever. You must be logged on as an administrator or a member of the Backup Operators group to back up a computer or data.

The best method to recover data is backup.

Restoring Previous Versions of Files and Folders

Backup and Restore (Windows 7) was designed to protect a computer in the event of a system failure by storing data on another medium (hard drive, network folder, or CD/DVD). It can also back up a system image of a computer, including applications.

Certification Ready

Which tool allows you to perform a traditional Windows backup of a drive? Objective 6.1

Backup and Restore (Windows 7), previously called Windows Backup and Restore and Windows 7 File Recovery, is available in Windows 10. However, because this feature has been superseded in favor of the new File History feature (discussed later), Microsoft does not recommend using both features at the same time. File History has been designed to check for an existing Windows Backup schedule. If one exists, it disables itself. To use the File History feature, delete the Windows Backup schedule if one has been enabled.

File History is designed to only back up personal files. To back up applications and system files, consider using Windows 7 backups or System Restore. If these tools do not meet your needs for managing your system and application files, the Backup and Restore (Windows 7) tool can be used in Windows 10 as an alternative to a third-party backup program.

The following exercise details how to use the Backup and Restore (Windows 7) feature to make a full system backup, including a system image.

Schedule a Windows 10 Backup to Include a System Image

To schedule a full Windows 10 backup to an external drive, log on with local administrative privileges and perform the following steps:

1. Connect an external drive. This drive must have enough capacity to store the data files and a system image.

2. Right-click Start and choose Control Panel.

3. In the Search Control Panel text box, type **File Recovery**. From the results, click Backup And Restore (Windows 7).

4. In the Backup And Restore (Windows 7) window (see Figure 8.1), click Set Up Backup.

FIGURE 8.1   Opening the Control Panel Backup and Restore (Windows 7)

5. On the "Select where you want to save your backup" screen, click the external drive, as shown in Figure 8.2.

FIGURE 8.2 Setting a location for the backup

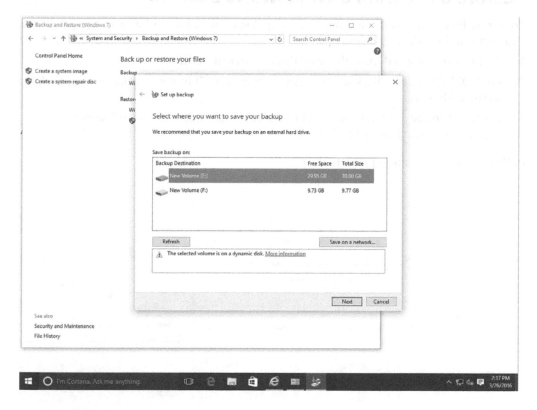

6. Click Next.

7. Click Let Windows Choose (Recommended) and click Next.

   Windows backs up data files saved in libraries, on the desktop, and in default Windows folders. It also creates a system image (only one per computer can be kept in the backup location), which can be used to restore a computer in case of failure.

   Another option is to select the "Let me choose to select specific libraries and folders" option and specify whether you want to include a system image as part of the backup.

8. Review the Backup Summary and click Change Schedule.

9. Click "Run backup on a schedule (recommended)" and click OK to accept the default settings.

   The backup is now scheduled to run every Sunday at 7:00 p.m.

10. Click the Save Settings And Run Backup button.

    Create a system repair disk to restore a system image if you do not have your Windows 10 installation media. Create this disk from within the Backup and Restore (Windows 7) control panel by clicking Create a system image.

Restore a File from a Windows 10 Backup

To restore files from a full Windows 10 backup, log on with local administrative privileges and perform the following steps:

1. Connect the external drive that contains the backed-up files.

2. On LON-CL1, using Backup and Restore (Windows 7) in the Restore section, click Restore My Files.

3. On the "Browse or search your backup for files and folders to restore" screen (see Figure 8.3), click Browse For Folders.

FIGURE 8.3   Restoring files

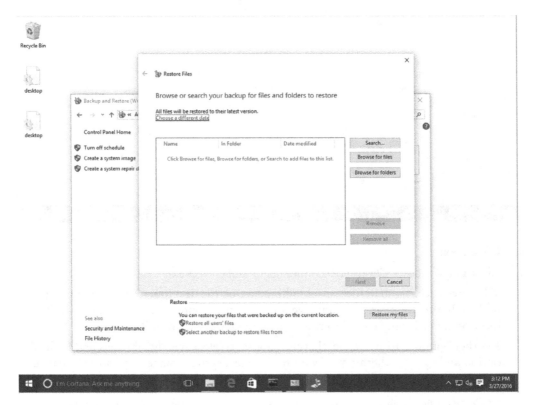

4. In the "Browse the backup for folders or drives" dialog box, click Administrator's Backup and click Add Folder.

5. Back on the "Browse or search your backup for files and folders to restore" screen, click Next.

6. When you are prompted to identify where to restore the files, confirm that the "In the original location" option is selected. Click Restore.

7. In the Copy File dialog box, select the "Do this for all conflicts" check box and click Copy And Replace.

8. Click Finish.

9. Close Backup and Restore (Windows 7).

Configuring System Recovery

There is no good time for a system to fail. But when it happens, you need to be ready. And the best way to be ready is to know the available recovery options and what steps to take before the problem occurs. However, the best method for system and data recovery is back up, back up, and back up some more.

A backup or the process of backing up refers to duplicating data so that these duplications can be accessed if you need to restore the original files after a data loss event. Backups can be used to restore entire systems following a disaster or to restore a small set of files that were accidentally deleted or corrupted.

When planning backups, decide where backup files will be stored. If files are stored at various locations throughout a corporation—including users keeping their files on their local computers—it is very difficult to back up all of these files. Therefore, you will most likely need to use some form of technology that will store files in a limited number of locations. For example, configure the user profiles for file redirection for the desktop and for My Documents so that files can be stored on a file server.

Configuring a System Restore

Windows 10 System Restore is a computer recovery option that backs up the settings and registry, but does not back up personal data.

Certification Ready

What is the simplest method to roll back settings when an application installation causes Windows instability? Objective 6.1

Windows 10 System Restore saves information about drivers, registry settings, programs, and system files in the form of restore points for drives with system protection turned on. A *restore point* is a representation of the state of a computer's system files and settings.

Use the restore points to return these items to an earlier state without affecting personal files. Create restore points prior to performing any major system event, such as installing a program or a new device driver.

By default, Windows 10 automatically creates restore points every seven days if no restore points have been created during that time period. Windows 10 also allows you to create restore points manually at any time.

Configure a System Restore

To configure a System Restore, log on with local administrative privileges and perform the following steps:

1. Click Start and type **System Restore**. From the results, click Create A Restore Point.

 Another way to access System Restore is via Control Panel ➤ System and Security ➤ System ➤ System Protection.

2. Click the C: drive, click Configure, and then make sure "Turn on system protection" is selected, as shown in Figure 8.4.

FIGURE 8.4   Confirming system protection is enabled

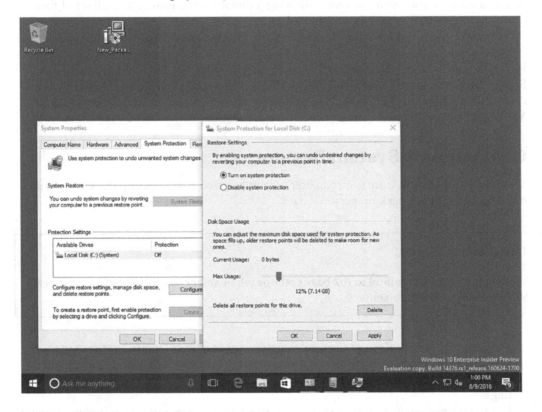

3. Drag the Max Usage slider to 10 percent. This adjusts the disk space for system protection. When the space fills up, older restore points are deleted to make room for new ones.

4. Click Apply and click OK.

5. Click Create to create a new restore point.

6. In the Description text box, type text that describes the name of the restore point.

7. Click Create.

8. When notified that the restore point was created successfully, click Close.

9. Click OK to accept the settings and close the System Properties dialog box.

In most cases, the most recent restore point should be used, but you can choose from a list of restore points if more are available. The best approach is to use the restore point that was created just before you started experiencing problems with the computer.

In the following exercise, assume that an application was installed and the system is not functioning normally. To return the computer to a functioning state, use the restore point you just created.

Perform a System Restore Using a Restore Point

To perform a System Restore using a restore point, log on with local administrative privileges and perform the following steps:

1. Click Start and type **System Restore**. From the results, click Create a restore point.

2. Click System Restore.

3. Click Next to start the System Restore Wizard. A System Restore does not affect documents, pictures, or other personal data. Recently installed programs and drivers may be uninstalled.

4. Select the desired restore point (see Figure 8.5) and click Scan For Affected Programs. After the scan is complete, Windows 10 lists any programs and drivers that will be deleted, as well as programs and drivers that might be restored.

FIGURE 8.5   Selecting a restore point

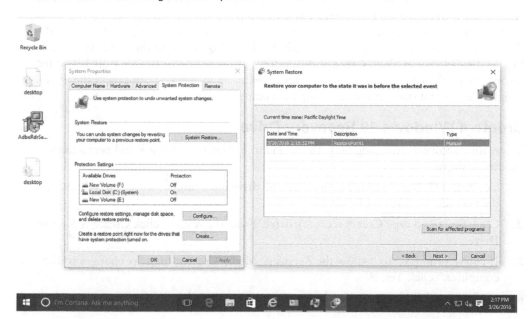

5. Click Close and click Next.

6. Click Finish.

7. If you changed your Windows password recently, create a password reset disk by clicking Start and then searching for "Create a password reset disk."

8. Click Yes to begin the System Restore process. Windows restarts the computer, restores the files and settings, restores the registry, and then removes temp files as part of the restore process.

9. After the restore process is complete, log back on to the system.

Configuring a Windows 10 File Recovery Drive

If a system fails to boot and Windows 10 installation media is not available, create a recovery drive that includes a Windows 10 boot environment and troubleshooting tools to regain access to the computer.

With improvements in operating system design, system crashes have been reduced over the years. The key word in that last sentence is *reduced*, not eliminated; therefore, it's important to have the right tools in place to recover from a system failure even when you can't start the Windows 10 system.

A *Windows 10 File Recovery drive* can help by providing enough of a boot environment to get back into the system to begin the troubleshooting process. It can be used to refresh or reset a computer, restore a computer to a previously created System Restore point, recover a Windows installation from a specific system image file, automatically fix startup problems, and perform advanced troubleshooting from the command prompt.

If you create a Windows 10 File Recovery drive on a Windows 10 32-bit system, you cannot use it to repair a 64-bit system, and vice versa.

After creating the recovery drive, you need to enable the system to boot from a USB device in the basic input/output system (BIOS). When booting into the drive, the Windows logo is displayed on a black screen and Windows prompts you to choose your keyboard layout. Next, the Choose an Option screen appears, on which you can access the troubleshooting tools and start troubleshooting the computer.

Create a Windows 10 Recovery Drive

To create a recovery drive, log on with local administrative privileges and perform the following steps:

1. Connect a USB drive to the computer. The drive must hold at least 256 MB and all data on the drive must be deleted.

2. Click Start and type **Create recovery drive**. From the results, click Create A Recovery Drive.

3. If you're prompted to "Allow the Recovery Media Creator to make changes to the computer," click Yes.

4. Click Next. Windows 10 searches and displays the available drives.

5. Click Next to use the drive you inserted.

6. After reviewing the "Everything on the drive will be deleted" message, click Create.

7. Click Finish.

Configuring File History

The File History feature provides options for backing up and recovering access to personal files in case of a system problem.

File History is a feature in Windows 10 that is designed to keep personal files safe. It enables users who are not administrators to select an external drive or a folder on the network, and it automatically backs up and restores their personal files.

In Windows 10, File History simplifies the process of protecting personal files. It eliminates the need to use a more complicated backup process included with previous releases of the operating system and introduces a process that is automatic and transparent to the user. It is disabled by default, so enable it to take advantage of its features.

File History scans for changes to your personal files. When a change is detected, the file is moved to an external location you specify, so you can recover previous versions of files if necessary. To optimize performance, File History consults the NTFS change journal to determine whether a file has changed instead of scanning, opening, and reading directories on the volume. By default, File History backs up everything in your libraries, desktop, and favorites. The libraries contain items such as My Documents, My Music, My Pictures, and Public document folders. File History does not back up your system and application files.

File History does not require administrative privileges to set up and run. The user can decide when to turn it on and off, select the external drive to use, and restore files without having to contact an administrator. Although File History does not back up files to the cloud as OneDrive does, it can be used to back up the OneDrive folder if you are using the OneDrive desktop app for Windows.

The following exercise describes the process to turn on File History, which automatically begins scanning and copying all your files to an external USB drive.

Enable File History

To enable File History, log on with a domain user account and perform the following steps:

1. Connect an external drive.

2. Click Start and type **File History**. From the results, choose "Restore your files with File History."

3. Click Turn On (see Figure 8.6).

    This option creates a folder named FileHistory on the selected drive and automatically begins copying the files to the drive.

FIGURE 8.6   Turning on File History

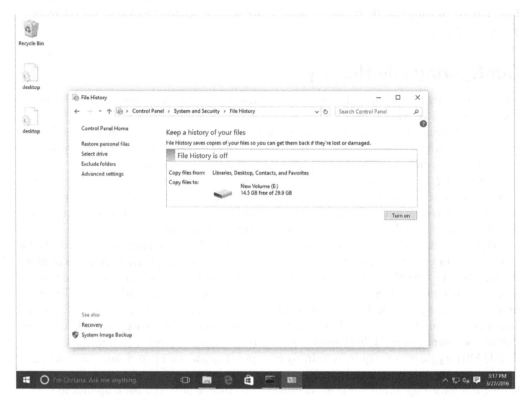

4. Close the File History window.

5. Right-click the desktop and choose New ➤ Text Document.

6. Type **FileHistoryTest** for the name and press Enter.

    This file will be used in the next exercise.

The File History window also includes the following two settings:

Exclude Folders   If you don't want to save copies of specific folders or libraries, specify them here.

Advanced Settings   You can identify the folders to exclude, the frequency with which they are backed up, and the amount of cache space to set aside for them.

When you click the Advanced Settings link, the Advanced Settings window opens (see Figure 8.7).

FIGURE 8.7   Configuring Advanced Settings

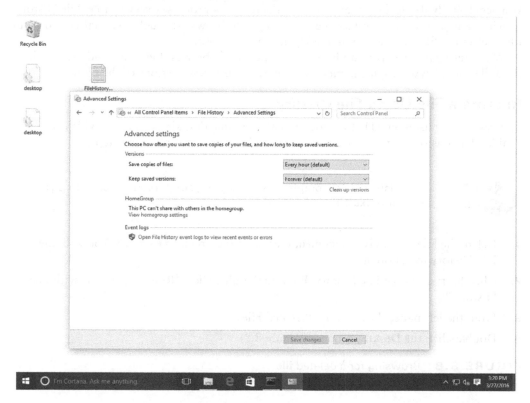

The Versions section includes the following settings:

- **Save Copies of Files:** The default is set to copy files every hour. Options include every 10, 15, 20, or 30 minutes; every 3, 6, or 12 hours; or daily.

- **Keep Saved Versions:** The default is Forever, but you can also set it to keep until space is needed; 1, 3, 6, or 9 months; or 1 or 2 years.

- **Clean Up Versions:** Settings here are used to configure when files and folders older than a certain age are deleted. Files and folders/versions that were excluded or removed from your libraries are also deleted. Options here include: All but the latest one; Older than 1, 3, 6, or 9 months; Older than 1 year (default); and Older than 2 years.

If you have a HomeGroup, use the HomeGroup section to recommend the drive to other HomeGroup members. Each HomeGroup member can decide whether to accept the recommendation. If they do, their information is automatically backed up to the network share you set up.

Windows 10 enables you to restore files through a familiar File Explorer interface after File History has copied all files to an external location.

As files are created and deleted over time, File History keeps track of each version. If you accidentally delete a file that you need, the recovery process is very simple. File History provides a new recovery interface that enables you to browse through a virtual view of your files, select the file you want, and quickly get back to work.

When restoring files, you can browse your personal libraries, files, and folders; search for a file using keywords, file names, and dates; and preview versions of the files.

Restore a File Using File History

To restore a file using File History, log on with the same domain account in which you enabled File History in the previous exercise, and perform the following steps:

File History must complete its backup of your personal files before you start this exercise.

1. Delete the FileHistoryTest document created in the previous exercise. You will now use File History to restore it.

2. Click Start and type **File History**. From the results, click "Restore your file with File History."

3. From the left pane, click Restore Personal Files.

4. Double-click the Desktop icon (see Figure 8.8).

FIGURE 8.8   Browsing for a deleted file

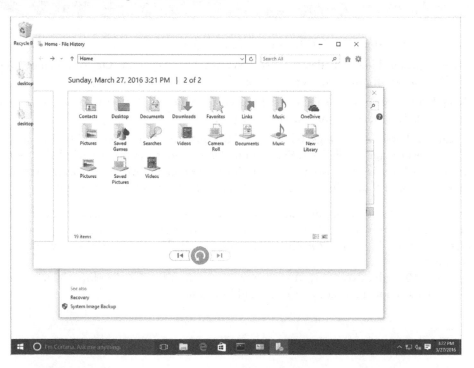

5. Double-click the FileHistoryTest document.

   You can now view its contents. If there are multiple versions of the same file, use the left and right buttons to see each version before choosing the file to restore.

6. Click the Restore To Original Location button (see Figure 8.9).

FIGURE 8.9 Clicking the Restore to Original Location button

7. Confirm that the FileHistoryTest.txt document has been restored and then close the Desktop window.

Performing Recovery Operations Using Windows Recovery

The *Windows Recovery Environment (Windows RE or WinRE)* can be used to repair common causes of unbootable operating systems. It is based on the Windows Preinstallation Environment (Windows PE).

To access WinRE, boot the computer with the Windows 10 installation disk. When the Windows setup program starts, click Next. Then, click the Repair your computer option. Alternatively, if you are logged into Windows, run the Shutdown /r /o command. To reset the PC or access advanced options, click Troubleshoot. If you click Advanced options, the following options are available, as shown in Figure 8.10.

FIGURE 8.10   Accessing Advanced Options

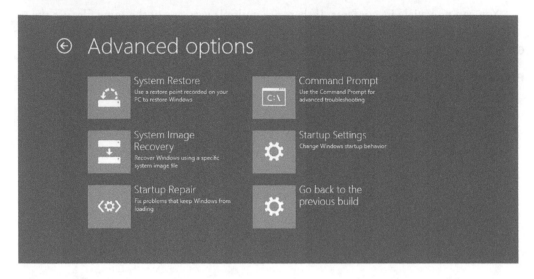

- **System Restore:** Can restore your system to a chosen restore point.
- **System Image Recovery:** Can use a system image file that you create with the recimg. exe command.
- **Startup Repair:** Reboots into a specific Windows Recovery Environment program known as Start Repair and runs a diagnosis and repair routine that seeks to make the PC bootable again.
- **Command Prompt:** Allows you to access a command prompt while in safe mode.
- **Startup Settings:** Reboots Windows and provides a list of advanced boot options (see Figure 8.11), such as safe mode, change video resolution, start debugging mode or boot logging, run in safe mode, disable driver signature checks, disable early launch antimalware scans, and disable automatic restart after failure.
    - **Enable Debugging:** Starts Windows in an advanced troubleshooting mode intended for IT professionals and system administrators.
    - **Enable Boot Logging:** Creates the file ntbtlog.txt that lists all the drivers that are installed during startup and that might be useful for advanced troubleshooting.
    - **Enable Low-Resolution Video:** Starts Windows using the current video driver and using low resolution (640 x 480) and refresh rate settings. Use this mode to reset the display settings.
    - **Enable Safe Mode:** Starts Windows with a minimal set of drivers and services. If you make a change to the system and Windows no longer boots, try safe mode.
    - **Enable Safe Mode With Networking:** Starts Windows in safe mode and includes the network drivers and services needed to access the Internet or other computers on the network. It should not be used if you suspect malware.

- **Enable Safe Mode With Command Prompt:** Starts Windows in safe mode with a command prompt window instead of the usual Windows interface.

- **Disable Driver Signature Enforcement:** Allows drivers containing improper signatures to be loaded.

- **Disable Early Launch Antimalware Protection:** If problems are caused by an antivirus program, stop the early launch antimalware protection, which allows you to update your virus definitions and perform further scans.

- **Disable Automatic Restart After Failure:** Prevents Windows from automatically restarting if an error causes Windows to fail. Choose this option only if Windows is stuck in a loop where Windows fails, attempts to restart, and fails again repeatedly.

FIGURE 8.11   Accessing Startup Settings

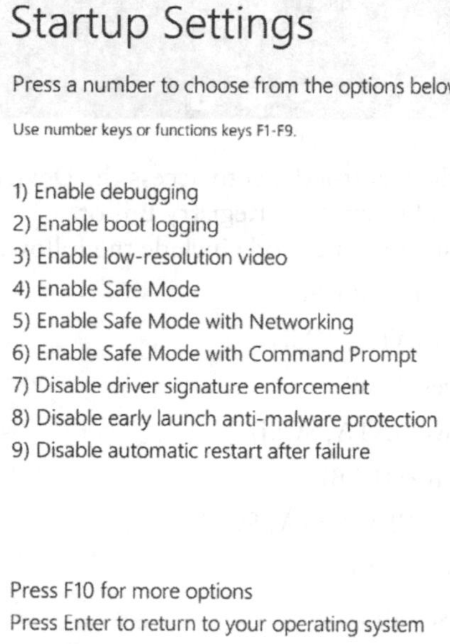

Startup Settings

Press a number to choose from the options below:

Use number keys or functions keys F1-F9.

1) Enable debugging
2) Enable boot logging
3) Enable low-resolution video
4) Enable Safe Mode
5) Enable Safe Mode with Networking
6) Enable Safe Mode with Command Prompt
7) Disable driver signature enforcement
8) Disable early launch anti-malware protection
9) Disable automatic restart after failure

Press F10 for more options
Press Enter to return to your operating system

Safe mode is useful for troubleshooting problems with programs and drivers that might not start correctly or that might prevent Windows from starting correctly. If a problem doesn't reappear when you start in safe mode, eliminate the default settings and basic device drivers as possible causes. If a recently installed program, device, or driver prevents Windows from running correctly, start the computer in safe mode and then remove the program that's causing the problem. See Figure 8.12.

FIGURE 8.12   Windows 10 safe mode

While in safe mode, use the Control Panel to access the Device Manager, Event Viewer, System Information, command prompt, or Registry Editor.

Devices and drivers that start in safe mode include the following:

- Floppy disk drives (internal and USB)
- Internal CD-ROM drives (ATA, SCSI)
- External CD-ROM drives (USB)
- Internal DVD-ROM drives (ATA, SCSI)
- External DVD-ROM drives (USB)
- Internal hard disk drives (ATA, SATA, SCSI)
- External hard disk drives (USB)
- Keyboards (USB, PS/2, serial)
- Mice (USB, PS/2, serial)
- VGA video cards (PCI, AGP)

Windows services that start in safe mode include the following:

- Windows event log
- Plug and Play
- Remote procedure call (RPC)
- Cryptographic Services
- Windows Management Instrumentation (WMI)

Devices and services that start in safe mode with networking include the following:

- Network adapters (wired Ethernet and wireless 802.11x)
- Dynamic Host Configuration Protocol (DHCP)
- DNS
- Network connections
- TCP/IP NetBIOS Helper
- Windows Firewall

Using Advanced Boot Options

The Windows 10 advanced boot options can be used to troubleshoot any errors that prevent Windows 10 from booting properly.

FIGURE 8.13   Advanced Boot Options screen

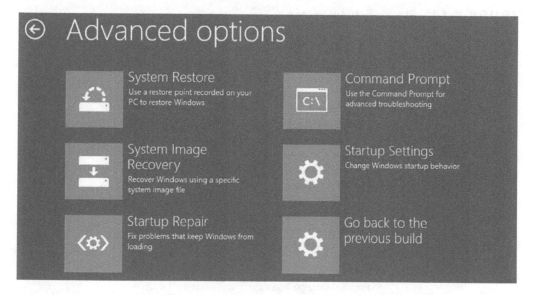

To access the Windows 10 advanced boot options, start or reboot the computer and press the F8 key after the firmware POST process but before Windows 10 is fully loaded. This brings up the Advanced Boot Options menu, which provides options for booting Windows 10.

Starting in Safe Mode

When a computer does not start, one of the troubleshooting techniques is to try to simplify the configuration. This is important when there is an unknown cause and you have a complex configuration. If the issue is in the basic configuration, you have a starting point for troubleshooting.

If Windows 10 does not load, an administrator can attempt to load the operating system in Safe Mode. When running in safe mode, an administrator can simplify the Windows configuration. Safe Mode only loads the drivers that are needed to get the computer up and running.

The drivers that are loaded with Safe Mode include those for the mouse, monitor, keyboard, hard drive, video driver, and default system services.

Safe Mode is considered a diagnostic mode, so you do not have access to all of the features and devices.

Windows 10 offers a few settings when trying to repair a Windows 10 system.

FIGURE 8.14   Startup Settings screen

Startup Settings

Press a number to choose from the options below:

Use number keys or functions keys F1-F9.

1) Enable debugging
2) Enable boot logging
3) Enable low-resolution video
4) Enable Safe Mode
5) Enable Safe Mode with Networking
6) Enable Safe Mode with Command Prompt
7) Disable driver signature enforcement
8) Disable early launch anti-malware protection
9) Disable automatic restart after failure

Press F10 for more options
Press Enter to return to your operating system

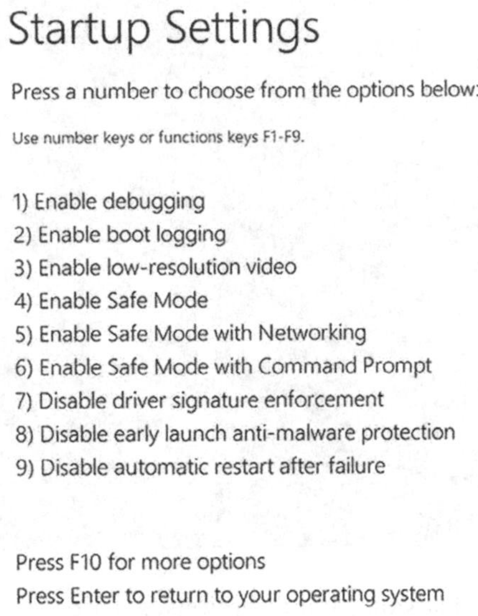

When the Startup Settings screen appears, you can choose to enter Safe Mode. Once a computer is booted into Safe Mode, you will see the text Safe Mode in the four corners of your desktop.

FIGURE 8.15   A computer running in Safe Mode

If you boot to Safe Mode, check all of the computer's hardware and software settings in Device Manager to try and determine why the machine will not boot properly. After steps have been taken to correct the problem, try to boot to Windows 10 normally.

Booting Your Computer to Safe Mode

1. Turn on the Windows 10 system.
2. During the boot process, press the F8 key to access the Boot Options menu.
3. At the Recovery screen, choose See Advanced Repair Options.
4. At the Choose An Option screen, choose the Troubleshoot option.
5. At the Troubleshoot screen, choose Advanced Options.
6. At the Advanced Options screen, choose Startup Settings.
7. At the Startup Settings screen, click the Restart button. The system will reboot into the Startup Settings screen.
8. At the Startup Settings screen, choose 5) Enable Safe Mode With Networking.
9. When Windows 10 starts, log in.

Recovering Files from OneDrive

Microsoft OneDrive is built into Windows 10 by default and is a subscription-based storage system. OneDrive is a cloud-based storage subscription so users can store their documents and then access those documents from anywhere in the world (provided there is Internet access).

OneDrive was designed for a home user who wants to store data in a safe, cloud-based environment. OneDrive, when initially released, was also for corporate environments, but, with the release of Windows Azure, OneDrive is directed more towards home users or corporate users to store personal documents in the cloud.

Configuring OneDrive

1. Open OneDrive.

2. Log into OneDrive using your Microsoft account.

3. You will see a screen that shows where files will be located on the system. Click the Next button.

4. At the Sync Files screen, choose what folders to sync with Microsoft and click Next. A screen will appear telling you that your OneDrive is set up and ready to go.

5. Click the Open My OneDrive Folder button to open your folders and Microsoft OneDrive.

6. Close OneDrive.

Using Last Known Good Configuration

The Last Known Good Configuration option was available in Windows XP, Vista, and 7 only. In Windows 8, 8.1, and 10, use Safe Mode instead.

The Last Known Good Configuration was used to load the last working version of Windows. However, it was replaced every time you logged on to the computer.

In Windows 8 and Windows 10, the Last Known option is no longer included.

Skill Summary

In this lesson, you learned:

- A backup is a properly secured copy of files and folders—and sometimes settings—usually saved in a compressed format. A backup is created so you can restore the files and settings in the event of data loss from a hard disk failure, accidental erasure or disk formatting, or natural events.

- Backup and Restore (Windows 7) was designed to protect a computer in the event of a system failure by storing data on another medium (hard drive, network folder, or CD/DVD). It can also back up a system image of a computer, including applications.

- Windows 10 System Restore saves information about drivers, registry settings, programs, and system files in the form of restore points for drives with system protection turned on. A restore point is a representation of the state of a computer's system files and settings.

- A Windows 10 File Recovery drive can help by providing enough of a boot environment to get back into the system to begin the troubleshooting process. It can be used to refresh or reset a computer, restore a computer to a previously created System Restore point, recover a Windows installation from a specific system image file, automatically fix startup problems, and perform advanced troubleshooting from the command prompt.

- File History is a feature in Windows 10 that is designed to keep personal files safe. It enables users who are not administrators to select an external drive or a folder on the network, and it automatically backs up and restores their personal files.

- The Windows Recovery Environment (Windows RE or WinRE) can be used to repair common causes of unbootable operating systems. It is based on the Windows Preinstallation Environment (Windows PE).

Knowledge Assessment

You can find the answers to the following sections in the Appendix.

Multiple Choice

1. Backups of data can be stored on which of the following devices or media? (Choose all that apply.)

    A. CD/DVD

    B. The same drive on which you are storing the backup

    C. USB

    D. Hard drives

    E. Network

2. Which program allows you to perform a standard backup of Windows including the System image?

    A. File History

    B. Windows 10 Restore

    C. Backup and Restore (Windows 7)

    D. Windows 10 File Recovery drive

3. Which of the following is a representation of the state of a computer's system files and settings?

    A. Restore point

    B. File History backup

    C. Windows 10 File Recovery drive

    D. Windows Recovery Environment

4. Which of the following options are likely to restore a system in which a System Restore was performed from a restore point, but the issue was not resolved and now the computer doesn't boot? (Choose all that apply.)

    A. Roll back to another restore point.

    B. Manually delete all files that changed.

    C. Undo the System Restore.

    D. Restart the machine.

5. What can be used to repair common causes of unbootable operating systems?

    A. Device Manager

    B. File History

    C. Backup and Restore (Windows 7)

    D. Windows Recovery Environment

6. Which of the following is the Windows Recovery Environment based on?

   A. Windows Backup

   B. DOS boot disk

   C. Windows PE

   D. Windows installation ISO

7. Which of the following recovery boot options should be avoided when the affected computer has been infected by a virus?

   A. Safe Mode

   B. Safe Mode with Networking

   C. Repair Your Computer

   D. Safe Mode with Command Prompt

8. Which of the following indicates how often Windows 10 automatically creates restore points by default?

   A. Every day

   B. Once every 3 days

   C. Once every 7 days

   D. Once every 30 days

9. Which Windows 10 feature is used to protect personal files by automatically backing up those files?

   A. File History

   B. File Recovery

   C. System Restore

   D. Windows backup

10. Before installing some new inventory software, which of the following precautions can be taken to protect a system so that if something goes wrong, the changes can be undone?

    A. Install the application in safe mode.

    B. Create an image with the recovery disk.

    C. Perform a Windows backup.

    D. Create a restore point.

Fill in the Blank

1. The best method for recovering data is performing regular _____.

2. When you change your Windows password, you should create a _____ disk.

3. A _____ is a properly secured copy of files and folders—and sometimes settings—usually saved in a compressed format.

4. A user must be logged on as an administrator or a member of the _____ to back up a computer or data.

5. Use _____ to restore an earlier version of a file.

6. To back up a drive in Windows 10, open the Control Panel and click _____.

7. If a new device driver has been added and the system is not responding, boot to the Advanced Options menu and choose _____.

8. To find the text file that contains your driver information after enabling boot logging, look in the _____ folder for a file named ntbtlog.txt.

9. A Windows 10 _____ can provide enough of a boot environment to get back into the system to begin the troubleshooting process.

10. Use a _____ to roll back a computer system to an earlier point in time.

True/False

1. Windows 10 enables users to choose exactly what to back up to a folder.

2. The traditional backup program that comes with Windows 10 is called Windows 10 File Recovery.

3. Windows 10 allows users to control how much hard drive space backups can use.

4. File History can be configured to back up the registry files.

5. Users can restore individual data files from a system image backup.

Case Scenarios

You can find the answers to the following sections in the Appendix.

Scenario 8-1: Scheduling File Backups

You provide technical support for PBJ&S, a small environmental consulting firm. Dina, the graphic artist, creates a lot of maps for client reports. Her Windows 10 Professional computer automatically backs up files every Sunday starting at 7:00 p.m. Dina reported recently that her computer was still backing up files when she arrived for work the last two Monday mornings. What can you do to help ensure that Dina's files are backed up by Monday morning?

Scenario 8-2: Installing from an Image

The owner of PBJ&S approved funds to purchase a new computer for Dina because an upgrade to her main mapping software requires more memory than her current computer's motherboard can handle. The new computer will be the same make and model but will have more memory and will have a much larger hard disk. You also ordered a 1 TB external USB drive for backups. When the new computer arrives, describe how to quickly get it up and running for Dina.

Scenario 8-3: Creating a System Repair Disc

Stanley works for your organization from his home office on a company-owned computer. He called your cell phone while you were at a restaurant having lunch. He said his computer has been having all kinds of problems lately and that it takes a long time for Windows to start. You suspect his Windows system files have become corrupted. Describe how to recover his system.

Scenario 8-4: Resolving a Driver Problem Using Recovery Boot Options

You recently installed a new video adapter in Jeffrey's desktop computer using the driver supplied on the CD in the adapter packaging. When Windows starts, the words on the screen are unreadable. Describe your recommended solution.

Appendix

Answer Key

Lesson 1: Installing and Upgrading Client Systems

Answers to Knowledge Assessment

Multiple Choice Answers

1. b, c, d. Windows 10 Pro, Windows 10 Enterprise, Windows 10 Education

2. a. Windows 10 Media Creation tool

3. c, d. Education, Enterprise

4. b. BranchCache

5. b. Activation

6. c. ZTI

7. b. LTI

8. b. Windows 10 Home

9. c, d. Open the System window, Run the System Information utility.

10. d. In a confirmation email received after purchasing and downloading Windows 10 online.

Fill in the Blank Answers

1. upgrade path
2. Activation
3. 32
4. upgrade
5. High Touch Installation (HTI)
6. Pro
7. Enterprise
8. Zero Touch Installation (ZTI)
9. Windows Deployment Services
10. operating system as a service.

True/False Answers

1. F
2. F

3. F

4. T

5. F

Answers to Business Case Scenarios

1. Install the new computer with Windows 10. You will also have to install all of the user's programs on the new machine. You can then use USMT to transfer the files and settings from the Windows 7 machine to Windows 10. User State Migration Tool (USMT) requires that you run ScanState to gather the settings and data files and LoadState to copy the settings and data files to the new system.

2. Danielle should back up files and settings on all computers. She can then perform in-place upgrade installations to Windows 10 Pro on the computers running Windows 7 and 8.1.

3. Randi can run a word processor, spreadsheet application, a web browser, and an email client on a computer with a 2 GHz processor, 4 GB of RAM, and at least a 250 GB hard drive. The computer should run Windows 10 Pro. Pooja's graphics programs may require at least 8 GB of RAM and 500 GB or more of hard disk space, and should run Windows 10 Pro. Danielle should acquire a tablet for Stan. The network would run Windows 10 Pro.

4. The organization will need a total of 175 Windows 10 licenses. The computers can be upgraded to the same edition. Therefore, Windows 7 Pro and Windows 8.1 Pro can be upgraded to Windows 10 Pro. The 32-bit machines can be upgraded to the 32-bit versions of Windows 10 and the 64-bit machines can be upgraded to 64-bit versions of Windows 10.

To deploy Windows, you can use the Windows 10 Media Creation tool to create multiple 32-bit and 64-bit installations of Windows 10 on USB devices. You can then go from system to system to deploy Windows. If you have more experience with Windows servers, you could configure a Windows Deployment Server (WDS).

Lesson 2: Understanding Operating System Configurations

Answers to Knowledge Assessment

Multiple Choice Answers

1. b. Limited user

2. d. Hybrid mode

3. a. Uninstalling a program

4. c. Administrative Tools

5. b. Notify me only when users try to access my files

6. a. Shake

7. d. Windows theme

8. d. System Configuration

9. b, c, d. Professional, Education, Enterprise

10. c. Virtual Hard Disk

Fill in the Blank Answers

1. user account
2. standard user
3. User Account Controls (UAC)
4. Ease of Access Center
5. Show Desktop
6. Control Panel
7. Administrative Tools
8. Screen Resolution
9. Client Hyper-V
10. File Explorer

True/False Answers

1. F
2. F
3. T
4. F
5. F

Answers to Business Case Scenarios

1. You may use the default Administrator account to perform maintenance tasks on the computer, but the account is currently hidden (disabled). To use the default Administrator account, open a command prompt window in administrator mode: click Start, type cmd in the Ask me anything search box, right-click cmd.exe in the resulting

list and choose Run as administrator. In the command prompt window, type net user administrator /active:yes and then press Enter. Perform the maintenance tasks, and then disable the account when you're finished: open a command prompt window and type net user administrator /active:no.

2. Programs that accommodate the visually impaired are found in the Ease of Access Center. You could enable Magnifier, Narrator, On-Screen Keyboard, and High Contrast as a start. Be sure to train Alexandra on how to use each feature that you enable.

3. You should install client Hyper-V, which will allow you to run a virtual machine running Windows XP. To run client Hyper-V, you will need to have a 64-bit Windows system running on a 64-bit computer. Of course, you should test the application to ensure that it runs as expected.

4. To enable Oscar to start Microsoft Excel quickly, pin the program to the taskbar. You should also unpin Windows Media Player from the taskbar per his request.

Lesson 3: Understanding Native Applications, Tools, Mobility, and Remote Management and Assistance

Answers to Knowledge Assessment

Multiple Choice Answers

1. a, b, c, d. Print Management, System Information, Computer Management, Event Viewer.

2. a. Annotate an image with the pen tool

3. d. Run as adminstator

4. a, b, c, d. Stream video files over the Internet, Rip music from a CD, Play a slide show, Create playlists

5. a. Internet Options Security tab

6. c. Windows PowerShell

7. a, b, d. Event Viewer, Performance Monitor, Disk Management

8. b. Remote Desktop Connection

9. c. Easy Connection

10. b. Windows PowerShell Integrated Scripting Environment

Fill in the Blank Answers

1. Microsoft Edge
2. 3389
3. InPrivate Browsing
4. SmartScreen Filter
5. Snipping Tool
6. Tracking Protection
7. offline files
8. Remote Desktop Connection
9. snap-in
10. Windows PowerShell

True/False Answers

1. F
2. F
3. T
4. T
5. T

Answers to Business Case Scenarios

1. In Internet Explorer 11 on her computer, you should increase her Internet zone security level to High (Tools > Internet options > Security tab). Ensure that Pop-up Blocker, ActiveX Filtering, and the SmartScreen Filter are enabled. Download and install at least one Tracking Protection list. Finally, instruct her to use InPrivate Browsing when she accesses any websites by selecting Tools > Safety > InPrivate Browsing.

2. You should show the sales staff how to initiate a Windows Remote Assistance session. With this program, you can view their desktop and watch while they perform an action, giving them advice over the phone or through a chat session. You can also take control of their desktop to show them how to perform an action.

3. You can use a Computer Management console (or Event Viewer console) on your machine to remotely connect to Joe's computer and access the logs.

4. You can use Windows Media Player to rip the music to the receptionist's hard drive (or attached storage). Then you can set up a playlist in Windows Media Player. Show the office manager and the receptionist how to launch Windows Media Player and start the playlist.

Lesson 4: Managing Applications, Services, Folders, and Libraries

Answers to Knowledge Assessment

Multiple Choice Answers

1. b. Uninstall an application

2. a, c, d. Restrict user access to an application, Update an application, Install applications from a network location

3. b. The Boot tab

4. d. Tools

5. d. 256 TB

6. c. Local System account

7. b, c, d. Striped volume, Simple volume, Spanned volume

8. b. Window Certificate database

9. a. Two small arrows pointing toward each other

10. a. Trusted Platform Module

Fill in the Blank Answers

1. application
2. Group Policy
3. services
4. MSConfig
5. NTFS
6. assign
7. Microsoft account
8. Encrypting File System (EFS)
9. Compression
10. BitLocker Drive Encryption

True/False Answers

1. F
2. T
3. T
4. F
5. F

Answers to Business Case Scenarios

1. On Mizuki's computer, open Disk Management and create a mirrored volume with the two disks. Mirrored volumes store an exact copy of data from the first member of the mirrored volume to the second member. Because the data is written across both drives, Mizuki will get redundancy and fault tolerance.

2. You should turn on BitLocker Drive Encryption on Henry's new laptop. BitLocker will prevent unauthorized use of the system should the laptop be lost or stolen.

3. Advise Henry to close all open programs and windows, and then right-click Start and choose Control Panel. Then instruct him to click Programs > Programs and Features. Next, he should browse the list of programs, click the voice transcription program, and then click Uninstall on the toolbar. Henry should follow the prompts that display until the program is removed. He should restart the computer and then try using a few programs to ensure the uninstallation process did not affect any other programs.

4. You can run the Program Compatibility Troubleshooter and select Windows 10 to emulate a Windows 10 environment. You can also check to see if this application requires administrative access and you will need to determine if your account has administrator access to the new system. You should also look for updates for the software package and check the vendor website for additional information about running the application on Windows 10. If the application still does not run, you can consider installing client Hyper-V and run the application on a virtual machine running Windows 7.

Lesson 5: Managing Devices

Answers to Knowledge Assessment

Multiple Choice Answers

1. b. Using the OneDrive Recycle Bin

2. c. 30 days

3. c. Send a notification after sharing the document or folder

4. d. Print queue

5. a. Internet Printing

6. b. Device Manager

7. b. Devices and Printers flder

8. a, b, c, e. Update a driver's software, Disable a driver, Uninstall a driver, Scan for hardware changes

9. b. Print job

10. The device is disabled.

Fill in the Blank Answers

1. Device Manager
2. print job
3. device driver
4. print queue
5. Device Manager
6. Plug-and-play (PnP
7. OneDrive
8. SharePoint
9. network printer
10. print spooler

True/False Answers

1. F
2. T
3. T
4. F
5. T

Answers to Business Case Scenarios

1. First, make sure that the printer is connected properly, and that the printer is on, and has paper. Next, you should open the print queue to see if the print jobs actually got to the print queue. If the print jobs are in the print queue, you can try to restart the printer server service. If the print jobs do not print, delete the print jobs and try reprinting the smaller print jobs. Then, if everything is working properly, try printing John's large print job.

2. Instruct Axel to install the printer software from the CD or DVD that came with the printer. Better yet, he should visit the printer manufacturer's web site and download the latest software. Axel should run the installation file from the CD/DVD or the downloaded file just as he would any other application. He could also open Devices and Printers, click Add a printer, and then walk through the wizard to install the latest printer driver from the manufacturer.

3. This is most likely caused by loading the wrong driver. Return to the Canon site and look for the correct driver. You should then test printing with the new driver.

4. Store the files on OneDrive, which can be accessed anywhere there is an Internet connection. You can create personal folders for their own files that are not meant to be shared with the other users, and you can create a shared folder, which would include the graphical images, and the shared Word documents and PowerPoint presentations.

Lesson 6: Understanding File and Print Sharing

Answers to Knowledge Assessment

Multiple Choice Answers

1. b. Office

2. c. A workgroup

3. a, b. Share libraries, Share attached printers

4. d. Map a drive

5. b. Copied files and folders retain permissions of the source folder

6. Full control

7. d. Public Projects

8. a. Advanced sharing settings

9. a. Devices and Printers

10. b. Allow Full Control

Fill in the Blank Answers

1. network location
2. Public folders
3. Basic sharing
4. inherit
5. NTFS
6. public network
7. Advanced sharing
8. HomeGroup
9. restrictive
10. Effective

True/False Answers

1. F
2. F
3. T
4. T
5. T

Answers to Business Case Scenarios

1. Because Arnie wants to share only one file, the easiest method is to have him use Public folders. You should ensure that Public folders are enabled on Arnie's computer and have him move the spreadsheet to his Public Documents folder. Then ensure that the three co-workers' computers can access Arnie's Public Documents folder.

2. Meredith should create a homegroup on the computer with the attached printer. When using the Create a Homegroup Wizard, she should deselect the Music option and the Videos option so that those libraries are not shared.

3. The Full Control permission gives Bob and Aileen permission to execute programs, in addition to all other rights. You should change their permissions to Read, Write, and Modify. In that way, they can read files, change files, and create new files, but they cannot execute programs.

4. Map a drive to the \Projects\Documents\98-349\ folder on the network. Use a drive letter that is not already in use on Samuel's computer.

Lesson 7: Maintaining, Updating, and Protecting Windows 10

Answers to Knowledge Assessment

Multiple Choice Answers

1. b. Disk Cleanup
2. a. Disk Degragmenter
3. d. Create Basic Task
4. c. Partial
5. b. Virus protection
6. a. A red circle with white X
7. b. Once a week
8. c. The Malicious Software Removal Tool
9. a. Malicious Software Removal Tool
10. a. CB

Fill in the Blank Answers

1. fragmented
2. Disk Cleanup
3. trigger
4. Windows registry
5. Windows Update
6. Windows Update
7. Malware
8. service pack
9. Windows Defender
10. System Information

True/False Answers

1. F
2. T

3. T
4. F
5. T

Answers to Business Case Scenarios

1. Advise Maria to ensure that Disk Defragmenter is scheduled to run at least once a month, that Windows Firewall is enabled and operating correctly, that she has real-time protection installed such as an antivirus program or Internet security suite, and that Windows Update is enabled to check for updates automatically. She should configure Task Scheduler to run Disk Cleanup weekly, and set Internet Explorer 11 and Microsoft Word 2016 to start when Windows starts.

    To schedule Disk Cleanup to run weekly and the other programs to start when Windows starts, she should select the Create Basic Task in Task Scheduler. The wizard will guide her through the prompts. For the trigger, she should select Weekly. In the Weekly screen, she should select a start date, time, and the day of the week Disk Cleanup will run. In the Start a Program screen of the wizard, she should click Browse, click Disk Cleanup, navigate to the Disk Cleanup program, select it, and then click Open. (Disk Cleanup is located in the Accessories/System Tools folder.) When she completes the wizard, Disk Cleanup will be added to her scheduled tasks list.

    The same general steps apply to Internet Explorer 11 and Word 2016, but for each program, she will select When the computer starts as the trigger. She will need to browse to locate the Internet Explorer 11 executable file and the Word 2016 executable file.

2. Tell Rajeem to download and run the Microsoft Windows Malicious Software Removal Tool. Have him perform a full scan of his computer and remove any infections the tool detects. When his system is clean, ensure that he has a reputable, current antivirus software program installed on his computer, such as Windows Defender.

3. On the affected computer, open System Information. Expand the Software Environment category, click the Startup Programs category, click File > Export and then save the file to the desktop or another location that's easy to access. Open the .txt file, highlight all information, copy the information, and then paste the information in a reply to the support forum moderator, along with a short message.

4. Implement WSUS on the Richman Investments server and set up a test client computer that's configured exactly as the broker's computers. When new updates and hotfixes are available through Windows Update, test them on the test computer. Install only approved updates and hotfixes over the network to client computers.

Lesson 8: Understanding Backup and Recovery Methods

Answers to Knowledge Assessment

Multiple Choice Answers

1. a, c, d, e. CD/DVD, USB, Hard drives, Network

2. c. Windows 7 File Recovery

3. a. Restore point

4. a, c. Roll back to another restore point, Undo the System Restore

5. d. Windows Recovery Environment

6. c. Windows PE

7. b. Safe Mode with Networking

8. c. Once every 7 days

9. a. File History

10. d. Create a restore point

Fill in the Blank Answers

1. backed it up
2. password reset
3. backup
4. Backup Operators group
5. Previous Version
6. Backup and Restore (Windows 7)
7. Safe Mode
8. C:\\Windows
9. File Recovery drive
10. restore point

True/False Answers

1. T
2. F
3. T
4. F
5. F

Answers to Business Case Scenarios

1. To ensure that Dina's files are backed up by Monday morning, reschedule her Windows 10 backup to begin sometime on Saturday. Another option is to increase the frequency of the backups from weekly to daily beginning at 7:00 p.m. When Windows 10 backup starts, it will back up only new files or files that have changed. Backing up files on a daily basis will reduce the amount of time that's currently needed to back up her files once a week. In addition, a daily backup better protects her data. Currently, anything she creates or modifies on Monday through Friday might have to be re-created if her computer fails before the next backup occurs.

2. Create a system image of Dina's old computer system to the external USB drive. Install that image onto the hard disk of Dina's new computer. Test the new computer to ensure it operates properly before transitioning Dina from her old computer to the new computer.

3. To help provide a boot environment, create a Windows 10 File Recovery drive. Insert a USB drive into your system, click Start, and execute the Create a Recovery Drive command. Select the USB drive and click Create. Once the disc is created, restart the computer with the Windows 10 File Recovery drive with the USB drive. You might be prompted to press any key to start the computer from the system repair disc. Next, select his language setting and then click Startup Repair from the list of recovery options.

4. On a properly functioning computer, visit the website of the video adapter manufacturer. Download the latest video adapter driver and save it to a USB flash drive or burn it to a CD/DVD.

   Shut down Jeffrey's computer. Then restart the computer with the Windows Recovery Environment, access the Advanced Boot Options menu, and select Safe Mode. Select Safe Mode. When Windows starts, use Device Manager to update the video adapter driver from the USB flash drive or CD/DVD. Then, restart the computer and let it start Windows normally.

Index

E

F

G

X–Y–Z

9781119650744: Networking Fundamentals

- Understand wired and wireless networks
- Work with fiber optic and twisted pair cables
- Learn Internet protocol (IP) and categorize IPv4 Addresses
- Validate your skills and knowledge with MTA Certification

9781119650669: Security Fundamentals

- Gain knowledge of essential IT security concepts
- Learn physical, Internet, and wireless security
- Identify different types of hardware firewalls
- Validate your skills and knowledge with MTA Certification

9781119650515: Windows Operating System Fundamentals

- Install and upgrade Windows 10 client
- Setup user accounts and account controls
- Customize user profiles
- Configure LAN settings and remote assistance and management
- Validate your skills and knowledge with MTA Certification

9781119650652: Windows Server Administration Fundamentals

- Install and manage Windows Server
- Use Disk Management Tools
- Manage devices and drivers
- Optimize server performance
- Configure Windows Network Services
- Administer remote and virtual servers
- Validate your skills and knowledge with MTA Certification